MAKING THE

Making Theatre

From Text to Performance

PETER MUDFORD

THE ATHLONE PRESS
LONDON & NEW BRUNSWICK, NJ

First published in 2000 by
THE ATHLONE PRESS
1 Park Drive, London NW11 7SG
and New Brunswick, New Jersey

British Library Cataloguing in Publication Data
A catalogue record for this book is available from the British Library

ISBN 0 485 11551 4 HB
0 485 12158 1 PB

Library of Congress Cataloging-in-Publication Data
Mudford, Peter.
  Making theatre : from text to performance/Peter Mudford.
    p.   cm.
  Includes index.
  ISBN 0–485–11551–4 (cloth : alk. paper)
  ISBN 0–485–12158–1 (pbk. : alk. paper)
  1. Drama—Explication. 2. Theater—Production and direction.
3. Music in theaters. 4. Musicals. 5. Opera. I. Title

PN1707.M83 2000   792′.023—dc21   00–055882

Distributed in The United States, Canada and South America by
Transaction Publishers
390 Campus Drive
Somerset, New Jersey 08873

Typeset by RefineCatch Limited, Bungay, Suffolk
Printed and bound in Great Britain by
Cambridge University Press

This book is dedicated to the past, present and future students
of the Department of English at Birkbeck College
in the University of London.

Contents

Acknowledgements   viii

List of Illustrations   x

List of Abbreviations and References in Text   xi

Foreword: A Personal Note   xiii

1 The Stage and Performance   1
2 Words   45
3 Vision   102
4 Music   165

Index   229

Acknowledgements

I would like to record my thanks for permission to reproduce the copyright photographs in this book as follows: Ralph Richardson: Peer Gynt (Naomi Campbell/John Vickers). Laurence Olivier: Macbeth; John Gielgud: Prospero (Angus McBean, The Harvard Theatre Collection, The Houghton Library). Michael Frayn: *Copenhagen*, (Conrad Blakemore). Janáček: *Jenufa*, (Mike Hoban); Anouilh, *Ring Round the Moon* (Victoria and Albert Museum Picture Library). Shakespeare, *A Midsummer Night's Dream; Henry V* (The Shakespeare Centre Library, Stratford-on-Avon). Brecht: *Gallileo*, (McDougall/Group Three Photographs). Shaffer: *The Royal Hunt of the Sun* (Angus McBean, The Harvard Theatre Collection, The Houghton Library). Wagner: Götterdämmerung (Ray Dean), Loesser, *Guys and Dolls* (John Haynes).

I would also like to express my thanks to Dr. Vesna Goldsworthy who made invaluable comments on the first draft of this book; and to Harriet Bagnall who, through her knowledge of the theatre, made many useful suggestions to improve and clarify it. Professor Katharine Worth made many further useful suggestions and corrections as well as encouraging me in the project. Over many years I have been helped by conversations with Professor Willard Pate of Furman University, South Carolina whose knowledge of the theatre in London, and whose enthusiasm have always been stimulating. Discussions with colleagues at Birkbeck have given me many insights. The positive support and encouragement of Professor Leonée Ormond has also been invaluable. Finally, I would like to record my thanks to my wife, who has accompanied me to many productions, and whose interest and response has been a constant help.

I am also grateful for support from the special fund of the English Department at Birkbeck College in the publication of this book, and to David Atkinson for compiling the index.

List of Illustrations
(between pages 80 and 81)

1. Ralph Richardson: Peer Gynt (1945): see p. xvi.
2. John Gielgud: Prospero. (1957): see p. 34.
3. Laurence Olivier: Macbeth (1955): see p. 38.
4. David Burke, Sara Kestelman, Matthew Marsh in Michael Frayn's *Copenhagen* (Royal National Theatre), 1998: see p. 47.
5. Designs by Sally Jacobs for *A Midsummer Night's Dream*, (Royal Shakespeare Company), 1962: see p. 115.
6. Set by Oliver Messel for Jean Anouilh: *Ring Round the Moon*, Act Two, (Globe Theatre), 1950: see p. 139.
7. Janáček: *Jenufa*, set by Tobias Hoheisel, Act One (Glyndebourne Opera), 2000: see p. 150.
8. Set by Tanya Moseiwitch for Shakespeare's Histories (Richard II–Henry V) (Stratford-on-Avon), 1951, see p. 141.
9. Set by Jocelyn Herbert for Brecht's *Gallileo*, Act One, (Royal National Theatre), 1980, see p. 146.
10. Set by Michael Annals for Peter Shaffer's *The Royal Hunt of the Sun*, (Royal National Theatre) 1964, see p. 147.
11. Set by Josef Svoboda for Wagner's Götterdämmerung, Act Three, Scene One (Royal Opera House, Covent Garden) 1976, see p. 160.
12. Finale of *Guys and Dolls*, setting by John Gunter, (Royal National Theatre), 1996, see p. 206.

List of Abbreviations and References in Text

Barrault, Jean-Louis Barrault, *Memories for Tomorrow*, translated by Jonathan Griffin, Thames and Hudson, London, 1974.

Billington, *Ashcroft*, Michael Billington, *Peggy Ashcroft*, Mandarin Books, London, 1989.

Billington, *ONS*, Michael Billington: *One Night Stands*, Nick Hern Books, London, 1993.

British Theatre Design: British Theatre Design, The Modern Age, edited by John Goodwin, Weidenfeld and Nicolson, London, 1989.

Brook, *ES*, Peter Brook, *The Empty Space*, Methuen, London, 1968

Brook, *Ring*, 'Preface' to Jean Anouilh, *Ring round the Moon*, translated by Christopher Fry, Methuen, London, 1950.

Brook, *SP*, Peter Brook: *The Shifting Point, Forty Years of Theatrical Exploration, 1946–1987*, Methuen, London, 1988.

Burian, Jarka Burian, *Svoboda: Wagner* Wesleyan University Press, Middletown, Connecticut, 1983.

Callow, Simon Callow, *Being an Actor*, Penguin Books, Harmondsworth, 1984.

Cole, *Playwrights on Playwriting*, edited by Toby Cole, MacGibbon and Kee, London, 1960.

Cox, *Shakespeare Comes to Broadmoor*, edited by Murray Cox, Jessica Kingsley, London, 1992

Duff, Charles Duff, *The Lost Summer: The Heyday of West End Theatre*, Nick Hern, London, 1995.

Eyre, Richard Eyre, *Utopia and other Places*, Vintage Books, London, 1994.

Gielgud, John Gielgud, *An Actor and His Time*, Pan Books, London, 1996.

Guinness, *Blessings*, Alec Guinness, *Blessings in Disguise* Hamish Hamilton, London, 1985.

Guinness, *My Name*, Alec Guinness, *My Name Escapes Me*, Hamish Hamilton, London, 1996.

Guthrie, Tyrone Guthrie, *A Life in the Theatre*, Columbus Books, London, 1960.

Hall, *Peter Hall's Diaries*, edited by John Goodwin, Hamish Hamilton Paperback, London, 1983.

Herbert, Jocelyn Herbert, *A Theatre Workbook*, Art Books International, London, 1993.

Holden, Anthony Holden, *Olivier*, Sphere Books, London, 1988.

Mahabharata, *Peter Brook and the Mahabharata*, edited by David Williams, Routledge, London, 1991.

Meyer, Henrik Ibsen, *A Doll's House*, translated by Michael Meyer, Hart-Davis, London, 1965.

Miller, John Miller, *Ralph Richardson*, Sidgwick and Jackson, London, 1995.

Mortimer, John Mortimer (ed.), *Three Boulevard Farces by Georges Feydeau*, Penguin, Harmondsworth, 1985, pp. 9–11.

Pilbrow, Richard Pilbrow, *Stage Lighting Design*, Nick Hern, London, 1997.

Shaffer, Peter Shaffer, *The Royal Hunt of the Sun*, Pan Books, London, 1964.

Spoto, Dennis Spoto, *Tennessee Williams*, Bodley Head, London, 1985.

Stanislavsky, *Stanislavsky on the Art of the Stage*, translated by David Magarshack, Faber, London, 1950.

Tynan, Kenneth Tynan, *A View of the English Stage, 1944–1965*, Methuen, London, 1975.

Foreword: A Personal Note

My love of theatre began in 1943 with Ralph Richardson's *Peer Gynt*. On the radio. Every house in England was blacked out. Each night the German bombers rumbled over the sky. In a Gloucestershire valley, lit only by lamps and candles, a wireless crackled. As Bristol burned, voices told tales of other worlds, other places, of a mountainous ride on the back of a reindeer, of dreams and visions, which turned out to be lies, and some other truth.

The following year *Peer Gynt* was performed by the Old Vic Company in London. I asked to be taken. It was a strange request from a boy of seven whose family had no interest in theatre, to whom Ibsen meant nothing; but my godfather took me. London was still a dangerous place, with the doodle-bugs falling. The theatre meant excitement and danger, the actors whose names I never forgot – Ralph Richardson, Laurence Olivier, Sybil Thorndike, Margaret Leighton, Nicholas Hannen – inhabited enchanted worlds which bombs could not destroy.

Since that first afternoon in war-time London, the theatre has always been for me a place of exploration. The following book attempts to revisit these imagined worlds, and to recall some of the extraordinary richness of the English stage in the last fifty years, through plays performed, performances given and productions which bring words alive through the various arts which theatre uses.

These arts involve scene design, costume, lighting, music, movement within very different stage spaces, and with resources from those of the simplest kind to those of techno-logical wizardry which as in *Peter Pan* can make actors seem to fly. Books of many kinds have been written about the history of the drama, its trends in the twentieth century, and the work of individual dramatists. Very few books of any kind have been written about the visual and physical languages of theatre, except as technical guides for those who work in the theatre, or are involved in play production. Critics, writing in newspapers and journals, comment on the qualities of particular productions and performances; but their comments are inevitably confined to the production under review. As a teacher of drama in the University of London for more than thirty years I have always been aware of how difficult students find it to relate what they have read on the page to the interpretation of a play in performance, even if they have seen it on the stage. The analysis of plays often reads as though they are novels or tracts, and seldom as though they are living things, performed by actors in front of an actual audience in a particular space; or that every performance is an interpretation.

Audiences for many forms of theatre are growing all over the world. Drama and Performance play a large part in school and university courses in many different countries. But much that is written shows little sense – apart from books by directors and actors – that the languages of theatre bring together many different arts; or that a play only comes to life when it is being performed. Even audiences may not be aware of the different forms of magic which are being used to arouse their response and interest. This book attempts to illustrate how these languages work. It is intended both for the student of theatre, and for the theatre-goer who may be helped to recall why some performances remain vivid and memorable.

The book does not attempt to be comprehensive in its coverage. Almost everything I have written about I have seen; but there is also much I have missed. The largest and most obvious omission is ballet and dance-theatre because they have influenced me less, and I know less about them. Theatre exists most profoundly for me in its relation between words, and its other languages. This book records and analyses those productions which have continued to resonate over a long a period of time, as a piece of music which once heard is never forgotten. Its principles of selection have been shaped by memory, and are inevitably subjective; but that does not prevent them, I hope, from illustrating qualities and values in the life of the theatre which have general application. The book attempts to probe the relation between theatre and life, between stage and audience, to rediscover why the theatre has mattered; and to offer a view of its creativity in the second half of the twentieth century. I admit the book's partiality, but can only write about that part of theatre's legacy, in which I have discovered the greatest riches.

The 'opening' or 'rising' of the curtain is itself a metaphor for what theatre does, whether or not it has a curtain. It *shows* (again, as in the phrase, 'we've been to a show'); *shows* but does not state; and what it shows will in one sense always remain indefinable, because each member of the audience will carry away some other memory. Dramatic images, created out of theatre's various languages, matter because they reveal and suggest. The theatre, even as it entertains, means always a search for meaning, a quest.

Among the many changes which have occurred in the last fifty years, none has been more significant than the diversification of types of performance, which theatre includes, and the spaces in which it is performed The pocket-size programme schedule (with its distinctive yellow cover) of the Shakespeare Memorial Theatre, as it then was, after the war was a treasure-trove of immense riches; but infinite riches in a small room. I went for the first time in 1949 to see Godfrey Tearle and Diana Wynyard in *Othello* and learnt (though I did not know the word till many years later) what Aristotle meant by catharsis: the power of a great dramatic performance to purge the emotions, and create a calm of mind, all passion spent. Though it can equally well disrupt, leave the mind jagged, or inspire joy.

The cycle of thirty-eight major Shakespeare plays would take a long time to revolve in a short Stratford season in one theatre. (The Old Vic undertook it as a five-year plan between 1953 and 1958.) Now Stratford has three theatres and, as elsewhere, the repertory has widened. Revivals are sometimes spoken of by critics with deprecation. But revivals, if they are good, reinterpret the plays of the past, giving them a new life and necessity. A revival, just as much as a new play, can explore the contemporary.In both, the languages of theatre forge new ways of looking at reality, or the realities, in which we live. The 'live' theatre belongs to the present.

The theatre has also become international. As I started to write this book, *A Midsummer Night's Dream* was being performed by a visiting company in Japanese; at the Edinburgh Festival, Chekhov's *Uncle Vanya* was being performed in Italian, directed by a German, Peter Stein. Since then there have been memorable productions of Racine's *Phèdre* with Diana Rigg (in English) and with Valerie Dréville (in French), of Schiller's *Don Carlos*, of Victor Hugo's *The Prince's Play*, of Goldoni's *Le Baruffe Chiozzotte*, directed by Giorgio Strehler, and Eduardo de Filippo's *Filumena* with Judi Dench, to mention just a very few.

'All the world's a stage' has become true in a different sense. The modes of drama in different cultures, languages, historical periods have become familiar and, like Puck on his travels, girdle the earth, confronting audiences with images drawn from cultures and societies different to their own.

In the last act of *Peer Gynt*, Peer, peeling an onion, in search of the Gyntian self, finds that it lacks any heart, and writes his own epitaph, 'here no one is buried'. Drama has remained for me an attempt, shared between actors and audience, to peel away the layers of the onion, to see if it has a heart, to ask what it means to write 'here someone is buried.' The question is asked of each member of the audience, and of the society to which we belong. What are the unique contributions which theatre makes to a culture? What does it enable us to see about our lives, and our times? Why in the end is it necessary?

As a way of beginning, something needs to be said about the nature of plays, the stages on which they are performed, and the art of performance itself.

1
The Stage and Performance

In the last half-century, the theatre has often been described as being in a terminal state. Silent movies, then talkies, television and videos have all threatened the live theatre. The expense and risk of productions have escalated; the cost of going to live theatre has risen. How much easier to stay at home and watch a video where there is no sense of implicit formality or communal participation.

But the living quality in the theatre, watching people perform, in front of an audience whose response is audibly felt, has unquestionably helped to ensure that it does not die. Theatre always aspires to the excitement of watching the artist on the high trapeze. When it falls flat it does so because it has not taken the risk, shown the dazzling skills of performance and daring which the great actor shapes. The theatre is a dangerous craft, composed of many different kinds of language. Because it involves danger, it offers the opportunity for greatness; and no one knows when, or if, it is going to happen. We cannot know whether the performance we are watching, which the previous night might have seemed a skilful impersonation, is going to touch greatness.

Once the curtain falls on a play, it is over; but it is also unfinished. The action continues in the mind of the audience. What will happen to Denmark after Hamlet's death under the rule of Fortinbras? Will the Three Sisters ever get to Moscow? Are Vladimir and Estragon still waiting for Godot? These questions forbidden by some critics who argue that nothing exists outside the text overlook the living presence of the actor whose performance does not end with the play any more than his own existence does. Unlike a film where the

words 'The End' mean what they say, what we have shared
with those on the stage has created a continuing life of its
own. The Muscovites, who on cold winter nights used to say
outside the Moscow Art Theatre, 'let's drop in and see how
the Three Sisters are getting on', spoke perhaps more wisely
than they knew.

But the darkened theatre is also a place where something
has ended. The performance can never be repeated; and the
production once closed has vanished into air. Unlike the film
which can be viewed any number of times, and where particular shots or sequences can be reviewed and analysed as
long as the celluloid lasts, the performance and the production of a play is always transient, ephemeral. This is not just
because a production comes to an end; but because every
performance depends on a relationship between the actors
and audience.

An audience makes no difference to the showing of a film
because a film once made is finished. A play, as Thornton
Wilder once said, 'is what takes place . . .'. It exists in the
simultaneous present of actors and audience. A play only exists
in the living present of the performance, creating its sense of
inner vibration between audience and stage. The darkened
auditorium and the illuminated space create a different relation, and make quite different demands on the audience to the
projection of a film in the cinema. A play comes closer to life:
a film tells us what to see, while the theatre plays on, and with,
the inner worlds we inhabit.

'To go on the stage' remains a common colloquialism for
becoming an actor. Unlike to go on stage which merely
implies an entrance, the little word 'the' suggests an ascend-
ancy, makes us imagine at least a raised platform, on which the
performance takes place. But this image raises the most fundamental questions about the nature of theatre, about the
physical relationship between performer and audience, about
the architecture of theatres, and the importance of illusion.
What happens on a stage, the nature and kind of performance
given is shaped by the space to be filled.

In many modern plays, the audience will constantly be reminded that they are in a theatre, but as well as making them question the relationship between what they see on the stage and the world outside, this may paradoxically intensify the power of the illusion.

To a modern audience the dimming of the lights in the auditorium (and often the rising of the curtain) means the compulsion of silence, and the expectation of being 'transported' (literally carried across into another world) for as long as the action lasts. The darkening of the auditorium only became possible in the mid-nineteenth century with the introduction of gas, and then electricity. Sir Henry Irving, one of the great Victorian actor–managers, was the first to believe the lighting more important than the scenery, and to hold lighting rehearsals with his actors. Charles Garnier's Opéra which opened in Paris in 1867, contained 28 miles of piping and 960 gas-jets. The technology of the theatre in the last one hundred and fifty years has radically altered the nature of dramatic art in the Western world. Radically or superficially? The answer is both. And both are related to the nature of stage-space.

Greek theatres were cut into a hill-side, and the audience looked down on the acting area. The performance started early in the morning, and the watchman who sees the sun rising at the start of Aeschylus's *Agamemnon* would have been inviting the audience to do so too. But this was the start of no ordinary day. Agamemnon was about to return, after ten years absence, from the Trojan War and, stepping down on the purple carpet, reserved for the gods, make his entrance to his palace, where his wife, Clytemnestra and her lover Aegistheus will murder him. The pride of Agamemnon will result in his downfall, as *hubris* results in *nemesis*. What is invisible has been made visible. And thus from the very start, performance arouses the most fundamental of all dramatic emotions: wonder. It is sometimes argued that art is a matter of observation; but equally it depends on making visible, often through silence, a gesture, an image, what we had not seen before.

What the characters in a play say, and what the play means to us, the audience, are two very different things. From this very simple fact, there grows gradually the theatre as a place of illusions; and in the twentieth century, the theatre as a place of anti-illusion. The history and nature of the stage is inseparable from the debate about these two views.

The engineering skills of the Romans enabled a theatre to be built with free-standing walls, as opposed to being cut from a hill-side; the *scaena* (or scene building) then rose to the same height as the seating. The *scaena* allowed for appearances at different levels, for emperors and gods to be given a different symbolic relation to the mere humans on the *pro-scaena*. Vitruvius, writing in the first century AD, gave instructions for the design of a Roman theatre, in which he describes painted scenery, with perspective effects. Visually, the relationship between actors and audience had been altered, and with it the possibility of stage illusion. The theatre had become an amphitheatre in which audience and performers were enclosed. The difference between the Greek and Roman theatre can easily be seen by comparing the theatre at Epidauros in Greece with the Roman theatre at Orange in France, both still in use for summer festivals.

In the Middle Ages, a stage was made out of any open space: a street, a hall, a tavern, a field, a church; and the performance could move with the audience from one to another, freeing the relationship between performer and audience, and making one more involved with the other, as still happens in many forms of theatre today, in pubs and warehouses, converted attics and nissen huts.

The Elizabethan thrust or apron stage, with tiring houses behind, enclosing the audience as at the Globe, sustained and intensified a personal and intimate relationship, compelling the actors to make themselves heard over the clamour of those who had come to the theatre for many other purposes than watching the play. This made visible one interpetation of drama as metaphor ('all the world's a stage, and all the people on it merely players'), while at the same time intensifying another, that drama itself was an illusion, a performance, a coming together of many different talents, in which clowns were as important as tragedians, musicians and tumblers as important as either, and those who found, made or borrowed the costumes central to the creative endeavour. The actors as a company, itself a metaphor for the idea of community outside the theatre, became well known in Shakespeare's time, as the 'Lord Chamberlain's Men' or the 'Admiral's Men'. Scenery was still unimportant, except in the form of a bank or trees; but voice ('speak the speech trippingly upon the tongue, I pray you ') gesture (sometimes in dumb-show) and properties of various kinds had become essential. You can't have alarums and excursions without drums! All were capable of provoking wonder at the spectacle; and wonder belongs to the subliminal, the threshold of perception, where drama occurs at the meeting-point between the imagined and the actual.

The increasing complexity of the spectacle has dominated the history of the theatre in the post-Renaissance period; and still does in the musical theatre of the late twentieth century in *The Phantom of the Opera*, *Cats* and *Les Misérables*. All this sophistication half-conceals the fact that, for theatre to occur, all that is required is a space, an audience and someone performing in that space so that the audience wonders at their skill. At its simplest, this may be the skill of appearing to eat fire; at its most complex, the power to make the audience see in imagination what they had not seen before, whether a wood outside Athens, or Prospero's sea-girt isle. As many contemporary productions prove, lavishness and expense do not 'make this magic', though the technological resources of the modern theatre can help. Stage design remains the art of pruning, because the simple allows the imagination free play; the over-elaborate deadens and restricts because it states too much.

In Shakespeare's theatre, the performance beginning in the late afternoon would continue as the evening drew in, so that the rush-lights and tapers could cast their flickering shadows over the tragedies of blood which were frequently performed. Natural light was beginning to give way, however simply, to the light and shadow which the enclosed space of a theatre like the Globe made possible. But it was in the fully enclosed space of the Hall, where Royal performances occurred, that in the course of the first part of the seventeenth century, particularly in Italy, and the masques of the Caroline court, the scenic theatre began to evolve; and with it the theatrical form, in which music becomes as important as any of the other creative talents: opera.

In the Court masque for which elaborate stage machinery was required, costing then as now immense sums, the clouds could part, and Heaven be revealed. But the illusion could only be sustained if the machinery was concealed; and the machinery did not interfere with the audience's illusion. For this the proscenium arch, like a picture-frame, was indispensable, as were the wings which gave depth and perspective. All this radically altered not just the stage for opera but the theatres for all kind of performance, and the dramas which came to be written for them. Even the names given to the tiers of the theatre, the stalls, the royal or dress circle, the gallery (and gods) invoked a new formality in the relationship between stage and audience, which the rise of the high bourgeoisie in cities, mainly capital cities, intensified.

Whatever the shape of the stage, including its rake, the size of the auditorium and the position of the spectators, the only purpose of any arrangement is to facilitate the performance. To perform means literally to complete by adding what is wanting. The performing arts do this; and the more fully they complete what is written down – whether a musical score, a choreographer's design or the script of a play – the more an audience will be aware of a 'great performance'. The act of completion requires an audience. As the Chorus puts it at the start of Shakespeare's *King Henry V*:

> O! for a muse of fire, that would ascend
> The brightest heaven of invention;
> A kingdom for a stage, princes to act
> And monarchs to behold the swelling scene.

Without the monarchs – or the substitutes for them – the scene would not swell, because the completion occurs in their imagining.

Since the proscenium arch was removed at the Shakespeare Memorial Theatre in Stratford-on-Avon, and Tyrone Guthrie insisted on an arena theatre in Stratford, Ontario in the 1960s the debate has continued about theatre-space. Tyrone Guthrie has been among the few practitioners – like Richard Wagner at Bayreuth – who has been able to see a theatre built which matched what he thought to be the right conditions for a performance. Unlike Wagner, Guthrie had to produce his first festival in a specially designed tent, later replaced by a permanent structure. 'The relation of the stage to the auditorium is such that a large audience – nearly two thousand people – can be accommodated so near the actors that the farthest spectators are only thirteen rows from the front. In a proscenium theatre of similar capacity those in the back rows would be more than twice as far from the stage.' (Guthrie, pp. 300–1). In positioning the audience two-thirds of the way round the stage, Guthrie realized his own conception of what a performance was intended to be and do; and unlike Wagner who made his orchestra invisible so that nothing should interfere with the stage-illusion, Guthrie started from the opposite conviction:

I believe that the theatre makes its effect not by means of illusion, but by ritual.

People do not believe that what they see or hear on the stage is 'really' happening. Action on the stage is a stylised reenactment of real action, *which is then imagined by the audience* [my italics]. The re-enactment is not merely an imitation but a symbol of the real thing. . . . It [the audience] should, however, participate in the ritual with sufficient fervour to be rapt, literally 'taken out of itself', to the extent that it shares the emotion which the actor is suggesting. It completes the circle of action and reaction; its function is not passive but active. (Guthrie, p. 313)

In this active participation, the performance will determine not only the degree to which the audience is 'rapt' but also when the play is done what it reflects on, what it has been moved by, what it rationally assents to. A performance continues in the mind after the performance is over; and we ask ourselves what we have witnessed. The power of the actor to draw the audience into the stage illusion creates at the same time the shock-waves which continue after the performance has ended. A somewhat crude distinction is possible between the emotions aroused in us at the time, and the reflection upon those emotions which occur after we leave the theatre. Wordsworth's 'emotion recollected in tranquillity' inspires him to write poetry. A re-creative act of another but not altogether dissimilar kind occurs for an audience, which crystallizes from the performance a view of what has occurred.

All the arguments which continue about the shape of the stage, the position of the audience, and the size of the auditorium are only of interest in their relation to the resonance and clarity of the truths which the audience carry away with them into the night: the sword has many edges, but they must be sharp.

The three stages of the Royal National Theatre in London – the arena in the Olivier, the proscenium arch in the Lyttelton, and the studio in the Cottesloe – can be seen as three commentaries on this debate; and each has proved its strengths in different productions. But the Olivier, for all its openness, remains the hardest to fill with meaning. In the Olivier an audience is much more likely to 'go to see' than to 'participate in' a performance. Not surprisingly, young directors prefer to work in the Cottesloe which, while an awkward space compared to the Swan at Stratford-on-Avon, draws its audience into each move on the stage. 'Theatre [as Peter Hall has remarked in his diaries] is about people not buildings. Buildings are fine, they give you opportunity, a foundation, but they are the second priority, not the first.' (Hall, p. 332).

★

The stage is an illuminated space which we can be made to imagine is any place, any time. Within the wooden O of Shakespeare's theatre as in any other, we can be transported to the vasty fields of France, and hear the very casques that did affright the air at Agincourt. At one moment we can be in the Rome of Octavius Caesar, and the next in the Egypt of Cleopatra. All that is required is a 'Muse of fire, that will ascend the brightest Heaven of Invention'. This Muse may take the form as in Shakespeare's prologue to *Henry the Fifth* only of words; but we may also be transported by a set, or music, or silence into some other land. Just as space can be girdled very fast, as Puck knows, so time too is the stage's domain. Arthur Miller in *The Death of a Salesman* (first called *Inside his Head*) created a drama in which there was a 'mobile concurrency of past and present'. Spatially and temporally, the stage mirrors the processes of consciousness. Between birth and death, waking and sleeping, consciousness is like an illuminated space, pained, humorous, joyful, questioning. Every minute consciousness presses against the ceiling of self-knowledge, trying to make 'sense', find 'pathways' of whatever sort, and is limited by closed doors through which it cannot pass. Consciousness has its own sight-lines, is enclosed and boundless; and like a stage action can shift rapidly in time and space, but cannot move beyond its own sight-lines. We can explore our consciousness, our consciousness can develop or shrink, but we can never stand outside it, just as, although people and events exist off-stage, they only do so in relation to an action we are watching on stage. The action of a play cannot be other than it is; its details are variable; but not its substance, any more than an identity is variable. (Even when someone goes mad, the change occurs only within certain limits; they are still recognizably themselves in many aspects of their bearing and behaviour, as Blanche always reminds us in *A Streetcar Named Desire*.)

Samuel Beckett's *Play* makes brilliant play of this relationship between stage and consciousness. The three characters, up to their necks in urns, only speak when the light shines on them. The spotlight is an interrogator; it compels them, by shining on them in turn, to speak, which is to say, reflect, remember, feel pain, attempt to come to terms with what they have done, make sense of experience, when it would be more peaceful to be left in the dark; but once the light shines, they have no choice, just as on waking we have no choice but to resume consciousness, and find another way of surviving 'another happy day'. So the spot is also an internal light: the light of awareness pressing against its own limitations. When it goes out, sleep once more relieves the pain. But we are also aware in this post-Brechtian theatre that the spot is just a spot: *Play* is play; and like all theatre is a liberating release of energy, a coming together of multiple skills. We see the relevance of the action to a waking–sleeping world; but we can also find relief in watching the spots create the action, reminding us that this is theatre, not life.

What happens on the stage, and everything which is on the stage throughout the performance is part of an action abstracted from experience – not in the sense that it is abstract, on the contrary it is (or should be) vivid, concrete in every detail – but an abstraction in that it is an action complete in itself: isolated, and held up before us in that illuminated stage space, in which we become participants. Here too it differs from the cinema, in which we are always taken in by moving images: and everything which moves, moves from somewhere to somewhere. The essence of a moving image is that it is not where it was five minutes ago; and so the cinema is always concerned with passage. The camera tracks, moves in and out of close-up, pans from left to right and right to left, changes in focal length and depth. A movie is built up from sequences. Its success (or failure) depends on the way those sequences are edited together, cut short, held, juxtaposed; its art is an art of moving at variable speeds, in a process where we are always losing the previous sequence, like a ship which loses in its wake the water its passage has just churned up. A play is an act of simultaneity, even if divided into acts and scenes, a 'whirlwind of concurrent events'; a play in performance is always in the present; a film has been 'engraved', a play is always being 'painted'.

Sophocles in his late play, *Philoctetes* increased the number of actors from two to three, so that the conflict became not as previously a battle of wills but of characters acting and reacting with each other; and so working out their fate. Sophocles set his play on a desolate part of the island of Lemnos, where Philoctetes has been abandoned by his companions on account of a foul-smelling wound, until they have need of his bow to win the Trojan War. Writing three hundred or more years after the Trojan War, Sophocles abstracted from it an action which questions man's nature and the standards by which we judge it. As he wrote eleswhere, 'many things are strange, but nothing is stranger than man'. Shakespeare's *Antony and Cleopatra* has forty-two scenes; and observes none of the unities of which Aristotle approved, but in an action also abstracted from experience, and even more remote from the Elizabethan world, asks whether the world is well lost for love. What matters is the action as whole. The images before us we know to be imaginary, and they ask us to question their relationship to the world in which we live, where the value we place on public roles and private lives remains equally divisive, and open to censure. A play, abstracted from experience, offers a way of getting one's bearings on the world, an orientation in space.

The nineteenth-century play with its three-act structure, each act being in its way complete in itself, attempts to conceal this fact (out of deference to an audience wishing to refresh itself). This risks fracture, but does not conceal that the play succeeds or fails by the significance of the action overall. Every Greek play has this in common with a play by Samuel Beckett or Arthur Miller; and all of them differ in this from the art of the cinema. When an attempt was made to film Arthur Miller's *Death of a Salesman* it failed because the cinema did what it has to do, in moving from location to location, while Miller's play has only one location, inside Willy's head, where the action moves freely, as in consciousness between past, present and future. But this very restriction is also what makes a stage action boundless; it has the freedom of the mind at play, while the film is bound by a visual narrative, which in recapturing the past depends on the crude device of flashback. The cinema is also dependent on what can be captured on film. The camera cannot see at night, while a darkened stage can be boundlessly suggestive, as in the first scene of *Hamlet*. The ghost is here, is there and gone. The camera has to see something, even if it is only swirling mist. The theatre compels us to imagine what we do not see.

★

A dramatic action, because of its brevity, presses towards a climax, a goal, even if not a resolution. In this whirlwind motion we see the content of the world as simultaneous, a cross-section of inter-relationships in what appears to be a single moment, though we know it not to be. In a dramatic action there is always a triumph over time, for 'speed is the single means for overcoming time in time', of making time disappear. Stage time and 'real time' bear little relation to each other, even when they are meant to be related. This matters little even if as in *Othello* the time-scheme makes Cassio's seduction of Desdemona impossible, since they travel to Cyprus on separate ships, and spend no time together, a fact which neither Othello, nor the audience, notices.

The axe which falls on Chekhov's cherry orchard cuts down a way of life, a set of relationships which cannot be restored. The poignancy felt at the end of *The Cherry Orchard* is not to begin with political or social, but the feeling left by the absence of the familiar, of what gives a sense of assurance and identity, and arouses in the audience an affection for lives as distinctive and familiar as those of friends. Gayev, like any uncle, has an affection for a bookcase, enjoys his boiled sweets and playing billiards. The transience of things is as inseparable from the theatre as from life itself. Until a family moves, the life of a house appears to have permanence; the particularities of a way of life, the cars in the drive, the curtains in the window signal how it is; until one morning they have all disappeared, as though they have never existed. As Linda tells her sons in Arthur Miller's *Death of a Salesman*: 'You've got to get it into your head now that one day you'll knock on this door and there'll be strange people here.'

And so it is with theatres which when we pass them in the street can only offer the ghosts of 'insubstantial pageants faded'. The two or three hours' traffic of the stage plays on a deep recognition of life outside the theatre. All that is here today, is gone tomorrow. A part of the theatre's hold comes from this translation. Cinema and televison can in no way rival or reproduce this effect, which rises from the presence of actors and audience in a living relationship, bonded by the knowledge that 'we are such stuff as dreams are made on, and our little life is rounded with a sleep'. All too are but shadows: an awareness which Shakespeare shares with Sophocles, and both with those who go 'dancing' at Lughnasa, or find with Tom in *The Glass Menagerie* that they are more faithful to their memories than they intended to be. As the wily Odysseus, the counterfeiter and actor asks: 'Are we not all, All living things, mere phantoms, shadows of nothing?' (Sophocles, *Ajax*, lines 116–17). Seen like this, the theatre is always a metaphysical art.

The wind and the rain to which we are returned on leaving Illyria suggests a transportation from a land we have come to know and love to another of deeper uncertainty. The play at one and the same time takes us to a place where nothing can ever be other than it is, and then dissolves it, when the curtain falls, with the finality of death.

★

Plots differ from stories in novels in that their juxtaposition of scenes adds up not to a sequence in time, but to a single picture of how things are. Plot and sub-plot (Lear's mental suffering and Gloucester's physical suffering in *King Lear*) are both parts of a single action. Even Ibsen's *Peer Gynt* the most sequential of all plays, representing Peer's life from youth to old age, does not dramatize Peer's life as in a *Bildungsroman* but

Peer's self. The enigma of the action revolves around the 'gyntian self'; and whether the self, like the onion, has any heart? Is Peer right to say his epitaph should read, 'Here no one is buried'? What actually happens to Peer becomes increasingly unimportant. In the Egyptian lunatic asylum he is crowned 'the emperor of self'; and selfhood becomes a *reductio ad absurdum*. In Dickens's *David Copperfield*, unlike *Peer Gynt*, one cannot speak of the unimportance of events. A play is in this sense much closer to a poem than a novel.

A play also differs from a novel in another fundamental way. A play, like life, is always concerned with roles, and role-playing, with masks and masking, with identities which shift and are fixed. Eugene O'Neill once expressed this duality, like this: 'One's outer life passes in a solitude haunted by the masks of others; one's inner life passes in a solitude hounded by the masks of oneself' (Cole, 67). An actor is cast in a part; and for the run he will play that part, however much the performance differs from night to night.

Jean Anouilh's *Antigone* (1942), one of the great plays of the Second World War, written in occupied France, sees this as being central not just to tragedy as a dramatic form, but to life as tragic. Antigone will continue defying Creon and burying her brother against his orders because that is what it means to be Antigone. She can do no other night after night. That is what Antigone is born to do. In life too, all are 'given' roles, which they cannot change; no one can become someone else; and though they may not be entirely the same person they were yesterday, they are much more the same than they are someone else. Characters in a play also change only within limits. Cleopatra, 'the serpent of old Nile' puts on 'immortal longings'; but she is still Cleopatra; and the Duchess of Malfi, tortured, forced to endure the sight of her murdered lover and children, subjected to the worst forms of mental and physical suffering 'is Duchess of Malfi still'. However much they change, people, like characters in a play, remain the same.

Nonetheless, identity is not a fixed, simple or stable thing. And the theatre plays on this in many ways which neither the cinema, nor the novel can. An actor in a film is always seen as the camera perceives him to be; the angle from which he is shot, the length and nature of the sequence will determine how we see him; and that cannot be changed. The camera is a private eye which observes and records, under the complete control of the director. Apart from the interference of studios and censors, the director fixes the work for ever.

The novelist can only write about events which have happened, since they cannot be written about as they occur. In the theatre, there are no private eyes, only the palpable presence of someone playing a role in the present, shared by the audience for as long as they remain in the theatre, and sustained by the actor only as long as he or she remains in the theatre. For a time, on both sides of the 'footlights' something has been shared, which involves an awareness of the roles we play, and of their shifting nature: that what people say may not reflect what they feel, or like mountain tops rising above the mist may misrepresent it.

The adoption of roles in both cases is far from being a conscious process, though for the actor it is more radical and self-aware, a separation of what he does from what he is; and may involve as Lynne Redgrave has recently shown in her great solo performance of *Shakespeare for my Father* in England and the United States the disappearance of the person behind the disguise or disguises, so that he becomes even to his own daughter the roles he plays, a Richard, or Hamlet, or an Antony.

A great deal has been written by actors and directors about this talent for transformation. To Stanislavsky, it involved a method which had to be acquired, a discipline not unlike a spiritual exercise, requiring complete submission and involving the imagination of characters' past and future lives. Brecht in his dislike of empathy, and his belief in the *gestus* wanted the actor to distance himself from the part, so that he could always signal to the audience its provisional nature, its social conditioning. Accordingly, his characters lacked any 'focused inner life'. But between these two grand conceptions lies a more particular landscape of observation, and imitation, which the actor practises all the time. When preparing a role Laurence Olivier 'always tried to hit on some external starting point – be it a false nose, a wry smile, a specific person or just a pair of old boots – as a prop on which to build the rest of his performance' (Holden, p. 3). As the Captain in Strindberg's *The Dance of Death* he strutted like an officer on parade through his marriage, with all the assurance and insecurity which the non-promoted may often personify. Olivier's greatness arose out of many things which were physically calculated, however unconsciously acquired; he built the part inward from the outward thing. The terrible cry which he uttered as Oedipus when he realized the truth about himself was achieved like this: 'He read in a magazine of the way ermine are trapped in the Arctic: the hunters put salt on the ice, the ermine licks it and its tongue freezes to the ice. It was from the unique torment of the trapped ermine that Olivier conjured his devastating Oedipus scream. To him, the technique justified his belief that "it is next to impossible to produce the effect of great suffering without the actor enduring some degree of it."' (Holden, p. 249). Ralph Richardson built outward from an inward question such as 'what would he sound like?' The magic of a Richardson performance came from a feeling that however much observation had gone into the part, there was always something just out of reach in the role, for which he was searching, trying to pluck the heart out of the mystery which was someone else. And as we all do with ourselves, let alone other people, falling just short of the goal. Richardson's dissatisfaction with his acting, with his continued working at a role after the play had opened came perhaps from a profound, if unexpressed awareness, that we are strangers to one another, and to ourselves. When he was eighty, he still believed he had not achieved much.

At times – perhaps at all times – acting may depend on some intangible symbiosis between the role and the performer, as in this analysis of Peggy Ashcroft's relationship with Hester Collyer in Terence Rattigan's *The Deep Blue Sea*. 'She was married [at the time] to an eminent QC, Jeremy Hutchinson, and one of her two earlier marriages had been sexless. She was, by all accounts, a most passionate and amorous woman, whose enjoyment of sex with many lovers also shocked her sense of respectability. There is conflict between Hester's conventional manner and her relish of sex. Maybe Aschcroft truly found no common denominator between herself and the character [as she claimed] or maybe, like Hester, she had difficulty in acknowledging it' (Duff, p. 131).

Role-playing, masking, putting on costume and make-up have always been things which theatre has played with; and in the twentieth century drama has become more self-consciously aware of them. The theatre which held a mirror up to nature has also enjoyed holding a mirror up to itself. This is not something entirely new. Jaques in *As You Like It* knew that all the world's a stage, and all the people on it merely players. Coriolanus never forgets, or Shakespeare never forgets in writing *Coriolanus* the difference between political rhetoric, and the man within. In speaking at all, we are playing roles created by the language we command. Wittgenstein was right in saying, 'the limits of our language are the limits of our world'; but language is not the limit of our identities, and is frequently a concealment of our selves which are not unitary, shifting with our circumstances and our environment, physical and human. In this century, and particularly in the last fifty years, the language of drama has become more audaciously concerned with itself, and with this fact.

One of the great plays of the twentieth century, Pirandello's *Six Characters in Search of an Author* is about just this. At the start, the actors are rehearsing an earlier play by Pirandello, *The Rules of the Game*. Their rehearsal is interrupted by a family of characters whom their author has created, and then abandoned. They are looking for a play to be in; and, understandably, the director and his actors are irritated by this sudden invasion of their rehearsal. On the spaces of the Olivier stage in 1984, when Richard Pasco played the part of the Father, the family emerged mysteriously from the bright illumination of the stage door into the shadowy areas of the rehearsal space towards the front of the stage. Moving as a group, they seemed to find assurance from each other's proximity – ironically in terms of the subsequent action – as they advanced into a world which they did not understand, and was hostile to them. They demand to be heard, to find the author who has created them, and to understand the play for which their parts have been written. They come as supplicants who will not be ignored, and who interrupt the action which already is in rehearsal. They are both afraid of coming into the light, and at the same time are compelled to do so. The emergence of these visionary figures depends for its effect on their distancing at the outset from the actors on the stage – an effect which was destroyed in Franco Zeffirelli's production, when he filled the stage with movement and confusion.

The characters come to the dramatist out of the dark in an action which is not yet complete; whose meaning he does not yet know. Imaginative truth and truth to life are inseparable here, since we are all in search of an author, of a key to understanding the action in which we are involved; and are also surrounded as these characters are here by those who think, or appear to think, that their roles have been given in a play which is complete. We all emerge on a stage where the 'rehearsal' has been going on a very long time; and into which we insert ourselves, demanding to be heard, to speak our lines and to find ourselves truly represented. The irony of the action as it subsequently develops is that the actors in trying to play the roles of the characters turn them into people they are not, ascribe to them actions and feelings which they deplore, and turn their truth into a fiction. Only the characters in search of 'their' author have a certain identity; and their tragedy is that it is fixed; they are born to play themselves. The action of the play is created out of that gap which exists between what cannot be changed and what cannot be interpreted with finality.

This tension between what is fixed and subject to change

(Hamlet is always Hamlet, and always different) is grounded in the metaphor of the stage itself which is at one time the most limited and bounded of spaces: bounded by sight-lines (what the audience can see from all parts of the auditorium), and by the relation between stage and audience, whether in the round, on an apron or behind a proscenium arch. When we go to the theatre, our attention is focused on that illuminated and restricted space, the stage or acting area. But the stage is also the most boundless of spaces; it is finite, and also without an end, bounded without a boundary. What is happening off-stage may affect those on stage, as in Harold Pinter's *The Dumb Waiter* where the instructions placed on the dumb-waiter come from above, without those on the stage (or the audience) knowing who sends them. What the audience, and the characters can know about off-stage action is always limited; here too the stage reflects the determined and indeterminate nature of things. In Samuel Beckett's *Act without Words, 2* Beckett uses the stage as metaphor to suggest this:

Desert. Dazzling light.
The man is flung backwards on stage from right wing. He falls, gets up immediately, dusts himself, turns aside, reflects.
Whistle from right wing.
He reflects, goes out right.
Immediately flung back on stage, he falls, gets up immediately, dusts himself, turns aside, reflects.
Whistle from left wing.
He reflects, goes towards the left wing, hesitates, thinks better of it, halts, turns aside, reflects.
A little tree descends from flies, lands. It has a single bough, some three yards from ground and at its summit a meagre tuft of palms casting at its foot a circle of shadow.
He continues to reflect.
Whistle from above.
He turns, sees tree, reflects, goes to it, sits down in its shadow, looks at his hands.

A pair of tailor's scissors descends from flies, comes to rest before
tree, a yard from ground.
He continues to look at his hands.
Whistle from above.
He looks up, sees scissors, takes them and starts to trim his nails.
The palms close like a parasol, the shadow disappears.
He drops scissors, reflects.

The man when we first see him is being flung back on the
stage from the right wing (this is the stage, not a desert but the
desert is also a stage) by something, someone off-stage, and
what is off-stage we can never know; no more can he. When a
whistle summons him to the left, he tries that too, but hesitates
and thinks better of going out left. What is the nature of these
forces, which throw us to the ground, whenever we attempt
anything, and which nevertheless we resist by picking ourselves up, dusting ourselves down, reflecting and having
another go? Genetic, psychological, social, historical, economic? Or some complex combination of them all? We
cannot know. In life, as on the stage, you also cannot make
your exit until the author lets you go, if as here the means of
self-destruction are denied you. The meaning of what is happening cannot be fixed with certainty, just as life itself cannot
be fixed on a pin.

But stage space is also space to be played with. 'A little tree
descends from flies': the space above the stage where a piece of
scenery is concealed from the audience until it is required in
the play. Who causes it to be lowered, or subsequently flown
again? What it stands for, what it offers – temporary relief, or a
new torment? – these remain open questions. But it is
indisputably a stage effect, determined by design and lighting.
The meagre tuft of palms casts at its foot a circle of shadow;
and it is into this circle of shadow that the man will temporarily move, and where he will seek refuge from the pitiless desert sun. So playing with space is not just playing with stage as
space, but playing with space on the stage, and in doing so
establishing relationships between inner and outer worlds.

In deciding (though this is probably too conscious a word) what to illuminate in this stage-space, the dramatist may use as Shakespeare and Brecht do the distancing of historical time. In Brecht's *Mother Courage* set in the Thirty Years War of the seventeenth century, the progress of war 'in time' matters little. The town of Halle, which features in the final scene of the play, might be any town which the progress of the war threatens. The action of this so-called chronicle play is not a chronicle at all; its episodes resemble a series of superimposed snap-shots which reveal the effect of war on the lives and relationships of Mother Courage and her family. By the end of the action, she will have lost all three of her children, and will have to drag her cart, relentlesly on, over a windswept landscape, alone. In the final image of the Berliner Ensemble production, the cart receding into a frozen stillness, we are left simultaneously with an image of courage and loneliness, of courage and despair, of courage and baseness. Mother Courage has lost all and changed nothing. She has risked everything to survive, and survived alone. She has fed off the bones of war, and received her just reward. In a world, and a war, where necessity goes unchallenged, according to Brecht, out of ignorance, the repetitions of time only reflect the lack of a critical spirit which demands to know why. War as an implosion within human territory is being questioned, not war as a sequence in time. When this play begins, the war has already begun; when it ends, the war still goes on. The central image of the play is that of human society at war with itself, where dog eats dog. The figures of the seventeenth century speak to us out of the past, asking whether a world which has not changed at all, by 1939 (when Brecht wrote the play) or by 1996, has to be like this. The space which is illuminated is that of a space between people; a national and personal no-man's land, which becomes the territory of violence.

Brecht uses his illuminated space to show a social order which, whatever the names or the place, does not change. Timberlake Wertenbaker in the more recent *Our Country's Good* (1988) suggests that, while human nature changes very

little, the stage is a space where change can occur. Set in a
convict colony in Australia in 1787, the action of *Our
Country's Good* revolves around a debate as to whether the
proper entertainment for convicts is watching a hanging, or
whether the violence done to them by the society from
which they have been sent into exile might not be exorcised
by getting them to put on a play – the first Australian performance of Farquhar's *The Recruiting Officer* – whether they
might not be humanized by 'fine language and sentiments': a
tenuous enough argument, it might be thought. The action
begins with the savage flogging of one of the convicts on
the voyage out; it ends with laughter and clapping, and the
triumphant music of Beethoven's Fifth Symphony, as the
audience (or audiences in the convict colony and the theatre)
begin to watch the performance. Both have been recruited
into an action which moves from sullen cowed silence to
victorious affirmation. Convicts who begin without words
have been restored to language. The action has moved from
one state of feeling to another with that whirlwind motion of
which the drama is capable; and has sent the audience (both
audiences) away with the knowledge that inarticulate rage
and despair can be turned at least temporarily into something
other: that the illuminated space can not just question, but
transform (possibly) the 'nature of our little society'. 'The play
is a world in itself – a tiny colony we could almost say.' *Our
Country's Good* is concerned not just with what a play says,
but what a play can do; and in arguing the transformation of
which theatre is capable argues also by analogy for the same
possibility in society. 'The theatre is like a small republic, it
requires private sacrifices for the good of the whole.' The play
itself is an enactment, not so much of what it says, but what it
is: and it exploits the resources of the language of the theatre:
physical action, music, silence, lighting, costume and
suggestiveness.

★

Every production, and performance, has its moment. Even

though video recordings make possible a record, it can only be a historical record, interesting for its technique and its style. Theatre's power to take the audience out of itself, rises out of a mutual recognition between stage and audience, which is created out of the moment, and at the moment. A production and a performance may to a greater or lesser extent affect us like a dream. But every production has one thing in common with a dream. No one dreams yesterday's dream: the essence of dreaming, whether by day or by night, is of the moment, images fusing from past and present in a new apprehension. A performance, like a dream, is always something being worked out. Whether the play has been written six months or two thousand five hundred years ago, theatre is always born of this truth, which the producer and the actors discover. Peter Brook puts it like this:

> it became clear that a play of Shakespeare, and therefore a production of Shakespeare, could go far beyond the unity that one man's imagination could give, beyond that of the director and designer. And it was only through discovering that there was far more to it than that my interest moved from just liking the play, and therefore showing my own image of the play, to another process, which starts always with the instinctive feeling that the play needs to be done, now.
>
> This is a big change of attitude; without thinking consciously or analytically, there is this sense that this play is meaningful in many ways at this moment which opens a new awareness. It's not only that it's meaningful for me autobiographically at this moment. At certain points in one's life one can identify and wish to do a youthful play, a bitter play, a tragic play. This is fine, but one can then go beyond to see how a whole area of living experience that seems close to one's own concerns is also close to the concerns of the people in the world around one. When these elements come together, then is the time to do that play, and not another. (*SP*, pp. 78–9)

Peter Brook's productions of *King Lear* (1962), *The Mahabharata* (1988) and *The man who* (1994) mirror these transitions. Brook was drawn to *King Lear* as the 'the prime example' of the Theatre of the Absurd (*Waiting for Godot* had first been produced in England by Peter Hall in 1955). The barbarism and ferocity of the Second World War, and the almost unimaginable depths of cruelty in human nature that it revealed were still being absorbed into the consciousneness of Europe. Brook's production reflected this sense of horror and absurdity. By the time of *The Mahabharata*, a new global consciousness, created out of the migration of people, the mixing of cultures, the questioning of national identities made the moment right for its appearance, and its performance by actors themselves drawn from many different countries and cultural backgrounds. The production attempted to suggest both how Indian (and culturally different) *The Mahabharata* will always be, and its power to echo feelings which have been true for all mankind. As Yudhishthira says: 'Each day, death strikes and we live as though we were immortal' (p. 105). *The man who*, dramatized from Oliver Sacks's book on neurological disorders, reflected a quite different and growing preoccupation of the nineties, with the frontiers of human perception and behaviour, with the relations between mind and body, with the bizarre and inexplicable in human nature, at the crossing-points of consciousness. The last decade of the millennium seemed to combine a growing interest in science and medical research (Oxford University now has a Chair in the Public Understanding of Science) with a return to a sense of how mysterious and inscrutable human beings are; and the new frontiers into other spaces which the human brain may yet cross: space travel in both senses.

Productions do not reflect conscious intentions of this sort. Theatre, like other forms of art, is intuitive, catching things on the wing, only fully realized for what they are when they have passed. We have the experience, and only later know the meaning. There is an irony here, peculiar to theatre in all its forms. Although by its very nature theatre is transient, it is the transient thing which lives in the memory as a presence. Some productions seem, as the scroll moves on, to define a moment with a symbolic relation to past and future by the particularity with which they belong to the moment of their conception.

What Peter Brook identifies as the moment for a production applies equally to the preparation of a role. Every actor and actress goes about this in his or her own way, needing more or less direction from the director. Out of the subtle and complex chemistry between the roles of performer and director has grown the often aggressive argument in the last forty years beween those who resent a director's theatre, and those who applaud its achievements. In both roles the English stage has been inspired with a huge amount of talent since the Second World War. Its creative diversity, of which the country has every reason to be proud, has enabled the theatre to remain a place of exploration and invention, including directors as different as Peter Brook and Peter Hall, actors as different as John Gielgud and Steven Berkoff, companies with styles as different as those of the Royal Shakespeare Company (though the style is now that of a production, rather than that of a company) and Cheek by Jowl or Théâtre de Complicité. Whatever the relationship between actor and director, however the actor prepares his or her part, and whether or not the director has an idea or a concept for the production, all that matters in the end is the truth of the result; and this again is something which only the audience judges when the theatre has gone dark.

'Shoot first, ask questions afterwards' defines how theatre works, as Peter Brook has said. And the same is true of the actor who has to find within himself those other beings who temporarily he (or she) becomes. With the greatest actors this can become an almost physical transformation not just through make-up and costume; but as though another of the many selves we all bear within us has risen to the surface, like the Kraken from the deep, and transformed one person into someone else: the actor is quite literally a shape-shifter. Laurence Olivier's acting was memorable for this physical transformation, which became the inscape of the character. As Astrov in *Uncle Vanya*, Solness in The *Master Builder*, James Tyrone in *Long Day's Journey into Night*, Tattle in *Love for Love*, and the Captain in *The Dance of Death* he drew upon resources and strengths of an always shifting kind which affected his posture, his manner of walking, his physical deportment, down to the smallest detail. In his famous performance as Othello (1963), he took infinite pains in the training of his voice, to reproduce the intonations, the gestures, the rolling eyes which represented for him not just Othello's character as a Moor, but as a 'negro'. He belonged more to the Caribbean than to Cyprus, reflecting the words of the play 'Haply for I am black', but also what he saw around him in London. 'He would look and talk and walk like a negro – yes, a contemporary negro, of the kind now commonplace (if only recently) on the streets of London', drawing the play not always comfortably into 'the arena of race relations' (Holden, pp. 462–4). The performance as well as the production belonged to its moment.

The physical strain of giving such a performance is immense, as Tyrone Guthrie has pointed out:

It is not perhaps generally realized what a great physical, as well as intellectual and imaginative, effort is involved in the performance of a great role like Macbeth, Lear or Othello. A series of 'arias' have to be performed which, if they are to be adequate, make elaborate demands on the breathing apparatus, under the full resources of the voice from top to bottom. At some stage of the evening, athletic demands will be made – Lear must carry Cordelia, Hamlet must carry the body of Polonius; there are duels, battles. Othello must, after a violent struggle with Iago, feign epilepsy. In mere casual movement hither and yon upon the stage an actor will walk several miles in the performance of a big part, often in armour or dragging a great cloak; there will be several changes of costume, all of which have to be accomplished under the strain of very limited time. An important

thing to learn in the course of rehearsal is where and how
to rest, how to eke out the limited resources of energy so
that there will still be enough in reserve for the critical last
lap. All these are problems which do not arise in the film
studio. (Guthrie, p. 11)

Films are almost never shot in sequence; and actors may
have little sense of the performances being given by those in
scenes other than their own. Even rehearsals, as they occur in
the theatre, with the possibility of experimentation and rejection of the excessive are rare. Only the director really knows
when he has got what he wants; and then the scene is finished
In the theatre everything has to be recreated every night.
Whether it works, or how well it works, depends on a
dynamic between the actor, his fellow actors and the audience: a dynamic which changes every time the play is performed. Olivier, being congratulated on one occasion after a
performance of *Othello* replied angrily: 'I know it was great,
dammit, but I don't know how I did it. So how can I be sure
of doing it again?' (Holden, pp. 2–3) It depends, at least partly,
on the combination of an intense preparation and discipline
with an ability to let go and let the play perform. The pianist,
Alfred Brendel, writing about a concert performance,
summed up this interplay between preparation and spontaneity, demanding the utmost control and self-discipline, as it
applies to all the performing arts: 'You have to think and feel
in advance what you want to do and, simultaneously, to listen
to what you *are* doing, and react to that. You have to play to
satisfy yourself, and also play so that the people in the back
row will get the message' (Interview with A.Alvarez, *New
Yorker*, 1 April 1996, p. 55).

The impalpable element in a performance, the heart of its
mystery, which cannot be plucked out, or made to order, lies
in the imagination. As Stanislavsky realized, scenic truth is
not like truth in life. Stage truth is discovered by the actor
within himself, through imagination, and a 'childlike naivety
and trustfulness' which enables him to develop an artistic

sensitivity to the truthful in 'soul and body'. Simon Callow, describing the effect of a 'good performance', associates it with a 'dazzling mental clarity. The chambers of the brain open up one by one. The number of levels on which you are thinking is uncountable' (Callow, p. 200).

This sense of being totally present which all acts of imagination involve is brought by the great actor to every part, however small. 'No one can show, no one can really act what the audience sees a great actor do. He doesn't in point of fact do it. He suggests it to you and you do the work in your own imagination' (Miller, p. 4).

How a line is spoken – or can be spoken – depends on the actor's position on the stage whether he is sitting or standing – how near or far he is from everyone else on the stage. (These things matter very much less on film, where the camera angle, and sound-track determine the effect.) Simon Cadell (who died recently when he was only just over forty) recalled a lesson he had learned when he was twenty-two and acting with Richardson:

> When I got too close to him, within two feet of him on the stage, he said, 'Oh no. No. No, too close, you're in my bubble.' I understand it now totally. He knew that, unless one was playing an intimate scene with somebody, space on the stage is terribly important; and, if two characters who are not being passionately intimate get too close, the audience definition between the two disintegrates, and he called it his 'bubble'. It was in no sense ungenerous. (Miller, p. 246)

In 1978, five years before his death, Ralph Richardson played Firs in *The Cherry Orchard*. At the end of the play, when everyone is thought to have left the house which has been closed up for the winter, Firs suddenly appears again, abandoned, alone with his memories of the life and the lives he has known there. He is the sole survivor of a way of life which will not return. The axe is already starting to fall on the orchard trees; and the snapping of the string which symbolizes many different kinds of ending – including life itself – is about to be heard for the second and final time. What Richardson brought to this part had a special poignancy for those of us who had known and loved what he had brought to the theatre over many years. In playing Firs he created the dignity and eccentricity of the ordinary human being knowing he has to face his own death alone, and at a moment when the way of life which has given him his identity is also ending. As Kipling once said, there is something very lonely about the soul preparing to go away; and Richardson alone in the empty and silent house brought to those closing moments of the play the immense resources of an actor who could imagine what Firs was feeling. Not a feeling which could be articulated or expressed, but a feeling which everyone understood as inescapable, and to be confronted. His gift for perceiving poetry in the commonplace was joined here to silence – 'that paper on which the actor writes' – until broken by the falling of his stick at the moment of death.

This act of imagination which makes possible truthfulness in soul and body plays in turn upon the audience's imagination, and in doing so creates a sense of real presence more powerful than the presence of people in a room can often do.

Nora in Ibsen's *A Doll's House* has been played by many famous actresses, from Janet Achurch in 1889, to Eleonara Duse, Joan Greenwood, Anna Massey, Jane Fonda (in the film), Claire Bloom, Juliet Stevenson, and most recently Janet McTeer. How we respond to *A Doll's House* and what we think about it afterwards, depends to some extent on the degree of sympathy which we feel for Torvald: he can be anything, from odious bore to a man whose emotional intelligence is tragically limited by the conventions of his time. More crucially our response depends on the change which occurs to Nora in the middle of the fourth act. Here she changes from being Torvald's 'little song-bird' into a woman who realizes her survival depends on leaving her husband and children. As Shaw remarked, the sound of the front door

slamming was heard all over Europe. In the recent production
by Anthony Page (1996), with Janet McTeer, it was not heard
in the front row of the stalls. When Janet Achurch turned on
her husband, her performance was described like this: 'In the
last act this great actress would magnify herself into the magnitude of Boadicea, Brünnhilde and the Statue of Liberty
thrown into one' (Meyer, quoting James Agate, p. 112). In
overthrowing the petty tyrant, she became the champion of
women's emancipation (however much Ibsen denied it), the
expression of individual will and the charioteer, who, with
swords on her wheels, cuts down those who get in her way.
The type has not died out. Janet McTeer, creating the role in
1996, played Nora from the start as someone whose identity is
created by her role, and who discovers, to her cost, that the
two things are not the same. When the moment comes for her
to turn on Torvald, she does so not with triumph but with the
deepening pain of what she has to give up – her children and
her home – to discover who she is. She symbolizes a harsh
truth that sometimes it can be necesary to break down completely in order to discover a new self and a real identity. She
did not slam the door, because there was more pain in her
than anger; and the path she was going to take meant isolation,
hardship, and only perhaps renewal. In Janet McTeer's performance there was no triumph, only the hardening
recognition of what she had to do to survive. In the modern
world – without any obvious compass – that act of survival is
what most of us have to perform every day. Janet McTeer
created from the first moment of her appearance on the stage,
when she tore at the parcels she could not unwrap, the impression of a person under very great stress. This local observation
became part of her whole conception of the effect on people
of a close relationship proceeding to ruin, of reaching the
point where you know you can no longer cope. In every
gesture and movement she revealed a stress only partly understood, until it resolved itself into the deeper pain of knowing
she could not go on, without change. In reflecting the conscious and unconscious ways in which relationships disinte-

grate, Janet McTeer's performance was drawn from the air of its time.

The way in which an actor builds up a part depends on a combination of observation and technique, in which every actor likes to conceal a good deal of the mystery; and every actor has his or her own technique. As Richardson once remarked to a fellow actor about to be interviewed: 'Don't tell them how it is done!' In rehearsal, two processes occur, sometimes separately, sometimes together. Peter Hall has commented on this: 'I think more and more that rehearsal should be divided quite clearly between the learning of technique, and the creative process of the actor. We shouldn't confuse the two and that is what we always do. . . . There's teaching technique, and there's trying to provoke imagination, but separate them (Hall, p. 421). The learning of technique may include learning to sew, or appearing to play a musical instrument: in performance these acquired techniques may enable an actor to be 'absolutely present'; and at the same time free the actor so that the play 'performs'. As in many arts, not to appear to be doing it is the secret of doing it well.

Even the learning of lines presents an obstacle, and a technical problem which is overcome in different ways, for reasons which are far from technical. Noel Coward liked the cast to turn up to the first rehearsal word-perfect (not so difficult for him as he had often written the words) because otherwise so much time was wasted. Gielgud preferred a different approach:

> In my view, it is much easier to learn the words when you have the movements and the business. It is important to know how the other actor is going to speak his line so that both of you can react properly. If you start absolutely word-perfect, like a parrot, I think it makes every thing flat and dull. (Gielgud, pp. 45–6)

Some actors, even great actors, do not get to know their lines until the first night, and even then continue to be able to cover up lapses of memory by skilful ad-libbing, which the audience may even not notice, provided the rhythm of the performance is not broken. Edith Evans was notorious for not learning her lines, Ralph Richardson, for inventing when his memory failed him. 'One night when he was playing Sir Anthony Absolute in Sheridan's *The Rivals*, the cast heard him say: "So let me invite you to the Om-pom-pom-pom, where we will drink a health to the young couples and a husband to Mrs Malaprop. " But nobody in the audience seemed to notice. His inner rhythm . . . always preserved the metre . . .' (Miller, p. 207) Learning the lines is only part of the process of building a part in such a way that it relates to the performance of the company and that chemistry which can exist between stage and audience.

This process of transference can only occur when the technical skills of acting are matched with the profound imagining of the part, and its integration with 'the precise musical rhythm' of a production, through which we are constantly seeing what is not actually there. Alec Guinness takes enormous pleasure, quite rightly, in this power to conjure something out of the air.

It was during the rehearsals of *The Seagull* that I received, via Peggy Ashcroft, a sort of compliment that chuffed me no end. She returned early from a lunch break one day and found me, chewing an apple, in a corner of the stage. 'I've just had a squabble with Komis [the director, Komisarjevsky] about you', she said. My heart sunk a little. She went on, 'I said to him, "isn't it clever how that young man who pulls the rope to open the curtain makes you manage to see it?" and Komis said, "Not clever; he just pulls on a rope which hangs from the flies." When I pointed out that there isn't a rope he refused to believe me.' She looked at me almost doubtfully for a moment before adding, 'there *isn't* a rope, is there?' 'Of course not', I said. 'There's nothing.' 'That's what I told him. He'll be furious.' She moved away smiling; leaving me smiling too. Suddenly there was a new world hazily forming before my eyes; a world of mime which could create illusion; a world where props and scenery would be of minimum importance to the actor, an area where the actor's use of his body, his eyes, and above all his imagination, would create for an audience things they only thought they saw and heard. (*Blessings*, pp. 156–7.)

Alec Guinness defines here an essential element, not just in mime, but in all performance. You don't have to eat a meal in order to make an audience imagine you are eating it. In recent years, companies such as Shared Experience, Théâtre de Complicité, Theatre le Ranelagh, and those of Steven Berkoff and Robert Lepage have used this truth about theatre, and turned it into a style of dramatizing works as different as Tolstoy's *War and Peace*, George Eliot's *The Mill on the Floss*, Kafka's *Metamorphosis*, Oscar Wilde's *Salome*, Shakespeare's *Hamlet* and *Romeo and Juliet*; inventing concept productions, or reinventing plays like Dürrenmatt's *The Visit*. In the first production of *The Visit* by Alfred Lunt and Lynn Fontanne in 1960, Lynn Fontanne as the millionairess, who returns to her native village to buy the vengeance of the inhabitants on the man who had seduced her, had live leopards on stage as her pets. The savagery and vengefulness of Kathryn Hunter's looks some twenty-five years later dispensed with the need for their actual appearance. A single glance was as good as leash of leopards, and the simple act of mounting a step-ladder enough to suggest her power over the community she corrupts with her money. Performance in becoming more physical makes spectacular demands on the actors and also leaves more to the imagination of the audience. As Gregor Samsa who wakes up to find he is a beetle, Steven Berkoff suggested this physical change as he scuttled about the floor of his room, while conveying in his voice the increasing pain and loneliness of the son rejected by his family. Robert Lepage in *Seven Streams of the River Ota* (1996) staged an act of voluntary euthanasia in a silence which made the audience concentrate on the physical preparations for death, while at the same time

investing it with an unemotional dignity. Style in performance becomes a bore, when it becomes a routine, or predict-
able because it lacks the power to surprise, and only demands
of an audience that it watches what happens. A theatre
where the audience does not participate – to laugh, gasp, feel
terror, amazement, wonder – is dead. We go to be 'held in
thrall' by the skills of the performer, of whatever kind they
may be.

Skill in speaking lines, whether in verse or prose, has
remained one of the great strengths of English acting. It
requires immense control and discipline. No one, it was once
said of the young Olivier, could make blank verse sound more
blank. Gielgud was helped to learn his lines by trusting the
sweep of a whole speech, concentrating on the commas, full-
stops and semi-colons. 'If I kept to them and breathed with
them, like an inexperienced swimmer, the verse seemed to
hold me up and even disclose its meaning' (Gielgud, p. 78).
Gielgud's speaking of 'our revels now are ended' in Peter
Brook's production of *The Tempest* on the Drury Lane stage in
1957 will never be forgotten by anyone who heard it, as an
elegiac climax to an interpretation of Prospero in which
authority was never separate from the imaginative pain of
exercising it.

Every actor finds their own particular way of shaping a line,
and a speech; or is helped to do so by a director. Simon Callow
has recorded his debt to Peter Hall who showed him how in
speaking Shakespeare's lines, 'the meaning of the line often
resides in the second half, so go towards that, which has the
additional advantage of sustaining the forward movement of
the verse' (Callow, p. 125). The pulse of the line becomes a
window on the soul of the character being created. Every
human voice has its own timbre, pitch, range which is
unmistakeable; and how each performer uses that instrument,
makes use of its strengths and weaknesses differs. (A lightweight voice is unlikely to be right for the great tragic roles.)
In preparing a role, how a character sounds remains of central
importance. Peggy Ashcroft, rehearsing with Peter Hall the

part of Winnie in Beckett's *Happy Days* agreed on an 'Anglo-Irish lilt with a slight echo of her old friend Cecil Day Lewis' (Billington, p. 239). Judi Dench, playing the part of the well-known actress, Esmé Allen, in David Hare's *Amy's View* (1997) found a way of timing her lines to sound as though she was a very good actress speaking them off-stage: a precise combination of *rubato* and attack.

A successful performance is always 'well-judged': a subtle talent which combines an inner feeling for the part, and the ability to integrate it with the production as a whole. The director, and the actors, have to discover a way of speaking the lines which amounts to a vision, paring away ideas, however fertile, which do not fit, arriving at a consistency of feeling which relates every part to the whole. Dogberry, and the rest of the watch in *Much Ado about Nothing*, are indispensable to the plot as they succeed in arresting the villains, by 'comprehending all vagrom men'. Their persistent malapropisms (long before Mrs Malaprop) come like a breath of fresh air after the contests of wit between Beatrice and Benedict. (Oscar Wilde and Tom Stoppard do not provide such relief.) But Dogberry and Verges can easily become a bore, destroy the rhythm of *Much Ado*, if their performances are not 'well-judged', becoming caricatures of silly–funny men. Shakespeare's inventiveness with words must never be allowed to seem drunken.

Even more crucial because deeper feelings are touched, is the playing of the 'rude mechanicals' in *A Midsummer Night's Dream*. The carpenter, joiner, weaver, bellows-mender, tinker and tailor do not just provide comic relief; and the more they are over-played, the more tedious they become. They restore the human balance, with common sense and practicality, to the dreamy maze in which the lovers are lost; and, in their playing of *Pyramus and Thisbe*, they make us recall not just another kind of theatre with a doubtful seriousnes (to which the gentry, not to mention the intellectuals, are addicted), but the sheer fun of playing a wall, moonshine or a lion. They bring innocence to their playing, and discover for the first

time a love of theatre which shines over the play as a whole. As
Peter Brook has expressed it:

> the 'mechanicals' scene is often misinterpreted because the
> actors forget to look at theatre through innocent eyes, they
> take a professional actor's views of good or bad acting, and
> in so doing they diminish the mystery and sense of magic
> felt by these amateurs, who are touching an extraordinary
> world with the tips of their fingers, a world which tran-
> scends their daily experience and which fills them with
> wonder. (*SP*, pp. 100–1)

Peter Brook's sense here of something which must not be
violated by 'performance' applies equally to the speaking of
the lines. The nineteenth-century style of stepping forward,
and hurling the great speeches at the audience has sometimes
been replaced by shuffling them under the carpet as though
they do not exist, as though rhetoric is an embarrassment.
Because so many of Shakespeare's lines are well known, this
means depriving the audience of an anticipated pleasure,
whatever the intended gain in dramatic effect. You cannot go
to *Romeo and Juliet* without waiting to hear the actor say:

> O she doth teach the torches to burn bright!
> Her beauty hangs upon the cheek of night
> Like a rich jewel in an Ethiop's ear;
> Beauty too rich for use, for earth to dear!
> (Act I, scene 5).

If they are spoken without an instinctive feeling for their
sound, as well as their pace, their effect will be lost. But Shakespeare's plays must not become a series of operatic highlights,
because the drama as a whole requires a different musical
effect. Some 'classical actors', of whom Ian McKellen is the
most oustanding example, make the lines sound natural,
almost as though he is thinking aloud, discovering in them a
new emphasis and a natural rhythm. Tyrone Guthrie identifies

what happens when the right notation is found in this account of Edith Evans as Rosalind in *As You Like It*:

Edith Evans was nearer fifty than forty and I think that, for the first five or six minutes of her performance, audiences may have had reservations about the wisdom of this marvellous, but quite evidently mature actress playing the part of a young girl, wildly in love and masquerading as a boy. For my part I had no reservations whatever; from beginning to end the performance swept one along on the wings of a tender and radiant imagination. It was a comment upon womanhood and upon love, more interesting and moving, not less, because it had the ripeness and wisdom of experience. It was a feast of spoken music – a revelation to me of how Shakespearean verse, when wonderfully spoken, gilds the meaning of words – and opens the windows of the imagination in the way which the theatre uniquely can, but seldom does. This was a great performance.' (Guthrie, p. 166)

Only when words and performance are fused together can windows open on what lies within. Without this, Rosalind – like other Shakespearean characters – may simply seem to talk too much!

As well as an ear for the shape of a line, and a speech, an actor needs an attack which involves the whole being. Donald Sinden, recalling rehearsing with Peggy Ashcroft in *The Wars of the Roses* put it like this:

However well you know someone, there comes a moment when you're rehearsing when something changes. One moment it's 'Donald would you be awfully sweet and do this? And then there comes a point when you're not Donald but the character. We do it to each other. So in the death scene of the Duke of York – though we were getting on like a house on fire off-stage – suddenly I could see genuine hate in her eyes. I thought she can't hate me – we've just had a cup of tea together. But the character has completely taken over. So often you don't see it in the eyes. You simply see it in an attitude, a face, a voice. With Peggy you see it in furious close-up. (*Ashcroft* p. 201)

In some performances, for example, Olivier's Macbeth, this attack grew out of his whole conception of the role. He was guilty from the start: his single state of man shaken from before his first entrance by his thought, 'whose murder yet is but fantastical'. He grew in horror of himself, the more he put on kingly robes, reaching in the banquet scene, where he was clothed in royal purple, a crazed apprehension of the man he had become: a man who in acting out his fantasy shrank increasingly from the physical role this made him play. He conveyed, or held the audience relentlessly in the grip of, the widening gap between mind and body, so that as the outward trappings became more splendid, the inner life withered and died, appalled at its own extinction. Kenneth Tynan wrote in his review.

Last Tuesday, Sir Laurence shook hands with greatness, and within a week or so the performance will have ripened into a masterpiece: not of the superficial, booming kind, but the real thing, a structure of perfect forethought and proportion, lit by flashes of intuitive lightning. (Tynan, p. 157)

Ian McKellen's performance in 1976 was no less great, but an interpretation of an entirely different kind. His hair 'swept back like Toshiro Mifune in a Samurai epic' (Billington, *ONS*, p. 87), McKellen revealed the soldier who out of ambition turns into a killer, driven by his own inner evil. As with Olivier's performance, the shaping of the role grew out of its inner conception, which reached its climax in an 'epileptic frenzy' after the appearance of Banquo's ghost at the Banquet.

Physicality – the outward manifestation of the changing inner self as though the body bears the imprint of its inner notation – is one of the signs of performances which reach beyond the ordinary. When Michael Gambon in 1987 played Eddie Carbone, the New York lighterman who falls tragically in love with his own niece in Arthur Miller's *A View from the Bridge* his heavy shambling appearance reflected his occupation; but also quite literally a man who was being torn apart by emotions with which he could not deal, unable to conceal in his looks and his actions his jealousy of the young Rodolpho. As he moved around the room, or sat reading his paper, while his eyes followed the lovers, he became a man whose emotions had passed beyond all reason, making him dangerous to all those around him. His body expressed the emotions which his words could not reveal.

In 1998, Juliette Binoche played the part of Ersilia Drei in Pirandello's *Naked*, a role created on the London stage thirty years ago by another actress more famous in the cinema than on the stage, Diane Cilento. Ersilia Drei, not unlike Ibsen's Peer Gynt, feels herself to be nothing, to be naked, a woman whom people use without seeing anyone there. When she explains her attempted suicide she says: 'I couldn't believe that anything I might do . . . not even dying . . . would affect you. I thought I wasn't important enough. I thought I was nothing. And I wanted so much to be more than that. I wanted people to believe me. I wanted them not to pass by.' What was extraordinary in Binoche's playing came in the change from Act I, where she was still the hurt, confused woman just out of hospital, to the fierce defender in Act II of her own right to an identity, not just the person her lovers want her to be. As she told Franco, 'don't touch me', her eyes and her posture expressed the inner fury of a person who refuses to be saved by someone else's idea of them. In her clenched fierceness which seemed at times to be on the point of tearing her body apart, she expressed the loneliness and the courage needed not to give in to someone else's idea of her role. Binoche brought to this part the great star's sense of an inner emptiness and nakedness: the tragic relationship of acting to life where as Simon Callow has put it, 'life can sometimes seem a sad second'.

'Some plays (and productions) depend on bravura performances, in which the energy and technical skill dazzle on the surface, without suggesting any depths below (and no bad thing either!) Actors are entertainers; and their skills in entertaining give delight and hurt not. As with any artist, their talent for doing something supremely well communicates itself to the audience as a form of joy. The role of the Police Inspector in Eduardo de Filippo's *La Grande Magia* (1995) does not look much on the page; in the National Theatre production David Ross's postures and grimaces turned it into a comic impersonation of 'the great image of Authority' which is all gesture and no substance.

Sheridan's farce, *The Critic* depends for its success on timing, and technical skill: '*The two nieces draw their two daggers to strike Whiskerandos: the two uncles at the instant, with their two swords drawn, catch their two nieces' arms, and turn the points of their swords to Whiskerandos, who immediately draws two daggers, and holds them to the two nieces' bosoms.*' The timing, which needs to be musical in its precision, determines the impact of this entanglement. In *The Critic* as in Tom Stoppard's *The Real Inspector Hound* everyone has to perform with panache to make the play work at all; but the meaning of the play does not shift with the production. Congreve's *The Way of the World* is a much more socially complex play, though most of us go to see how Lady Wishfort, Mirabell and Millamant will be played; Margaret Rutherford's Lady Wishfort was immortalized in so far as a performance can be by Kenneth Tynan's account of it:

> Margaret Rutherford . . . got up as Lady Wishfort, the man-hungry pythoness. This is a banquet of acting in itself. Miss Rutherford is filled with a monstrous vitality: the soul of Cleopatra has somehow got trapped in the corporate shape of an entire lacrosse team. The unique thing about Miss Rutherford is that she can act with her chin alone: among its many moods I especially cherish the chin commanding, the chin in doubt and the chin at bay. My dearest

impression of this Hammersmith night is a vision of Miss Rutherford, clad in something loose, darting about her boudoir like a gigantic bumblebee at large in a hothouse. (Tynan, p. 124)

For a great Millamant, who could be loved not in spite of her faults but for her faults, we had to wait another twenty-five years when Maggie Smith played the part; and her words flowed, as Kenneth Tynan also said they should, whether 'tinkling like a fountain or cascading like Niagara' from a great height. Millamant is described just before she enters, in '*full sail, with her fan spread and streamers out, and a shoal of fools for tenders*'. Her performance has to fulfil these expectations.

The Importance of Being Earnest, like *The Way of the World*, continues to be revived partly because we want to see how every part, ranging from the moral priggishness of Jack to the innocent fatuity of Miss Prism, will be played. The appearance of Lady Bracknell is awaited with keen anticipation. How will she differ from the 'grande dame' immortally created by Edith Evans, and at least partially preserved on film? Her subsequent cross-examination of Jack as to his suitability for marrying Gwendolen delights, however many times it has been heard, by its combination of the Socratic with the absurd. One almost believes that only carelessness can account for having lost both one's parents. All the roles in *The Importance of Being Earnest* including Merriman the butler, are written to be performed with verve and style; they are all outward show and technique, and our pleasure is created from seeing how faultlessly, and how differently, they are done.

But there is another kind of performance, altogether stranger, which only occurs when an actor seems to bore deeper and deeper into the character as the play continues. It is made possible by a certain kind of dramatic writing; but the writing does not ensure – in fact nothing ensures – that it will occur. When Tennessee Williams's *The Glass Menagerie* (1944) went into rehearsal, Laurette Taylor had been cast to play the role of the mother, Amanda. She was then sixty and, although once a star, was living in retirement, in poor health and an alcoholic. With only a week to go before the opening, she 'attended the final rehearsals in what can only be called an alcoholic stupor, barely summarising the dialogue and so broadly defining the woman's southern accent and character that . . . she made the play sound like the Aunt Jemima Pancake Hour' (Spoto, pp. 110–11).

After a couple of half-empty performances – and thanks to a couple of reviews which recognized the spell of the play, and the poetry beneath its colloquial prose – something shifted.

> On the third night, Laurette Taylor was not simply dis-
> charging a half-formed role, she was creating a legend; she
> had begun to draw a more wonderful portrait than anyone
> could have imagined . . . she was continually working on
> her part, putting in little things and taking them out –
> almost every night in Chicago there was something new,
> but she never disturbed the central characterisation. Every-
> thing she did was absolutely in character.

She was to repeat the role in New York, establishing fame and fortune for Tennessee Williams, and creating a piece of American theatrical history. What reserves of strength and imagination Laurette Taylor drew on to create the role will always remain part of that mystery which makes actors – like all other people – tick. While playing Amanda in New York, she was diagnosed as having cancer, and frequently had to vomit when not on stage, during the performance. Four months after the production closed, she was dead. But, although Laurette Taylor in the view of the author almost came to direct some of the scenes in the play, the production had a wider significance which Arthur Miller expressed like this some years later.

> It is usually forgotten what a great revolution his first great
> success meant to the New York Theater. *The Glass Men-
> agerie* in one stroke lifted lyricism to its highest level in our

theater's history, but it broke new ground in another way. What was new in Tennessee Williams was his rhapsodic insistence that form serve his utterance rather than dominating and cramping it. In him the American theatre found, perhaps for the first time, an eloquence and amplitude of feeling. And driving on this newly discovered lyrical line was a kind of emotional heroism; he wanted not to approve or disapprove but to touch the germ of life and to celebrate it with verbal beauty. (Spoto, pp. 116–17)

Beauty was trapped not only in the net of words, but in those fragile glass animals so easily shattered, which symbolize all that the withdrawn and repressed daughter finds to love in her enclosed world. Walter Kerr, the well-known critic of the *New York Herald Tribune* was later to characterize Williams's gift in a way that links it with the success of Laurette Taylor's performance. 'What makes you an artist of the first rank is your intuitive gift for penetrating reality, without junking reality in the process; an intuitive artist starts with the recognisable surface of things and burrows *in*.' (Spoto, p. 188). Tennessee Williams's view that 'we're all of us sentenced to solitary confinement inside our own skins' became a motivating force and a *raison d'être* of his theatre in which writing joined to performance pierced that outer shell to reveal the living being beneath the skin. In 1994, Zoe Wanamaker recreated the role of Amanda in London, and showed once more how the steeliness and tenderness of Williams's writing survives the years, but requires that kind of performance which, like the mole, can work underground.

What happens on the stage, what an actors can do with the space in which they are given to act, depends on a dynamic relationship with the audience, which is being created, or destroyed every moment the show goes on. This dynamic is created from spatial relationships on the stage, and between the stage and the audience. As space is restricted, so is time. By its very nature a performance is transient. What happens between the audience and the performers can never be exactly repeated; and paradoxically this also gives a performance permanence: unique because unrepeatable. As with life itself, the moments as they pass cannot come again, and unlike the pages of a novel, can never be turned back.

Inventiveness, technical skill, discipline, control, daring and imagination are common to performers of every kind from the clown to the tragedian. The exclamations which greet the artist on the high trapeze make audible the silent wonder with which we respond to those who have mastered an art, and give to their audiences the shock of recognition at seeing how things are, by drawing us for a time into their illuminated space.

2
Words

KING: How fares our Cousin Hamlet?
HAMLET: Excellent. I'faith, of the chameleon's dish: I eat
         the air, promise crammed; you cannot feed
         capons so.
KING: I have nothing with this answer, Hamlet; these
         words are not mine.
HAMLET: No, nor mine now.

Hamlet (Act III, scene 2)

Silence, as has often been remarked, is the most effective thing in the theatre: 'the paper on which the actor writes'. The performance of a play begins with silence (the hush in the auditorium as the lights go down); and it ends in the silence of remembered images. The action of a play floats on silence. 'Drama', as Richard Eyre has said, 'is about the spaces between the lines' (Eyre, p. 34).

This may seem paradoxical, as the action of a play depends on dialogue. A chapter in a novel – Chapter 11 in Evelyn Waugh's *Vile Bodies*, for example – may be written entirely in dialogue, and be brilliantly funny as a result, but it draws attention to itself as a narrative device. Except in mime, characters on the stage converse: a fact which to the film buff, Dominic Tighe, in David Hare's *Amy's View* (1997) means theatre is outdated ('The image is much more important. The image has taken the place of the word.') Whether this is true or not, an ear for dialogue remains indispensable for the playwright; and his skill will often reveal itself with the greatest dramatic power at the point where words, phrases, exclamations shade into the inarticulate, leaving the audience to imagine what the character cannot fully express. Dialogue in a play needs to be

interesting to speak, to have its own rhythms and pitch; it also
needs to be interesting to listen to, which means what it does
not say, as often as what it does: to reflect the silence beneath
the lines. An actor has got to be able to speak the lines, inflect-
ing them in such a way that they become the voice of the role
as the actor feels it to be. He has to find a pulse which is
natural in them.

To find the pulse, the actor needs to be in complete control
of emphasis, rhythm and breath. And the second two go
together in creating pauses, which the audience will hear as
one form of silence. In the meticulously written plays of
Harold Pinter, where every comma and full-stop has the
equivalent of a musical value, the dramatist differentiates
between 'pause' and 'silence'. A pause controls, as a rest does
in music, how a phrase is played; but a silence is as much a
dramatic device as anything else which happens on stage. A
silence is like an exit or entrance. As Pinter has said, 'silence is
fear'.

This is so because an audience listens in a state of expectation. Silence is uncomfortable, disconcerting, painful, as it
can be off the stage. Whatever can he or she be thinking,
feeling, planning to do? Silence makes us all nervous; how
long we can bear it expresses our 'nerve'. In the theatre, the
audience fills the silence: 'each motionless listener is part of
the performance'. But silence is not just 'fear' as Pinter suggests. Michael Frayn in his profound play, *Copenhagen* (1998),
about the meeting between the Danish physicist, Niels Bohr
and Werner Heisenberg, the German physicist in Copenhagen in 1941 centres his action around the question about
what they actually said to each other concerning the possibility of creating an atomic bomb. The various possibilities about
the nature of that crucial conversation lead to the conclusion
that perhaps Bohr saved the West from a nuclear attack by not
asking Heisenberg the *one* question which would have made
him see the critical omission in his calculations. On such
'unsureness' and 'indeterminability' the fate of nations, and
people, often depends. Margrethe, Bohr's wife, who often acts

as a kind of choric commentator on their dialogue says at the end of what passes between them: 'Silence. The silence we always in the end return to.' It is an explosive comment on the nature of theatre, and the way in which performance interprets a text.

The action of a play takes place in the imagination of the audience; and during a silence that action continues, as it continues after the curtain has fallen. The silence in the theatre when 'you can hear a pin drop' is caused by the intensity with which that act of imagination continues; the audience is quite literally in a state of suspended animation. (The same effect is impossible in the cinema because the camera is always rolling, the sound-track never blank.) Here, we can see one reason why Brecht's rejection of empathy does not work. He wanted us not to empathize with his characters, so that we could judge their actions and ask ourselves why they acted as they did (for example, Mother Courage's dependence on the war); and whether things were necessarily like this. But it is not only a character or characters with whom we empathize; we become imaginatively involved with the action of the play, playing it out in our own mind's eye. And this does not result from a particular way of writing a play, as Brecht claimed, but from the nature of theatre itself. We go to see a play performed; but there are in fact two performances. The first we watch on the stage, the second is being enacted in the imagination of the audience. Silence in a play, whether written in by the dramatist, or played by the company, at the director's suggestion, allows this interaction a breathing space, a moment of drawing back so that it can then surge forward. To imagine an action we need time to see through it.

Like everything in the theatre, the writing of dialogue depends on a conjuror's magic. The banality of everyday conversation has to be transcended, in its verbal flatness, and its lack of a taut dynamic. Conversation drifts like smoke; dialogue in a play needs the strength of steel wire, to have an inevitablity which is constantly shaping the action, to have, though we do not realize it at the time, a goal. But at the same time we need to feel that this is how people speak, or have spoken. Keith Dewhurst, reviewing Ralph Richardson's performance in David Storey's *Home* (1970) where he and John Gielgud played two elderly men in a mental institution, put it like this: Richardson 'has a strange elegiac quality, a cadence of winds and weather, and seasons of the year, that enables him to express like no other actor something that is at the heart of English drama, and thus of *actually being English* [my italic]: something instinctive and involuntary in the rhythm of both phrase and situation that recurs whatever the style or generation' (Miller, p. 229). Winsom Pinnock in *Leave Taking* (1994), about a Jamaican family living in London, draws on the 'patwah' of a culture whose rhythms and colloquialisms have been influenced by reggae music. Words in a play reflect these heart-beats in a way that the dramatist cannot always explain. 'I learnt that when we no longer have the words to explain our choices we are on dangerous ground. It is this dangerous territory that is most exciting in the theatre' (Winsom Pinnock, Programme Note to *Leave Taking*). Tennessee Williams's ear for the intonations and rhythms of dialogue in the South of the United States needs to be interpreted with the accuracy of a musical score; an English actor who could not hear the beat would be unable to perform the part.

Dialogue always reflects and heightens the conventions of its time. Oscar Wilde's characters speak in witty and elegant epigrams, closer to a convention about how people should speak in 'high society' than would be the case today. Wilde was not alone in thinking that style was everything; he just had more of it than most of his contemporaries. At the opposite extreme, the breakfast conversation between Meg and Petey at the start of Pinter's *The Birthday Party* (1958) – which was eventually to establish his reputation – reflects and heightens contemporary banality, with an effect that is both very funny and disturbing. I saw the play in Oxford, before its disastrous failure in London. The humour and, later, the brutality of the dialogue made a lasting impression because nothing quite like this had ever been heard on the stage before.

What was not clear then was how deep-rooted and capable of development Pinter's originality was to prove:

> MEG: Here you are, Petey.
> *He rises, collects the plate, looks at it, sits at the table. Meg reenters.*
> Is it nice?
> PETEY: I haven't tasted it yet.
> MEG: I bet you don't know what it is.
> PETEY: Yes, I do.
> MEG: What is it, then?
> PETEY: Fried bread.
> MEG: That's right.

It isn't just a question of class or sharpness (though it is both of them) which distinguishes this piece of dialogue from another breakfast conversation between the Dangles at the start of Sheridan's *The Critic*:

> *Mr and Mrs Dangle are discovered at breakfast reading newspapers.*
> DANGLE *(reading): Brutus to Lord North. — Letter the Second on the State of the Army —* Psha! *To the first L dash D of the A dash Y. — Genuine extract of a letter from St. Kitts. — Coxheath Intelligence — It is now confidently asserted that Sir Charles Hardy —* Psha! Nothing but about the fleet and the nation! — and I hate all politics but theatrical politics. Where's the *Morning Chronicle?*
> MRS DANGLE: Yes, that's your Gazette.

Drama responds to the pulse of its time; and so it has to reflect 'in some way' an audience's conventions (and expectations) about how people speak to each other outside the theatre: the rhythms, if not the chosen words, reflect conventions of discourse. These are often exaggerated, as in Wilde, to give the audience a sharper version of themselves, and their society. In Patrick Marber's *Closer* (1997), characters' speeches are seldom longer than a line, and bring to the surface what is often felt but seldom articulated. As Hamlet knew, a play gives 'the very age and body of the time his form and pressure'.

As well as reflecting rhythms, and intensifying idioms of contemporary speech, a play draws upon the conventions of contemporary theatre, and the expectations of an audience about how people will speak on the stage. (The initial rejection of Pinter's *The Birthday Party* was caused in part by its failure to fulfil these expectations.) As Martin Esslin has shown in *Brecht: A Choice of Evils* (1959) Brecht 'achieved the rare feat of creating in his poetry and plays a language all his own, which suggested the rhythms and gave the feeling of real speech without being tied to any particular regional dialect. It is still not a language spoken by anyone in reality – with the exception perhaps of Brecht himself. But while it is a synthesis, this language is such a vital and original synthesis, so deeply rooted in a number of different traditions, that it creates the illusion of real speech' (Esslin, p. 96). This ability to draw upon the rhythms of contemporary speech without using the exact words is perhaps not so rare after all, but the basis of all dramatic dialogue. The gap between talent and genius lies in the vocabulary. Pinter has spoken about his interest in, his ear for, the oddities, of everyday speech, since boyhood; and at the same time his concern for the rhythm and harmony of a sentence. When writing he often speaks lines aloud to see if they please his ear. Brecht's case, like Pinter's, is only extreme because both are poets.

The soliloquies in Shakespeare's plays developed out of rhetorical conventions in earlier Elizabethan drama: speeches of lamentation and expectation, expressions of intent and reflection, of greeting and farewell, in which characters made speeches without reflecting the idiosyncrasies of individual accent. Elizabethan love of word-play, punning, new-minted words and phrases, aphorism and paradoxes were absorbed into these larger structural devices, and in Shakespeare's case assumed an individual accent. He drew his words from every level of society, from every age of man, from the countryman to the townie, from the courtier to the King, from whores to Queens, from tradesmen to merchants, from noblemen to the poor naked wretches who bide the pelting of this pitiless storm. He made everything out of living at a time when the English language was exploding, and human reflection about the self was going into a new orbit. Play with language, with syntax, rhetorical structures, and play with the nature of the self resulted in the sublimity of Hamlet's reflection:

> I have of late, but wherefore I know not, lost all my mirth, foregone all custom of exercises; and indeed, it goes so heavily with my disposition that this goodly frame, the earth, seems to me a sterile promontory; this most excellent canopy, the air, look you, this brave o'er hanging firmament, this majestical roof fretted with golden fire: why, it appeareth nothing to me but a foul and pestilent congregation of vapours.' (Act II, scene 2)

The interjection of the 'look you' breaks up the speech, making it suddenly colloquial, and provides the opportunity for varied interpetation by the actor.

Hamlet is of his time; but in his power of expressing himself transcends it.

In *Love's Labour's Lost*, love of language results in the comic pedantry of Holofernes:

> You find not the apostrophus, and so miss the accent: let me supervise the canzonet. Here are only numbers ratified; but for the elegancy, facility, and golden cadence of poesy, *caret*. (Act IV, scene 2)

Holofernes did not miss the accent of his time; but heightened and exaggerated it. The twists of the phrasing, the emphasis on selected words, and the onward thrust of the speech, require no less skill of the performer, than Hamlet's. Though both speeches are written in prose, both relish their own music.

Shakespeare still leaves to the actor the test of finding the pulse in the phrasing, turning the punctuation to pauses and discovering a pitch for the words which resonate with the rest of his performance and the rest of the cast. The words are like moving shuttles of the 'enchanted loom' which is the text as a whole.

Long speeches, whether sublime or pedantic, are not the modern manner. Those who make long speeches cause the eyes to glaze over: perhaps because we have lost even Holofernes's enjoyment of playing with words; perhaps because we no longer wish to listen to each other, except as a form of debate, or lack the necessary powers of concentration. Long speeches in life require an apology, though those who make them do not usually seem aware of the fact; counsellors and therapists are paid to listen. Long speeches in drama need a justification, and make special demands on the actor. Bernard, the English lecturer in Stoppard's *Arcadia* (1993), played by Bill Nighy with undashable self-admiration, likes nothing more than giving lectures, without the least interest in whether anyone wishes to listen. Speechifying is his *modus vivendi*; the longer he keeps talking, the more he prevents others from revealing his hollowness, or puncturing his vanity. In David Hare's *Amy's View* (1997) Esmé Allen, a famous actress, keeps talking to protect herself from the fear which, as she admits, touches all actors of not having a role, or a less good role, outside the play.

Outside the theatre, as inside it, making long speeches has become a suspect gift, practised, for example, by politicians, who by common consent do not mean what they say, and do not intend to practise what they preach. Making speeches may be a cover-up for charlatanism, or more simply a way of persuading others to let you do what you want to do, whether or not (which is more likely) you intend to do what you are asking their consent for. Conventions and attitudes outside the theatre determine what is said on the stage. The memorable long speeches in contemporary plays as in life are to be found in moments of self-confession, under the pressure of insupportable feeling, as in Lucky's outburst in Beckett's *Waiting for Godot* (1955) or Aston's account of electro-convulsive therapy in Pinter's *The Caretaker* (1960). But characters who make long speeches may not necessarily mean what they say. Words paper over the fear of silence.

The major transition from Shakespeare to the present day has been from the rhetorical, and expansive, to the laconic and monosyllabic; from the articulate to the 'unnameable'; from a society which loves and flourishes on its language to one which increasingly ignores it, or lets 'fuck' and 'fucking', as in the plays of David Mamet, express the weight of personal feeling.

> I know of no one who has caught more precisely than Mamet the pathos of the dim and unverbal in their desperate attempts to express themselves with language which is dead and repetitive. They say 'fuck' every other word, because that is their only way of getting emphasis. It is pathetic and moving. (Hall, p. 364)

In everyday speech the four-letter word has no such effect, and is merely boring in repetition. Mamet's skill comes from his placing of it in the rhythm of the line, his ear for the shape of a line and the imaginative resonance of the play as a whole, which Peter Hall is describing. Patrick Marber's *Closer* uses 'fucking' and 'coming' just as repetitively but for a different purpose. Although his characters have occupations (a doctor, a journalist, a photographer and a stripper), they have become their sex lives; and their vocabulary is mainly restricted to its gains and losses. As in an expressionist play, these characters express impulses, desires, drives, satisfactions and resentments, with an honesty more commonly felt than articulated. Their words define their identity; and that identity is constructed out of their sex lives. Marber is perhaps commenting on this reductiveness, and at the same time dramatising its compulsive honesty. Mark Ravenhill in *Shopping and Fxxxxxg* (1996) goes even further in making the language of sexuality, physical and verbal, an expression not of relationship but of transaction. Words, like money, become a form of surface exchange.

Dialogue in a play is not how people speak (though they might like to do so) outside the theatre; but it is not altogether separate from it. Just as the brushstrokes of a painter do not depict a leaf or ship, but suggest to us that we are looking at a thousand leaves in the wind, or a sailing ship on a choppy sea, so words spoken on a stage create an illusion of being drawn from life. The ways in which this illusion is created are as various as those of the painter's brushstrokes, but the further they seem to be removed from everyday speech the more artificial the action will become. Because dialogue is in this sense surrogate speech, the idiom has to be right for, seem natural to, the audience, however stylized it is.

New ways of writing dialogue create new dramatic forms. Konstantin Trepliev in Act I of Chekhov's *The Seagull* (1898) knows this, and attempts his own solution.

> *On a large stone sits Nina, dressed in white:*
> NINA: Men and lions, partridges and eagles, spiders, geese and antlered stags, the unforthcoming fish that dwelt beneath the waters, starfish and creatures invisible to the naked eye; in short, all life, all life, its dismal round concluded, has guttered out.
>
> (translated by Elizaveta Fen)

It will not be long before this new form of drama has been mocked off the stage by Konstantin's mother, Arkadina, the famous actress, who is irritated by these 'poetic ravings'. Arkadina's behaviour is cruel and rude; but she is right, this new theatrical form is going to become a bore and yet for a moment – as Nina will recall just before Konstantin kills him-self in Act 4 – the stage, the lake, the moonlight, even the language itself (in her final words to him she repeats the speech above) hovered, like the seagull itself, on the edge of something new. The feeling was of a new dramatic form, an image. But the problem, also apparent to Arkadina who as an actress understands theatre, lay in the absence of characters, of people who spoke to one another as people do; and Chekhov's triumph, the new form of drama which he created in *The Seagull* as a whole, was created from a new way of writing dialogue. The action which is created out of dialogue reflects discourse outside the theatre, but it is also a technical skill needed for writing a play that works, as Konstantin has discovered to his cost.

The characters in Chekhov's *The Seagull*, the dramatic images they compose, are not in themselves new; they could come out of his earlier plays, *Platonov* (the manuscript was not discovered till 1923, but it was written in the 1880s) and *Ivanov* (1887). In their secluded lives on a country estate, they are closely related to the characters in Turgenev's *A Month in the Country* (1850). The suicide with which Chekhov ends *The Seagull* repeats the melodramatic ending of *Ivanov*, which had given Chekhov his first theatrical success in 1888.

In *Ivanov*, characters speak about their inadequacies, sorrows, torments, illness, love; and they fritter away their days like their lives in games of cards, and idle romances. They tell us what is happening to them. In *The Seagull* we see what is happening to them. We see how empty or full their lives are, how sincere or pretentious their feelings; we see how life is not one thing or another, but made of a multitude of conflicting, irreconcilable things, feelings, desires, impulses. Arkadina can want as Mother to bandage Konstantin's wound, but she can bitterly resent him as son whose talent (if that is what it is) she does not understand and rejects. Arkadina wants to be a mother, and at the same time resents her son's demands for maternal affection and money. What is new lies in the intensity of our seeing, and feeling: the dialogue acts like a window through which we see; or one window, because the action is made from all that happens on the stage. (For example, the proximity *and* distance between mother and son, which Vanessa Redgrave and Jonathan Pryce played with physical endearment and violent repulsion.) Chekhov's stage is a very

Making Theatre

physical place, a head turned, a look averted can signal disaster. When Dorn says at the end of Act 1, 'how distraught they all are!' he confirms, like a Chorus, what we already know.

The transparency of Chekhov's characters becomes possible through a manner of writing dialogue which refracts light from different sources into a single focus on their inner isolation. This technique, like a fibre-optic cable, becomes capable of carrying more and more complex images in each of the three plays which succeed *The Seagull*.

In *Three Sisters* (1901), Masha knows that Vershinin, her lover, is leaving town with his regiment; and she will not see him again. There return to her memory, as often in such moments, some lines of poetry with no apparent connection:

> A green oak stands by a curving shore
> And on that oak hangs a golden chain

What we see is that the golden chain saves her from total breakdown, insanity. The images of the 'oak' and the 'chain' are all, quite literally, she has to hang on to; and the fragment of a tune which she and Vershinin had once hummed to each other. Between the lines of the text, the inner lives of the characters have to be performed.

The stage direction to *The Cherry Orchard* (1904), Act II, reads:

> *Open fields, a way-side shrine – old, crooked, and long neglected. Beside it – a well, large slabs which were evidently once tombstones and an old bench. A path can be seen leading to the Gayev estate. At one side rise the dark shapes of poplars; this is where the cherry orchard begins.*
>
> *In the distance is a row of telegraph poles, and a long way away on the horizon a large town can just be made out, visible only in very fine clear weather. The sun is just about to set.*

Here is a landscape of confused images, belonging to a half-forgotten past, and a future not yet created, both theatrical and of their time. Of the figures on stage, Charlotta, the German governess, is the most prominent. She has taken a gun off her shoulder.

> Where I come from and who I am, I don't know. Who my parents were – whether they were even married or not – I don't know. (*Gets a cucumber out of her pocket and eats it.*) I don't know anything.

Each one of these images, so different in kind, compels us to construct a mental picture of lostness, uncertainty and near-desperate loneliness: a world waiting to be born into certainty, on the edge of suicide and absurdity. Chekhov's dialogue reflects a time when outward confidence, the self-assurance of the individual belied an inner distress. His plays do not point, as has been suggested, to the need for a Russian revolution, but they do reflect an awareness of how people are trying to live without a compass, and need a new world to be born, to give them a goal which in life, if not in art, has been lost. He made his characters seem to speak as they would off the stage, but all the time he was compressing their speech to expose a new form of existential despair. He brought to this the wisdom of humour. This relationship between humour and despair needs to be reflected in the dress, deportment, spacing and lighting of the characters, both in their relation-ship with one another, and their unredeemable solitude. The text is like a scaffold through which the audience sees and feels.

Harold Pinter, in his early work, created a form of dialogue which expressed that sense of menace, far from specific, which hung in the atmosphere after the Second World War. How could it not do so, when 'subjectively all was possible'? The beginnings of Pinter's creative work lie close in time to the dramatization of *The Diary of Anne Frank*; itself an account of an imprisoned life, outside the walls of which a hideous barbarism prowls in search of its Jewish prey. A fear, as yet unknown, though even more terrible in actuality than imagination could conceive it, creates the fabric of Pinter's world, just as it had of Anne Frank's. And so it had for the world at large. No one since 1945 can live free from the fear of the depravity of which human beings are capable. And this fear infects feeling and language. Dialogue has come to live on the edge of the bestial. Theatre as always stalks its prey in the changes taking place in the world outside it; but, unlike that world, its dialogue moves to an end, the final curtain, relentless as a reaper.

*

Words in a play reflect the idioms of their time. Equally they are created by the conventions of theatre. Conflict in drama arises from the difference between the image characters have of each other, and the image they have of themselves. Words act as forms of self-protection, and self-revelation. When the first is inadequate, we are seen through; when the second misleads, words act as a trap for the unwary. The interest of a character on the stage, for the audience, involves a question about what he or she is really like. And the harder the question is to answer, the greater the dramatic interest will be (for a contemporary audience, at least). What does it mean for Hamlet to describe himself as mad 'but north-north-west'? How much the actor allows the audience to see into the soul of the character will determine at every moment the effectiveness of the interpretation. As with everything else about a performance, it must be 'well-judged', of a piece. Performance as a subtle art of self-revelation and self-concealment grows out of a much more ancient theatrical tradition: that of masking.

Masks, physical and metaphoric, are among the most ancient conventions of theatre. They continue to be central to performances throughout India and the Far East, in the Noh drama of Japan, as in the religious festival dramas of Bhutan. A mask enables a spirit to enter into the performer, and become what the mask presents, whether Krishna dancing under the stars in the theatre of the world, or Kali the destroyer.

In Greek tragedy the mask enabled actors to take on roles from the mythical past, and achieve the stature of heroes. In a recent production at Epidauros in Greece, and later at the National Theatre in London, Peter Hall used masks to suggest the archetypal nature of the drama which was being performed, as he had for the *Oresteia* in 1981. But, since there is no tradition of using physical masks in English drama, they present special problems for the performers, requiring special rehearsal techniques, and for the audience, who are unused to responding to the different notation of individual masks. To an unpractised audience, reading the visual signs of the mask, while listening to the complex flow of the words is a difficult task. In the Western European tradition, masks are more often felt than seen.

Shakespeare uses masks for local and psychological ends. In *Love's Labour's Lost* the ladies mask themselves to deceive the wrong men into making love to them, proving their infidelity. Romeo goes masked to the Capulets' feast to avoid detection as a Montagu. In the final scene of *Much Ado About Nothing* the lovers unmask when the moment for dénouement arrives:

HERO: And when I liv'd I was your other wife (*unmasking*):
And when you lov'd you were my other husband.
(*Much Ado About Nothing*, Act V, scene 4)

Masking arises out of the dramatic situation and has an important bearing upon the relationship of characters to one another. Juliet in the balcony scene expresses it like this:

Thou knowest the mask of night is on my face,
Else would a maiden blush bepaint my cheek
For that which thou hast heard me speak tonight.
(*Romeo and Juliet*, Act II, scene 2)

The image expresses the freshness and innocence of Juliet's young love; and this metaphorical form of masking – the invisible mask – is used by Shakespeare in many different ways.

Disguise itself is a form of masking. Viola in *Twelfth Night* and Rosalind in *As You Like It* disguise themselves as men in order to survive in a new world; Kent disguises himself as a poor man in order to continue to serve his outcast master, Lear. In *Much Ado About Nothing*, Margaret pretends to be Hero, and deceives Claudio into thinking that she is unfaithful the night before their wedding. Mariana pretends to be Isabella in Angelo's bed in *Measure for Measure*. Stage conventions about masks not being detectable are indispensable to the dramatic structure, requiring the audience's willing suspension of disbelief.

This form of masking, or disguise, soon disappears from the Western European tradition, except in *commedia dell' arte*. Elsewhere it becomes further internalized and psychologized, finding its expression in words. We are not simply the people we say we are; the self we present to one person remains different to the self we present to another. In the character of the young Henry V, Shakespeare dramatized this kind of masking too:

> I know you all, and will awhile uphold
> The unyoked humour of your idleness;
> Yet herein will I imitate the sun,
> Who doth permit the base contagious clouds
> To smother up his beauty from the world
> That when he please again to be himself
> Being wanted, he may be more wonder'd at,
> By breaking through the foul and ugly mists
> Of vapours that did seem to strangle him.
>   (*Henry IV, Part One*, Act I, scene 3)

From that moment on, we know that the identity in words and actions which Hal presents to his friends, Poins and Falstaff, involves a temporary concealment; and that, before

the play is done, he will reveal himself in new words and
actions, as he does in his rejection of Falstaff:

> I know thee not, old man: fall to thy prayers;
> How ill white hairs become a fool and jester!
> I have long dream'd of such a kind of man,
> So surfeit-swell'd, so old and so profane;
> But being awak'd, I do despise my dream.
> (*Henry IV, Part Two*, Act V, scene 5)

Much has been written about the rejection of Falstaff, and the
cold indifference of Hal to his former friends now he has
become King: the indifference of power which shores itself up
with a newly acquired morality. The complexity of our
response is born of the knowledge that however cynical and
mean Falstaff has become in the war, youth, festivity, life itself
is being rejected with him. The dream Hal now despises bears
little resemblance to the 'dream' he once had. Shakespeare
gives a clear insight into the nature of dramatic dialogue as
being composed of verbal identities which only partially represent the inner person; and which, when another identity
wishes to come out from 'behind the clouds' will need to find
another vocabulary to project itself.

The case here is extreme; Hal foresees the need at the outset; and then apparently forgetting it, though the audience
does not, continues to live out his youthful identity until his
father is dead, and the time arrives for him to assume the
crown. Then the new identity presents itself in new words,
and a new bearing which only his physical deportment on the
stage can characterize.

The passage of time, though scarcely referred to, from the
start of *Henry IV, Part One*, to the conclusion of *Part Two*
separates out these two identities with clarity. More normally
they are seen simultaneously. We see through the surface of
words to the person beneath, as the other characters on the
stage cannot. As Duncan remarks shortly before he is
murdered, 'There's no art to find the mind's construction in

the face.' We know what he does not. The art of performance requires that the audience should be aware to a greater or lesser degree of subterfuge.

In one case – that of Iago – this transparency is suddenly cut off like a shutter coming down; and the contrast of this shows up our normal expectations. When in Act V, scene 2, of *Othello*, Iago is unmasked by his wife, Emilia, as the architect of the tragedy, he replies:

> Demand me nothing: what you know, you know:
> From this time forth I never will speak word.

Although Iago has given several reasons during the course of the play for his envy of Cassio, and his hatred of Othello, his 'motiveless malignancy' remains one of the play's enigmas. When offered the chance to come clean at the end, he chooses to shut up. The audience is denied the transparency made possible through an articulated identity. This is not a criticism of *Othello*; on the contrary, it remains a source of its fascination. To say that Iago is cloven-footed, the devil personified, does not answer the case because Shakespeare does not throw in allegorical characters; his characters are created out of verbal surfaces which allow us to see the depths beneath them. Iago's silence has a special, if not unique, place in dramatic literature, in that even to the audience he refuses to reveal himself. Simply the thing he is has made him live. And his performance must remain enigmatic, the outcome of motives which are not self-consistent.

The tragedy of *Richard II* arises not out of his unwillingness to speak, but out of the inadequacy of words to represent who he is. As he knows, he sets the word against the word. The more he projects images of himself, the more he realizes their brittleness and shallowness: the mirror where he sees himself reflected, and which he breaks in despair, destroys the image of the man he has constructed, or tried to construct for himself and others.

Richard the Second whether played as poet–king by

Michael Redgrave or ironic self-mocker by Jeremy Irons is doomed to live and die without finding what lies behind the mirror. His words, however sonorous and beautiful to listen to (which they are) can never reflect what lies below; they only reflect themselves back to the speaker.

> 'Tis very true, my grief lies all within;
> And these *external* manners of laments
> Are merely shadows to the unseen grief
> That swells *with silence* in the tortur'd soul.
>
> *(Richard II*, Act IV, scene 1)

Words confer roles. In Richard's case to lose the name of king is to lose his role. But the word 'king' does not fit the character underneath: its tortured soul is doomed to silence.

An actor is sometimes described as completely miscast in a particular role. The phrase signals a profound relationship between role-playing and identity, and with a modern awareness that identity is not a single, but a multiple thing. We are made up of many selves, and our roles are determined by the stage on which we are playing. Some three hundred years after Shakespeare, Pirandello used this idea as a new way of thinking about theatre, and its mirroring of the masks which are worn in everyday life.

In *It is so, if you think so!* (1917) Pirandello, like Shakespeare in *Richard II*, poses the question of the mirror, and what it reflects. Laudisi, like Richard, finds when looking in the mirror his image mocking himself: 'Between you and me, we get along very well, don't we! But the trouble is, others don't think of you just as I do . . . I say that here, right in front of you, I can see myself with my eyes and touch myself with my fingers. But what are you for other people? What are you in their eyes? An image, my dear sir, just an image in the glass! They're all carrying just such a phantom around inside themselves . . .' (translated by Arthur Livingston). Irony and complex truth here demand a particular control of the actor.

The image we have of ourselves has no necessary or real

relation to the image which others have of us; nor is the image necessarily a reflection of the person underneath. So the daughter in this play finally discloses that she is nothing, only the image which others take her to be. The individual is imprisoned by phantoms of other people's other's making, like the actor in his make-up before his dressing-room mirror.

In *Henry IV* (1922) – a difficult play which nonetheless has been revived a number of times in recent years, with the central part played by actors as different as Rex Harrison and Richard Harris – Pirandello raises the question of identity even in the title. In an English audience it arouses the expectation of seeing a play about the Plantagenet King. Berthold, the new servant, who appears at the start of the play, has made a similar, though different mistake, in thinking that he is to serve in the court of Henry IV of France in the sixteenth century, when in fact he has come to serve in the court of Henry IV of Germany who submitted to the Pope at Canossa in 1071.

The scene is set in a secluded villa in Italy of the 1920s. In this villa (a set inside the set, like the person or persons underneath the mask), the salon has been made to look exactly like the throne-room of Henry IV at Goslar. The set is dominated by the imperial chair and baldaquin. All that is said and done in this room – the clothes which the servants wear, their deference to him – are intended to confirm Henry in his belief that he is the Emperor of Germany – a delusion he has been under since his fall from a horse twenty years previously, when dressed as the Emperor at a carnival. His sister and his nephew have preserved the illusion around him by providing him with servants who act as his courtiers.

The 'mad' identity of Henry is a frozen mask, a conception of his identity to which he has become tied. To begin with, the audience, like the servants, believe Henry to be really mad. His face is heavily made-up, with spots of rouge on his cheekbones, made up, as it were for his performance. But then – and it is a moment of great theatrical effectiveness – before his terrified servants, who have always assumed him to be really mad, he drops the mask.

> Oh, look at this imbecile watching me with his mouth wide open ! (*Shakes him.*) Dont't you understand? Don't you see, idiot, how I treat them, how I play the fool with them, making them appear before me just as I wish? Miserable, frightened clowns that they are! And you are amazed that I tear off their ridiculous masks now, just as if it wasn't I who had made them mask themselves to satisfy this taste of mine for playing the madman!

Words, he tells them, are what others impose, and from which they create an identity for you, which may, or may not, correspond to the reality within. He has been labelled with one of those words which everyone repeats: 'madman!' 'All our life is crushed by the weight of words!' which the past, and others give to us. What oppresses him most remains the impenetrability of others, and of himself to them.

> I would never wish you to think, as I have done, on this horrible thing which really drives one mad: that if you were beside another and looking into his eyes – you might as well be a beggar before a door never to be opened to you; for he who does enter there will never be you. (translated by Edward Storer)

Henry in the end will choose to confirm himself in his role of madman by killing the man who has always been his rival in love; and in this way fix for ever, in the eyes of the world, what his identity is. Rex Harrison brought to the part the immense vanity of a pathological self-regard; Richard Harris a murderous gloating instinct for self-preservation. In the Richard Harris production, a portcullis crashed down behind the throne at the end confirming the role which Henry had chosen, and from which now there could be no escape. He had become for ever his mode of survival.

Pirandello wrote plays in which the stripping away of masks caused as much pain as the tearing of skin from flesh, leaving a raw, bloody substance exposed; but he also proposed a witty, ironic explanation of the relation between plots of this kind, and theatre itself. The theatre, to which he came long after he had established himself as a writer of fiction, and with reluctance, was a place of illusion: the illusion of believing that identity is fixed, or that human motivations, desires, impulses have a more static relation than molecules in a cell which collide, jump, jostle, circulate, rearrange themselves with relentless energy. In writing with an ironic detachment about this, in using it to create the form and pressure of his drama, Pirandello exposed what had been true of much in the dialogue of Shakespeare's plays, in Ibsen, Strindberg and Chekhov, as in some later plays. Masks, as Oscar Wilde realized, are a way of creating illusion, and of stripping it off. This too is what making theatre means.

*

The effect of dialogue in a play depends on how it is written, and how it is played. After seeing Frank Benson play Hamlet, Tyrone Guthrie recorded the following impression:

> It was an intelligent performance, and, for the first time, I began to see why these plays were once considered master-pieces, to realise what great elaborate pieces of structure they were – dramatic cathedrals; to see how interesting they were as narrative, how, over and above and through the narrative were implicit meanings, like the echoes in a cathedral. (Guthrie, p. 82)

Tyrone Guthrie's final phrase says a great deal about how words work in a play, and what they leave to the actors. These 'echoes in a cathedral', implicit meanings and resonances which exist within a character and through the action as a whole, give dramatic dialogue in the greatest plays an open-ness to which the actor brings the whole power of his suggestiveness and imagination: the actor will hit the word, as the pianist does a note on the piano, creating a resonance within a character, as well as between characters, which the audience responds to, and amplifies. Everything which is said 'reverberates' through the play as a whole.

T.S. Eliot, writing about Shakespeare's *Antony and Cleopatra*, showed his own genius as a critic, as well as Shakespeare's as a playwright, in pointing out what Shakespeare had added to his source in North's *Plutarch*. In Act V, scene 2, Charmian, Cleopatra's attendant, has watched the queen commit suicide by applying the asps to her arm and breast. She follows her queen into death, as the guards rush in.

> FIRST GUARD: What work is here! Charmian, is this well
> done?
> CHARMIAN: It is well done, and fitting for a princess
> Descended of so many royal kings.
> Ah! soldier.
>
> (*Antony and Cleopatra*, Act V, scene 2)

Eliot pointed out that Shakespeare had added the last two words, 'Ah, soldier,' and commented, 'I could not myself put into words the difference I feel between the passage if these two words, "Ah, soldier," were omitted, and with them. But I know there is a difference and only Shakespeare could have made it.' Christopher Ricks – the finest critic of poetry writing today – pointed out again what Eliot had first perceived, adding 'it is an act of genius in the critic to see that the act of genius in the artist was the cry "Ah Souldier"'. (Geoffrey Hill quotes this in an essay on T.S.Eliot in *Agenda*, 34, 2, p. 16.) Shakespeare has left to the actress, and the audience the responsibility for settling upon the right response to a phrase which gathers up all the previous action in a final comment on the quality of Antony's love for Cleopatra. The resonance of the phrase illustrates the relationship between word, performance and audience as Shakespeare created it, and at the same time gave it freedom. In *The Tempest* Prospero's control and liberation of Ariel (leaving him free to work his magic) metaphorically suggests this tension and release at the heart of all dramatic dialogue.

In Act II of *Ghosts*, Ibsen writes a scene between Mrs Alving and Pastor Manders which might have been only a scene of confrontation and recrimination between a woman and the 'lover' who once spurned her. What Ibsen enables us to see goes far beyond that. We see mirrored in their dialogue the social conventions which Manders uses to protect himself from sexuality; and the blame which Mrs Alving attaches to him for expelling her into a loveless marriage, of which her son's inherited syphilis becomes the legacy. What happened between Mrs Alving and Pastor Manders is recounted by her: how she ran away to him, and was then rejected for the sake of convention, and respectability. The past is reconstituted in the present, as both have to face the ghosts which still haunt them. (The play's title in French, *Les Revenants*, suggests better than the English title these echoes within the characters out of which the larger action of the play is constantly growing.) The old dramatic device of putting the audience in the picture which Ibsen had used with some crudity in earlier plays resonates here with the anguish and resentment of all which has flowed from those past events,and with Mrs Alving's anxiety for Oswald's future in the almost unbearable present. We see the state of Mrs Alving's and Pastor Manders's souls in the silence beneath the words.

The ghosts of the title refer as much to this shadow life of the internal person, as to the ghost of Captain Alving who returns from the past in the form of his son's promiscuity. Vanessa Redgrave and Tom Wilkinson, playing this scene in the round at the Young Vic in London in 1986, revealed to the audience every registration of their accumulating inner distress. Wilkinson's shifty guiltiness when confronted with his rejection of love for respectability was matched by Redgrave's irresistible refusal to let him get away with it. In this small space, the victim could not evade the cobra's strike. Seeing what happened between their eyes allowed us to see what happened within and between them.

In later plays by Ibsen, this ability of the characters to locate and identify what has bugged their lives becomes obscure to them. Except in *The Lady from the Sea* where Ibsen writes about the curing of a psychotic obsession, he sees his characters as living in a mist where the desire for 'life-joy' founders on rocks which neither they, nor the audience, can fully perceive. Rebecca West and John Rosmer live together in Rosmersholm, but unable to marry out of inhibitions which are only partly to be explained by their guilt about the death of Rosmer's first wife, Beata, in the mill-chase. Freud in writing about Rebecca attributed her suicidal response to Rosmer's proposal of marriage as resulting from an incestuous relationship with her own father. Freud is perhaps right. If so, no such realization comes to Rebecca; her words, like Rosmer's, prowl around a problem which words cannot identify. Ibsen writes dialogue which knocks at doors that will not open. We, the audience, are aware of resonances now muffled and obscure, but equally life-threatening. The clouding of the focus is intensified when we can see, as in the Cottesloe production (1987) how closely the characters eavesdrop on each other, watch in 'unobserved' proximity, attempting to find a way through their repressions. The enclosed space becomes a space in which they are enclosed with their anxiety and their frustration, and begin as in the production of *Little Eyolf* at the Swan in Stratford-on-Avon (1997) to tear each other to pieces.

Ibsen's *John Gabriel Borkman* (1896) has been given two memorable productions in 1975 and 1996, the first with Ralph Richardson and Peggy Ashcroft, the second with Paul Scofield and Vanessa Redgrave. Love of money and power has once caused John Gabriel, the banker, to betray his love for Ella Rentheim; he has heard them as ore singing deep down in the mountains, which he is compelled to mine. Lured by them to social disgrace and exile, he will finally let the ore which still sings in the deep lead him to physical death on the cold of the mountain-side. For Richardson, this siren-call from within became the voices to which every artist must listen, even though they destroy him; for Scofield the final and doomed attempt to assert his own power: the pride and fear of the wolf who knows it is cornered by death.

Resonances such as this are made possible both by the performance, and the way in which the dialogue has been written. This is not a quality of poetic, as opposed to prose drama. Strindberg used it in a very specific way in *The Father*. No man, at least in Strindberg's time, could be certain he was the father of his own child. Bertha uses this as a means of tormenting and dominating her husband to the point of madness. The anger, hatred and anguish of the relationship between them reflects Strindberg's own experience of marriage. But the pain is seen as an existential problem: words cannot prove, cannot offer certainty; we cannot know whether or not they deceive. And once we fall into the trap of doubting language itself, we have fallen into an abyss from which there is no escape. Words are a *mise-en-abîme*; and thin as the paper on which they are written. As Lear discovers with his daughters, words and silence bear death within them. The performance of the text becomes a revelation of the impotence of language to resolve the insecurities of personality.

Strindberg admitted the influence of Shakespeare on him in writing *The Father*. Hamlet is called to revenge his father's death by killing Claudius; but he can never know the status of the ghost, whether it comes from Heaven or Hell, whether the words of this perturbed spirit tempt him to ensure his own damnation, or to settle a debt of honour, to see that justice, however wild, is done. No words, no 'knowledge' exists which can give Hamlet certainty, just as words cannot prove to the father that he is the father of his own child. By not giving his character a name, Strindberg licenses us to think of him not as a particular neurotic, but as an exemplar of what happens if we allow ourselves to fall into a state of extreme scepticism. There are no wings to buoy us up. The play, in growing out of this philosophical and emotional torment, discovers a dialogue between Bertha and her husband which founders on the inadequacies of words to represent their individual needs and impulses, or to express them in such a way that understanding and forbearance become possible. As the audience perceives, dialogue exists as a matchwood bridge over an abyss; and in doing so is compelled to confront the flaw in all human dialogue.

Dramatic dialogue created out of these echoing chambers of the soul – with all that it requires the actors to bring to the performance – continues to characterize a certain kind of play-writing which belongs to the Shakespearean tradition.

★

But there is another tradition where words do not create resonances, are not echoes in a cathedral, where they play – often joyfully – on the surface, like rain falling on a pool of water. This does not mean that the dramatic action lacks implications outside itself, or is not an action abstracted from experience; or is less interesting in itself; but it does determine how dialogue is written, and what actors have to bring to the performance. In the first kind of drama, the breaking of the ice lets us see how deep is the water beneath it; in the second reflections are thrown off the surface, the rain-drop appears to rise again and catches the light. Characters are what they say; and actors build the performance out of the words which they speak. The action is built from a surface of words which do not conceal hidden depths.

It might seem at first as though this distinguished drama written in prose from drama written in verse. But, as the illustrations from Ibsen and Chekhov in the previous section show, it does not. Equally, Keats, Shelley, Byron, Browning, Tennyson and Christopher Fry wrote plays in verse whose words do not echo with the depths beneath them. In much of their work verse remains a form of stage-rhetoric, where feeling belongs to the surface, not to the undertow.

Shakespeare's four plays from *Richard II* to *Henry V*, if performed in sequence, as they were in Stratford-on-Avon in

1953, and by the English Shakespeare Company around the country, and at the Old Vic in 1987, explore the state of England in courts and taverns, in peace and war, from kings to soldiers, from youth to old age; they reflect the image of a nation, and the 'discord' which follows once the 'string of order' is untuned. Whether in 1953, or 1987, they confront the audience with the idea of a nation, in which two old men discussing the price of ewes in a Gloucestershire orchard has as much place as the death of a king. They make play of the relationship between the gratification of individual desires and the health of the kingdom. They make us aware of the difference between order and anarchy; and the price which must be paid in individual freedom if order is to be preserved. While living with characters we never forget, we also sense how sovereignty, whether for the individual or the state, depends on the delicate balance between freedom from unjust interference, and freedom to live as we choose.

David Hare's plays, *Racing Demon, Murmuring Judges, The Absence of War* (1990–3) examine the institutions of State. But their dialogue only belongs to the surface; it states the case from different perspectives. The clash comes not from the fact that people are different (which is insoluble, as Shakespeare's language shows); but because they see things from different points of view which implies the possibility of change. David Hare, professional as always in stagecraft, offers only a dramatized debate about the Church, the Law and the Labour Party. No character is given a depth greater than the attitude he or she represents. The audience has no role but to listen and watch; agree or disagree at the end. David Hare wants us to see what kind of nation we live in, as his politics shows it. In Shakespeare's plays, the ideology does not precede the words; it flows from them.

Dramatic dialogue in which characters are what they say originates in the morality play. Knowledge presents himself to Everyman and says he will be his guide (in this world, virtue *is* knowledge). So too do Discretion, Strength, Beauty and Five Wits. Milton's *Comus* – a masque of extraordinary music, magic and power – includes both kinds of dramatic speech, creating a fissure which is never entirely healed. At its centre, the masque contains an extended debate between Comus and the Lady on the subject of Chastity. According to Comus, a very modern enchanter, 'Beauty is Nature's coin must not be hoarded,' while to the Lady

> Thou hast no ear, no soul to apprehend
> The sublime notion, and high mystery
> That must be uttered to unfold the sage
> And serious doctrine of virginity.
> (lines 783–6)

Even though these lines were written to be spoken by Alice, the 15-year-old daughter of the Earl of Bridgewater, which gives them an innocent radiance, they state the substance of her as a dramatic character. In the Attendant Spirit's opening speech, as in the song which summons up the nymph Sabrina to release the Lady from the Enchanter's spell:

> Sabrina fair
>   Listen where thou art sitting
> Under the glassy, cool translucent wave
>   In twisted braids of lilies knitting
> The loose train of thy amber-dropping hair,
>   Listen for dear honour's sake
>   Goddess of the silver lake,
>   Listen and save . . . . . .
> (lines 858–65)

Milton's verse reaches quite different levels of dramatic effect which holds us in thrall and 'spell-bound'. In writing a masque, Milton was not working within the bounds of ordinary stagecraft; but the speeches of the Lady reveal how declaration lowers dramatic power, unless it also sharpens character, as happens in Sheridan's *The School for Scandal*.

Lady Sneerwell at the drinking-table – Snake drinking chocolate

LADY SNEER: The paragraphs, you say, Mr Snake were all
                    inserted?
SNAKE: They were, madam, and as I copied them myself
              in a feigned hand, there can be no suspicion
              whence they came.

(Act I, scene 1)

In the first seconds of the play, the words of Lady Sneerwell
and Snake declare their credentials, as will those of Mrs
Candour, Joseph Surface and Sir Benjamin Backbite shortly
afterwards. Scandal itself is 'tittle-tattle', words for harming
'reputations', another verbal surface. What matters is the effect
made by words, not any concern for the truth or untruth of
what is said. As Joseph Surface himself remarks:

To be sure, madam, that conversation, where the spirit of
raillery is suppressed, will ever appear tedious and insipid.

The brilliance of the surfaces does not obscure, rather it
reflects the shallowness of the human and social feeling
beneath. Or to change the metaphor, you only have to break
the ice to feel the coldness of the water beneath it! When the
screen falls down in Act IV, scene 3 (the first time it did so the
roar of the audience was heard all over London) and Sir Peter
Teazle discovers his wife to be the 'little French milliner'
behind it, only a screen has fallen! Something has been
revealed to the Teazles, and to us; but it would be ridiculous to
ask whether at the play's end they will enjoy a happy marriage, even though Sir Peter is an ageing man married to a
young and spirited wife. In a play where words are surfaces,
the action stops when the curtain falls; when characters stop
speaking they cease to exist. If a character in *The School for
Scandal* said, 'the rest is silence', we know they would have to
start speaking again a moment later, or scandal itself would die.
And so too, in a rather different way with *The Importance of
Being Earnest* (1895), a play where nothing matters at all apart

from being ready with the *right* response, as Jack Worthing discovers when being cross-examined by Lady Bracknell as to his suitability for becoming engaged to Gwendolen.

Edith Evans and Maggie Smith remain the two most memorable interpreters of the part: Edith Evans for an hauteur almost stifled with surprise at being confronted, Maggie Smith for the preciosity of the ingenue whose husband has all the money. Each is compelled for quite different reasons to keep up appearances; and in each case the words are the appearances. The differences lie in the skill of the two actresses, in the precision of their technique in conceiving the detail of the character; but it scarcely affects the interpretation of the play. *The Importance of Being Earnest* cannot usefully be interpreted; it is simply there to be enjoyed, and played with all the skills which actors and actresses bring to it. No one in the play has a future or a past (whatever they have to say on the matter of handbags), only a brilliant present.

The plays of George Bernard Shaw occupy a special and unique position in the drama of words. They also remain big box-office draws. Major revivals of Shaw succeed in the West End as well as the state-subsidized theatres; and they have been frequent in each. Shaw's characters are played by stars, and his plays continue to be remembered for productions which figure prominently in the history of twentieth-century theatre. From the early performances at the Royal Court Theatre, associated with Harley Granville Barker and Mrs Patrick Campbell, through Sybil Thorndike's Saint Joan, to Laurence Olivier's Saranoff, Vivien Leigh's Cleopatra, Alan Badel's John Tanner, Richardson's Waiter (in *You Never can Tell*), Roger Livesey's and Paul Scofield's Captain Shotover, Brewster Mason's Undershaft and Judi Dench's Barbara, and Alan Howard's Higgins, the power of the plays to entertain and delight has proved enduring. *Pygmalion* made possible, and provided the source for many of the witty lyrics which Alan Jay Lerner wrote for, *My Fair Lady*.

But not everyone likes Shaw. Peter Hall directed *Man and Superman* for the fiftieth anniversary of the Third Programme, but admitted in a radio interview that he had never been drawn to directing Shaw before, because of the lack of feeling. (He has now (1998) directed *Major Barbara*.) Peggy Ashcroft, who had idolized Shaw when young only once appeared in a play by him: *Caesar and Cleopatra* in 1932. The controlled passion which provided a source for one aspect of Peggy Ashcroft's greatness as an actress could not be tapped in Shaw, because there is no passion beneath the surface of the words; the passion is in the words. They remain among the most musical plays ever written.

Man and Superman (1903), Shaw's longest play with the exception of his metabiological pentateuch, *Back to Methuselah* (1921), takes four and a half hours to perform, and through much of it John Tanner has been talking. It ends like this:

> VIOLET (*with intense conviction*): You are a brute, Jack.
> ANN (*looking at him with fond pride and caressing his arm*). Never mind her, dear. Go on talking.
> TANNER: Talking!
> *Universal laughter.*

Tanner as the author of the *Revolutionist's Handbook* has advocated a rejection of the social mores and economic principles by which he, like other members of the idle Rich Class, live. But he has done nothing to change his way of life. At the play's end, he will have lost the battle of the sexes to Anne Whitfield who, as the inheritor of the Life Force, intends to make him her husband. The stage is set for Shaw, some fifteen years later, to write in the last act of *Heartbreak House* (1919) of an air-raid as 'Heaven's angry growl of thunder at these "useless, futile creatures" who talk so much and do nothing'. Even Ellie, who represents the next generation, expresses in the last line of the play the hope that the bombers will come again. The universal laughter which covers all at the end of *Man and Superman*, in a tumult of talking, confirms an inadequacy in a drama where everything depends on what people say, and shows almost never what people do. As in Wilde's plays, there would be no play at all, if they did not speak so well.

Shaw's mind belongs to the eighteenth century where words still have their effect; in the twentieth century they often lack the power to cut ice. The more people talk, the more they show up the ineffectiveness of talking. Words are dwindling into 'mere' surfaces; and the people who use them mere ciphers, who mouth. Jean Giraudoux in his finest play, *The Trojan War will not Take Place* (1935) or, as it was called in Christopher Fry's translation, *Tiger at the Gates* (1955) shows how even as statesmen talk and express good-will, 'on a terrace in a garden overlooking a lake', war is preparing; and the following day will break out. In a more extreme form, this lack of grip of language on event becomes the absurd.

But Shaw is saved – and the effect of his plays is saved – because he never despairs of the universe. He continues to believe it is worth going on talking. In writing dialogue, he perceives the ineffectuality of talking, and at the same time the necessity of doing so. His characters remain embodiments of the 'will to live'. Alexander Pope, at the end of his mock-epic, *The Dunciad*, wrote, 'Light dies before thy uncreating word', and the words which Shaw gives his characters to speak, for all their intelligence and wit, for all the effervescent energy of their dramatic effect, remain confined within the bounds of the stages on which they are spoken, unable to touch what lies beyond. Our delight lies in seeing how words understood and misunderstood can be used to reverse a stage situation, but seldom a human one. The 'conversion' of Cusins and Barbara in the last act of *Major Barbara* (1905) remains among the least convincing, and most rhetorical which Shaw wrote. Cusins claims, 'I now want to give the poor man material weapons against the intellectual man. . . .' And we are left wondering what on earth he has in mind. Nonetheless, the performance has to make us continue wanting to listen.

Andrew Undershaft's success as an armaments manufacturer, enables him to create an ideal community with its schools, hospitals and good housing at Perivale St Andrews.

His bombs, when they fall, do so on Mongolia, as remote in those days as Mars, and so distancing Undershaft, and his audience from the effect of what he is causing to happen. Even the unethical source of the money with which he proposes to save the Salvation Army shelter, though vehemently rejected by Barbara with the cry, 'drunkenness and murder', affects only the surface of the drama, like wind on water.

Shaw's Prefaces and Plays, taken together, still retain the power to shape minds and inform attitude. John Tanner's rejection of moral disapproval at Violet's pregnancy (or what he takes to be her pregnancy) in favour of rejoicing at the creation of life remains one such Shavian touchstone. But, as always with Shaw, it is the utterance which matters, because the characters are what they utter. Again this is not intended as a comment on Shaw as philosopher or political thinker, but more circumspectly as a comment on the way he writes dramatic dialogue, and its power to explore how human beings feel and live. His desire for the theatre to be a 'temple of the ascent of man' – a hope clearly not realized yet! – was based on a wholly unrealistic view of human nature, not shared by the dramatist he most admired, Henrik Ibsen, that people understood what bugged them, that they could actually grasp who they were, as opposed to living in a mist, even when they thought they could see the stars. His reason did not recognize how partial all his consciousness is, or how much darkness exists even in its understanding of itself. Shaw's intelligence blinded him to the tragedy of human character, including his own, making his plays paradoxically artificial. The time for the saints, as he said in *Saint Joan*, had not come.

Verbal wit which gave Shaw's plays, like Wilde's and Sheridan's, their power to delight has continued to provide a source of inspiration in the writing of dramatic dialogue; but, for reasons which Shaw's plays suggest, it too has become increasingly edged with darkness. In Noel Coward's *Hay Fever* (1924), the Bliss 'family' are so blissfully unaware that they are incapable of attending to anything beyond their own personal concerns, including the guests whom they have independently invited for the week-end. They are unmade by the manners which they do not possess. In the last act the guests creep out of the house unnoticed, while the Blisses continue to talk, wrapped up in themselves, like bed-clothes. When David, the novelist father, attempts to reveal himself by reading his novel, he only succeeds in irritating his wife who claims he has forgotten the lay-out of Paris.

DAVID: 'Jane Sefton, in her scarlet Hispano swept out of the Rue Saint Honoré into the Place de la Concorde. . . .'

JUDITH: She couldn't have.

DAVID: Why?

JUDITH: The Rue Saint Honoré doesn't lead into the Place de la Concorde.

DAVID: Yes, it does.

SOREL: You're thinking of the Rue Boissy d' Anglais, Father.

DAVID: I'm not thinking of anything of the sort.

JUDITH: David darling, don't be obstinate.

DAVID (*hotly*): Do you think I don't know Paris as well as you do.

Beneath these polished, and finely crafted surfaces, what goes on? Coward never reveals or hints. In a farce, we may say, nothing goes on except for the situation. When the situation is over, it ends. But Coward who deserved to be called 'the Master' was much too good a writer to let his audience off as lightly as that. Bliss family life shuts out the whole world, just as each member of the family shuts out the others. As they would never ask the question – what are we Blisses like underneath? – the audience is left to ask it for them; and the answer is neither consoling nor pleasant. Words provide characters with a good pair of skates, oblivious that what they skate on is ice. The Bliss family do not know how funny they are, or how disconcerting. They need to be played absolutely straight which is much harder than it sounds.

Noel Coward in his preface to *Hay Fever* warned of the

difficulties of performing it because 'it has no plot and remarkably little action'. It demanded 'expert technique' from every member of the cast. As with all comedy, this depends on a sense of period: in dress, accent, intonation, posture (sitting and walking), gesture (for example, how you smoke a cigarette through a long holder, vertically as Maggie Smith did) and timing which brings out the 'tenuousness' and 'triviality' of what is being said, and in doing so liberates laughter. The characters themselves have to be created out of all these different forms of style; and style, like the words, belong to the surface. The person is not to be found in the feeling beneath the words, as for example with Malvolio ('What, are you mad, my masters!') because the words have no undertow. The superficial brittleness (scoring a point or losing one) is all. The dialogue is like a paper screen which you cannot walk through because the paper screen is all that exists. Dialogue written like this may disconcert not as some critics said at the time because of its triviality but because its triviality shows up a certain kind of performance: the emptiness of gesture when there is nothing to gesture to, and which leads in the end to the absurdity of late twentieth-century fashion.

Words as surfaces, like people as theatrical images without depth, have continued to inspire one form of dramatic writing which is funny and disturbing because it points to a void. Ionesco personified it in *The Bald Prima Donna* (1950) (which he described as an 'anti-play') in a certain form of Englishness:

MRS SMITH: Goodness! Nine o'clock! This evening for supper we had soup, fish, cold ham and mashed potatoes and a good English salad, and we had English beer to drink. The children drank English water. We had a very good meal this evening. And that's because we are English, because we live in a suburb of London, and because our name is Smith.

(*Mr Smith goes on reading his newspaper and clicks his tongue.*)

(*The Bald Prima Donna* Act 1)

1. Ralph Richardson: Peer Gynt (1945), see p. xvi.

2. John Gielgud: Prospero (1957), see p. 34.

3. Laurence Olivier: Macbeth (1955), see p. 38.

4. David Burke, Sara Kestelman, Matthew Marsh in Michael Frayn's *Copenhagen* (Royal National Theatre), 1998, see p. 47.

5. Designs by Sally Jacobs for *A Midsummer Night's Dream*
(Royal Shakespeare Company), 1962: see p. 115.

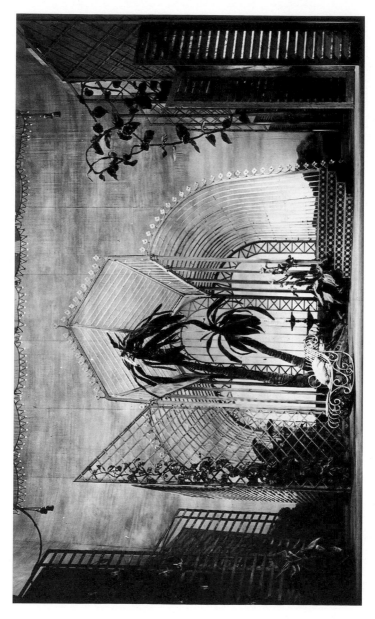

6. Set by Oliver Messel for Jean Anouilh: *Ring Round the Moon*, Act Two (Globe Theatre), 1950, see p. 139.

7. Janáček: *Jenůfa*, set by Tobias Hoheisel, Act One (Glyndebourne Opera), 2000, see p. 150.

8. Set by Tanya Moseiwitch for Shakespeare's Histories (Richard II–Henry V) (Stratford-on-Avon), 1951, see p. 141.

9. Set by Jocelyn Herbert for Brecht's *Galileo*, Act One (Royal National Theatre), 1980, see p. 146.

10. Set by Michael Annals for Peter Shaffer's *The Royal Hunt of the Sun* (Royal National Theatre), 1964, see p. 147.

11. Set by Josef Svoboda for Wagner's *Götterdämmerung*, Act Three, Scene One (Royal Opera House, Covent Garden), 1976, see p. 160.

12. Finale of *Guys and Dolls*, setting by John Gunter (Royal National Theatre), 1996, see p. 206.

In one state of consciousness Ionesco said he asked himself, 'what possible reaction is there left, when everything has ceased to matter, but to laugh at it all?' But in another, 'A curtain, an impassable wall stands between me and the world, betwen me and myself; matter fills very corner, takes up all the space and its weight annihilates all freedom; the horizon closes in and the world becomes a stifling dungeon. Language breaks down in a different way and words drop like stones or dead bodies; I feel I am invaded by heavy forces against which I can only fight a losing battle.' This combination of levity and heaviness, together with a feeling that the 'surreal' is present within the banality of everday speech conveys a quality present in the work of Joe Orton, Tom Stoppard and Alan Ayckbourn, all of whom continue to write dialogue in which the effect is reflected off the surface, rather than coming from beneath it.

Joe Orton's plays need to be acted, as he himself pointed out, 'perfectly seriously' and with 'absolute realism'. Like Wilde's characters, Orton's are never surprised by their own witty improprieties, they take them entirely for granted. They are spoken for effect, to reflect a pose – as well as to amuse – without feeling or moral content, in a world without feeling or moral content. A character may ask for a straight answer, as McCleavy does in *Loot* (1964), but he can be sure of not getting one. Words have no purpose except to advance the action. They cannot reveal because there is nothing to reveal. In *Loot*, a mother's funeral rites provide the opportunity for the son to stash the body in a cupboard and fill the coffin with banknotes which he and his partner Dave have acquired in a robbery. In this way they hope to evade the investigations of Inspector Truscott, who poses as a man from the water board. The dialogue is composed of *non sequiturs* and bizarre logic as when Truscott discovers the stolen banknotes in the casket.

TRUSCOTT: How dare you involve me in a situation for which no memo has been issued? In all my experience I've never come across a case like it.

Every one of these fivers bears a portrait of the
Queen.

A logical world without logic, a world where the effect of
every cause is random, creates a new kind of anarchic humour.
In Orton's last and funniest play, *What the Butler Saw* (1969),
the invention of the wit is joined to the pace of the stage-
action, set in a psychiatric clinic, where undressing and cross-
dressing provide a good deal of the fun; and the plot includes
nymphomania, incest, transvestism, blackmail and mistaken
identity. (Ralph Richardson was reviled for having taken part
in a play which caused old ladies to jump up and down on
their programmes in hatred.) Dr Rance, who is intended to
restore order in the clinic, proves to be madder than those
inside it; and like Inspector Truscott shows up the hollowness
and corruption of Authority. But as with *The Importance of
Being Earnest* the play only acts as play; it does not succeed in
referring outside itself: the action remains imprisoned within
the consciousness which created it. This gives Orton's plays
not the detachment of Ionesco's first form of consciousness,
but the heaviness of the second in which the world 'becomes
a stifling dungeon', refreshed only by laughter. The characters
at the end, 'pick up their clothes and weary, bleeding, drugged
and drunk, climb the rope ladder into the blazing light.' Or in
other words into the spot and the flies. Paradoxically, it may
seem, performance in this kind of theatre requires restraint.
Playing for laughs destroys the laughter.

Tom Stoppard's *Rosencrantz and Guildenstern Are Dead* took
the town by storm in 1967. In making Hamlet's two friends,
Rosencrantz and Guildenstern, whose only role is to wait, the
central figures of his play, Stoppard showed a brilliant inventiveness and power of parody. His imagination was nourished
by literature and drama; but not by anything outside it.
Rosencrantz and Guildenstern have been sent for to Elsinore;
but they do not know why; they pass the day spinning coins,
waiting for something to happen, something to do. They wait
for a role. As Guildenstern admits when the Player admon-

ishes them for questioninng their situation at every turn, 'we don't know what's going on, or what to do with ourselves. We don't know how to act.' They can only say for certain, 'we came'. They fill the time with verbal cleverness, games. Like the audience they are kept intrigued, without ever being enlightened. The only world they refer to, or can try to relate to is Hamlet's, creating around them a cold, dry air of intro-version. Denmark's a prison, and they too are imprisoned within the world of the play, with its verbal windows which only look inwards.

The contrast in the way words are used, dialogue is written and the action conceived is most apparent when it is com pared with *Waiting for Godot*, a play which in some ways it resembles: in both, two characters wait for something to happen. At the end, Rosencrantz and Guildenstern, as the title forewarns us, are dead; Vladimir and Estragon are still waiting for Godot. The play's eyes, however blinded or blind, are turned outwards. The action of *Waiting for Godot* takes place at the cross-roads where existing means getting through another day, and being means trying to find out what they are doing there.

VLADIMIR: Ah yes,the two thieves. Do you remember the story?
ESTRAGON: No.
VLADIMIR: Shall I tell it to you?
ESTRAGON: No.
VLADIMIR: It'll pass the time. It was two thieves, crucified at the same time as our Saviour. One –
ESTRAGON: Our what?
VLADIMIR: Our Saviour.

or

ESTRAGON (*suddenly furious*): Recognize! what is there to recognize? All my lousy life I've crawled about in the mud! And you talk to me about scenery!

These utterances are reflected back from the world outside the theatre, taking soundings in our own belief, or unbelief, or agnosticism. They are at the same time, funny and tragic. Rosencrantz and Guildenstern can only refer back to the world of theatre, from which they take their being, puppets within the 'real' tragedy of Hamlet. The languages of theatre are being played with to subvert, invert and anatomize each other, resulting in a curious, cold air of emptiness. Vladimir and Estragon are waiting for Godot; Rosencrantz and Guildenstern are waiting to die. In the meanwhile they are witty, clever, inventive and dangerous.

In *Arcadia*, written thirty years later, Stoppard continues to write dialogue with an unflagging zest for words, and how they can be played with, as the first two lines of the play between the the 13-year-old Thomasina, and her tutor Septimus makes clear.

THOMASINA: Septimus, what is carnal embrace?
SEPTIMUS: Carnal embrace is the practice of throwing one's arms around a side of beef.

So far, so clear! The next few lines contain a miniature Latin lesson, as well as references to the Gallic wars, onanism (or masturbation), algebra and poetry. As the action begins, so it will continue: not being learned for its own sake, but using learning for fun, to make play, to demand a response of the audience, and other characters which may, or may not be, forthcoming:

SEPTIMUS: Carnal embrace is sexual congress, which is the insertion of the male genital organ for purposes of procreation and pleasure. Fermat's last theorem, by contrast, asserts that when x, y and z are whole numbers, each raised to power of n, the sum of the first two can never equal the third when n is greater than 2.
(*Pause*)
THOMASINA: Eurghhhh.

The text exudes self-confidence which has to be reflected in the performance; being learned and witty is simply a sign of being alive.

The action takes place in the same house, Sidley Park, in the early nineteenth century, and at the present time, in scenes which interlock past and present to create a single dramatic image of how it is: an action abstracted from experience. In the eighteenth-century scenes, Thomasina and Septimus remain engaged – in addition to problems caused by sex – with problems of writing a formula.

> THOMASINA: . . . if you were really, *really* good at algebra you could write the formula for all the future; and although nobody can be so clever to do it, the formula must exist just as if one could.
> SEPTIMUS: (*Pause*) Yes.

In the contemporary scenes, Bernard, an English don, shows an equal persistence – though for much more questionable motives – in trying to prove that Byron fought a duel at Sidley Park with a minor poet called Ezra Chater, over his wife, killed him and was forced to leave the country in a hurry (which he did). In fact, as the play eventually reveals, Chater went to the West Indies where he died, after being bitten by a monkey.

A great deal of this verbal conjuring in both centuries is as Hannah, a historical biographer, points out, 'performance art'. 'Rhetoric! They used to teach it in ancient times, like PT.' Like PT it is energizing, involving the audience in intellectual gymnastics which they may, or may not, be able to do. The dialogue rushes on with tremendous momentum, throwing up ideas like rockets in a fireworks display. But, when the fireworks go out, they are seen to have flared in a dark night sky. The title is taken from the phrase, *Et in Arcadia ego* where the I is death. The idea which Thomasina hits on becomes a hundred years later the second law of thermodynamics: heat only passes in one direction, from hot to cold, from the more ordered to the less ordered; the energy of the universe is always decreasing, tending to stasis. In human life nothing is as certain as it appears to be: small things may lead to huge change, or huge things lead to no change, as with the weather. Randomness, chance (as with Bernard's success and failure with literary detection, or Thomasina's death by fire at the age of seventeen) rule individual life. But the play ends with a dance in which the characters from past and present participate, where feelings and 'carnal embrace' still matter. The human festival continues, but always in a universe ruled by death, and which itself is dying. In art, in theatre, the party continues, can be played again, dazzle with its brilliance, seem 'curiouser and curiouser', liberate tired spirits with laughter; but outside the ring of light on the stage, the darkness grows deeper, the cold grows worse. The theatre becomes a way of putting one's back to the night, but not by pretending that it isn't there.

Alan Ayckbourn gained his reputation through the writing of farce, plays written to brighten a rainy afternoon in the seaside town of Scarborough. As has often been said, his plays, while continuing to be very funny, have darkened in tone. Although he has now written more than forty plays, he has continued to invent new ways of using the stage, so that each play surprises in its stagecraft. Dialogue remains confined to a middle-class milieu, and restricted by practical everyday concerns. While Stoppard's characters never stop saying interesting things, Ayckbourn's characters can be relied on never to do so. Lacking depth, his characters need all the skills which actors bring to them in performance, where timing – an immediate relation between words, actions and audience – is of the essence. Ayckbourn is a master at putting his characters through their paces; and the fun derives from seeing how well they do them.

In *Man of the Moment* (1990), Douglas Beechey, created by Michael Gambon, has been brought to Spain to appear in a TV programme where he will be brought face to face with the bank robber whom he confronted eighteen years earlier. When the gun went off, it disfigured the woman whom

Douglas subsequently married, leaving them to a half-life of childless isolation and impoverishment. The robber, after a few years in gaol, has become a super-rich TV personality; and the programme has been set up in his Spanish villa to record their reunion. Beechey arrives unexpectedly, when the cameras are not yet ready to capture his reaction on seeing how the bank robber lives. Jill Rillington, the TV host, asks Beechey to make his entrance again.

> JILL: OK. Listen, I want you simply to come in through that gate – like this – (*She demonstrates.*) OK?
> DOUGLAS: (*Watching her intently.*) Yes. I came in the other way, originally. When I arrived. Does that matter?
> JILL: Not in the least.

She wants him to look 'a bit amazed – awed by it all.' But Beechey can't act, can't walk through the garden gate looking natural, can't speak as though he is not speaking lines, lacks all sense of timing. The discord which followed in Michael Gambon's performance, and the laughter it caused, grew from seeing a great actor act very badly. Ayckbourn has conceived Beechey as a man without desire, apparently incapable of wanting anything except what he has, and incapable too of playing himself. Whether this results from a lack of imagination, a loss of feeling or some terrible complacency in him are questions the play does not even begin to raise. When Jill tries to question him on camera about his marriage, she can get nothing from him; he won't give her a story because he has no story to give.

> JILL: Are you happy together, for instance?
> DOUGLAS: Yes.
> JILL: Truly happy?
> DOUGLAS: Yes.
> JILL: No problems?
> DOUGLAS: No. Not really. I can't think of any, off hand.

JILL: Despite the fact that she can't face leaving the house?
DOUGLAS: Well. That's true, yes. But we've both learnt to
          live with that, you see. . .
JILL: Doesn't it upset her?
DOUGLAS: No. She doesn't seem to mind. She doesn't want
          to go anywhere.

Dialogue develops the action, but it never reflects or suggests what lies beneath the surface, if anything does. It's a
meaningless question to ask what Ayckbourn's characters are
really like; they are as they appear. Words shock, surprise, cause
laughter; but do not involve – or seek to involve – the audience in imaginative exploration. Even in Act II of *Absurd
Person Singular* (1972), where Eva makes multiple attempts to
kill herself, thwarted by those who do not realise what she is
trying to do, our attention is focused on the causes of her
failure (for example, dropping the sleeping pills down the
sink), and the unawareness of those who interrupt (thinking
she is trying to clean the oven when she puts her head inside
it), not on her reasons – except human unhappiness, and the
blindness of others to its existence.

At the end of *A Small Family Business* (1987), duplicity,
sexual and economic, will have been extensively revealed,
through the use of a single set which we take to be different
houses according to the characters on stage. '*A Small Family
Business* takes place in the sitting room, kitchen, hall, landing,
bathroom and bedroom in the houses of various members of
the family over one autumn week.' Words and actions reveal
how these characters live; existence is what people do and say.
Their situation is all. But in these situations Ayckbourn shows
a good deal about attitudes, relationships, forms of behaviour,
personal and social, as the millennium draws to its end. And
he does so with a tireless originality in what can be done with
the stage. His performers need equally to have an acutely
observed sense of the social milieu, with all its nuances in
intonation and dress, to which his characters belong.

★

On 8 May 1956, when John Osborne's *Look Back in Anger* was first performed at the Royal Court Theatre in London, the 'climate of opinion' changed on the English stage, and with it the kind of dialogue which could be expected to be heard there. The theatre became overtly political, and the writer came to be judged by what was deemed to be his or her commitment. This reflected the conflict outside the theatre between left and right, marxism and capitalism, democracy and authoritarian regimes, north and south within England, and outside it. Words on the stage, what people talked about, what aroused their passions, caused conflict between them, were inspired by new emotions, reflecting a young generation, new social groupings, which in time became illustrative of the plurality of contemporary culture.

Kenneth Tynan, reviewing *Look Back in Anger*, attempted to estimate the size of the potential audience. 'I agree that *Look Back in Anger* is likely to remain a minority taste. What matters, however, is the size of the minority. I estimate it at roughly 6,733,000 which is the number of people in this country between the ages of twenty and thirty, and this figure will doubtless be swelled by refugees from other age-groups who are curious to know what the contemporary young pup is thinking and feeling.' (Tynan, p. 178) Tynan was right to be jubilant about the passion which had been restored to the English stage in Jimmy Porter's excoriating candour, after the soft water-colours of plays like N.C. Hunter's *Waters of the Moon* (1951) and *A Day by the Sea* (1953). But, as with all change, there was also loss. Terence Rattigan and Noel Coward in the previous generation wrote dialogue which had the effect of melting a solid sur-face with a volcanic eruption from underneath; the audi-ence 'felt' the disintegration of the person beneath the literal meaning of the lines. This came from a certain kind of English reticence – an embarrassment before too pro-nounced an avowal of feeling or of deep emotion – which Jimmy Porter's candour was to banish, and with it banish much of the poetry from the English stage as well. Landscapes of feeling are created by impulses, desires, inhibitions, represions which though unexpressed determine how characters act and react.

Terence Rattigan, who was homosexual at a time when homosexuality remained a criminal offence, and was constrained by the law, and by the censorship of the Lord Chamberlain, succeeded in transposing what could not be admitted; and in writing dialogue in which the tension comes from the unspoken. In *The Deep Blue Sea* (1952), Peggy Ashcroft, Vivien Leigh, Googie Withers and Penelope Wilton have all brought to the part of Hester Collyer, in various ways, a combination of intense outward control and inner suffering, implicit in the dialogue, but requiring immense technical skill and discipline in the performance. Hester cannot express her exorbitant sexual and emotional demands to the young ex-RAF pilot for whom she has abandoned the security of her life with a High Court Judge; nor can he respond to them. She in her middle-class English way lacks the words to express such feelings; he lacks the emotional commitment, as well as the sexual drive, consoling himself with booze and golf. The war was more exciting than Hester. Living in genteel poverty with Freddy, she is visited by her ex-husband who continues to treat her with an understanding and friendship which can never satisfy her needs. Seeing her living as she does, he does not have an inkling of what these are.

> HESTER: Oh, but he can give me something in return, and
> even does, from time to time.
> COLLIER: What?
> HESTER: Himself.

She can no more explain to her husband, or to herself (in words) what her lover, Freddie Page, means to her. But the audience knows – or which is more important, feels – the pressure of that almost unbearable desire to possess and be possessed, which nearly drives her to suicide, and which had driven Rattigan's young lover to kill himself in the auto-biographical events from which the play was derived. Rattigan's dialogue reflects the conventions of its time, with its taboos on self-expression, and observation of 'good taste', but also the inadequacy of language to express the complex interweaving of feeling in powerful emotions, reducing the sufferer to the monosyllabic, or the silence of a physical response. When the curtain rises at the start of the play, Hester is lying in front of the unlit gas-fire, and is only saved by the intervention of the doctor (himself struck off the register) who lives upstairs. The pressure in Rattigan's dialogue comes from the need to be secretive and surreptitious; and its dramatic effectiveness from all that this leaves for the audience to imagine of inner pain and loneliness. When words are always taking soundings from within, characters remain open to interpretation; and the resonances of the poetic remain part of the dramatic action.

More conservative critics than Kenneth Tynan complained of *Look Back in Anger* that they could not see what Jimmy Porter was so angry about. While it is true that his anger could be attributed to many causes, including the absence in his world of any 'brave new causes', the words of the play remain closed; they do not lead to hidden chambers, or unsuspected rooms. They remain what they say. Even Archie Rice, whom Osborne created for Laurence Olivier in *The Entertainer* – and Olivier returned the compliment by turning it into one of his most memorable performances – fails to be anything other than his own performance. The music-hall artiste who is dead behind the eyeballs cannot by definition be the window on anything else.

> ARCHIE: We're all out for good old Number One
> Number One's the only one for me.
> Good old England, you're my cup of tea,
> But I don't want no drab equality . . .

Why should I care
Why should I let it touch me
Why shouln't I sit down and cry
Let it pass over me.

Like the music-hall act, *The Entertainer* (1957) can be
interpreted – Archie becomes an image of post-imperial
sleaze and decay– but the meaning does not well up from
within the play. We are left with moral judgements we
impose from without. The sad family life behind the performance – and the death of Mick killed by the 'bloody
wogs' in Cyprus – do not startle with any new awareness:
they belong to the world of dramatic *reportage*. And this
remains true of much dramatic writing since 1956, however
profound its comitment to causes of many sorts. Plays in
which the meaning of the action is confined to what the
dialogue says do not often merit revival not just because the
message once heard does not need to be repeated, even if
the moment for it has not passed, but because a character on
the stage who is what he or she says offers little possibility of
reinterpretation. Every writer expresses an ideology in writing at all; but when the purpose of writing becomes the
expression of an ideology it hardens into rigidities which pre-
clude any depth of insight. Words are closed off from what lies
underneath them.

John Osborne in *Luther* (1961), owed a great deal to
Bertolt Brecht in stagecraft, as did many dramatists of the
sixties, seventies and eighties, who succeeded him. The episodic structure of the plays, the distancing of character and the
political commitment, as well as the constant reminders of
being in a theatre colonised English dramatic writing. But
Brecht had one gift which they did not possess and could not
be imitated; this gift distinguishes his work from that of almost
all those who saw him as the creator of a new form of theatre.
Brecht was a poet, a great master of the lyric. In prose and in
verse, his words are as sharp as a shark's teeth, even though his
plots often lack tension. Baal, his first major character (played

by Peter O'Toole in 1963 with an enormous relish for indifference and debauched excess) follows his instinct as poet, indulging his lusts and committing murder. He pays the price of exclusion from the normal human world by his indifference to everything except his own words. Brecht can create Baal who violently rejects the sexual mores and social niceties of middle-class society because he can write his poems for him.

In his first popular success, *Die Dreigroschenoper* (*The Threepenny Opera*), for which Kurt Weill wrote the music, Brecht, who had learnt a great deal from Kipling's *Barrack Room Ballads*, created lyrics which went with a new kind of operatic style based on jazz and folk-ballad. The Moritaten singer's ballad about Mack the Knife which opens the show, is raw and vibrant, a song to whistle, as it should be, on street-corners on a dark night:

> An dem schönen blauen Sonntag
> Liegt ein toten Mann am Strand
> Und der Mensch geht um die Ecke
> Den Mann Mackie Messer nennt.

> On a beautiful blue Sunday
> A dead Man lies on the beach
> And the man who goes round the corner
> Is the one they call Mack the Knife.
> > (Prologue)

In the Canonen-song, soldiers who live by the gun make 'beafsteak tartare' out of their enemies; and later Jenny reveals how she will only say yes to the man who is poor and rough and smells of sweat.

Brecht's words, always absolutely clear above the physically vibrant rhythms of Weill's music, create their effect through a controlled casualness:

Mac and Polly (singing together on the night of their marriage)

Die Liebe dauert oder dauert night
An dem oder jedem Ort.

Love lasts or does not last
In this or some other place.

Brecht's words always open themselves up to the audience's involvement, leaving them to make up their minds about what is being said. Here is how he writes the love-scene between Grusha and the Soldier when they are reunited, after the parting of war, in *The Caucasian Chalk Circle*:

GRUSHA: Simon!

SIMON: Is that Grusha Vachnadze?

GRUSHA: Simon!

SIMON (*politely*): A good morning, and good health to the young lady.

GRUSHA (*gets up gaily and bows deeply:*) A good morning to the soldier. And thank God he has returned in good health.

SIMON: They found better fish than me, so they didn't eat me, said the haddock.

GRUSHA: Courage, said the kitchen boy. Luck, said the hero.

SIMON: And how are things here? Was the winter bearable? Did the neighbour behave?

GRUSHA: The winter was a little rough, the neighbour as usual, Simon.

SIMON: May one ask if a certain person is still in the habit of putting her leg in the water when washing her linen?

Standing on opposite sides of a river, and speaking in a language so formal as to be almost impersonal, they leave the audience to imagine the feelings between them at this moment when Grusha is about to tell him she has married.

GRUSHA: How can I explain it to you? So fast and with the stream between us? Couldn't you cross that bridge?

(translated by Eric Bentley)

An emblematic setting (a piece of cloth for the river) and the simple words fuse here in a stage poetry, which is deeply erotic in its impersonality. In the dialogue of much English dramatic writing, influenced by Brecht, poetry on the stage becomes stage-rhetoric, as in Beatrice's long speech at the end of Arnold Wesker's *Roots*, with its vision of a socialist Utopia. Beatrice tells us what we should imagine; she does not leave us to imagine; words remains propaganda. Even more important, words alone fail to use the resources which theatre can use to play upon the audience's imgination. John Osborne's contempt and disillusionment at the neglect of his later work failed to see how uninventive his work had become in theatrical terms.

One play of the seventies, Trevor Griffiths's *Comedians* (1977), succeeded memorably in creating a poetry of the stage which owed much to Brecht, but was true to its own vision.

In Act II of *Comedians* a group of would-be cabaret-turns in a Manchester working-men's club try out their acts before a talent-spotter from London in the hope of getting a professional engagement. Their sexist and racist jokes play upon the audience's uneasy response, and awareness of the 'laceration of what ceases to amuse'. In the last turn, Gethin Price, created by Jonathan Pryce, is made up half clown and half street performer. He encounters two dummies in full evening dress, as it were outside a theatre, and offers to hail them a taxi. His act before their dismissive silence expresses the hatred of those who are disregarded because they are poor; and the laughter which it draws is intended to be as painful as it is funny. When Gethin pins a flower on the girl's dress, a blood-red stain spreads out behind it. Using the theatrical language of music-hall and clowning, *Comedians* explodes the idea that there can be 'one nation' where hatred is justified. To be poor in such a society is to be unworthy of notice because the rich have inherited the earth.

The act succeeds because of the number of theatrical languages it uses. Gethin holds a tiny violin which plays a piece of intricate Bach unaided, the bow catches fire, he smashes the violin underfoot; and with another plays a few bars of the 'The Red Flag'. The laugher literally draws blood from the girl. The political passion is expressed, not spoken. The very silence and disregard of the dummies, like the unaided playing of the violin, succeeds in being eery and funny. When in Act III the play turns into an argument between Gethin Price and his liberal humanist mentor, Eddie Waters, the play shrinks into a not very clearly articulated debate, about different kinds of hatred.

A play which lacks the resonance and compression which the poetry of the stage can create confines a play to being a stage-debate, often interesting as showing the conflicting and opposed points of view which exist in a modern society; but while this may clarify issues and attitudes, it catches little from the dark undertow where human action and reaction have their source. In doing this, it shrinks the area of the audience's imagining. David Hare's Trilogy – *Racing Demon, Murmuring Judges*, and *The Absence of War* (1995) – was a professional piece of theatre, in Richard Eyre's staging; it anatomized the Church, the Law and the Labour Party, and did so with compelling energy. But these were plays born of research which wore their heart upon their sleeve. David Hare's *Skylight* (1996) belongs to that other kind of dramatic writing in which words open up on constantly shifting landscapes of feeling. *Skylight* – with its title suggestive of a vision beyond, and of an upstairs room of confined space – is created out of an incandescent and transient encounter between two people whose lives had once been shared, and have now diverged. Unlike the later work of Pinter which conjures with memory as a theatrical device, where characters are never sure what they remember and, if memory itself is only a fantasy, not a record of what actually occurred, Kyra and Tom know what they shared. They also know what they've become.

Kyra used to live in Tom's house, while he was making his fortune as an owner of restaurants, and was his mistress. When his wife, who is dying of cancer, discovers their relationship by finding letters which Tom has 'carelessly' left around, Kyra immediately leaves him. The action of the play takes place during a single night when, a year after the wife's death, Tom calls to see her again. The dialogue of the play turns naturally around all that has happened to them since Kyra walked out; but the inner action of the play comes from a fencing-match between them in which each is trying to find out whether the solution to their solitariness would be to try living together again. They are well-matched. On both sides the hits are palpable, the pain greater than either admits. Only the sex is easy.

The apparent conflict between them often turns on contemporary political and gender issues: his Wimbledon house versus her cold, cheerless flat in north-west London; her life as a school teacher versus his as a wealthy business man; his 'eating out' in expensive restuarants versus her spaghetti at home; his desire to possess versus her need for independence and freedom. But David Hare has made these the exo-skeleton of an action in which we feel all the time the flesh beneath the bone. But unlike Strindberg with whose chamber plays *Skylight* has something in common, the struggle does not come from an elemental love and hate, but from a broader range of human sympathies and antipathies: friendliness, enjoyment of each other's repartee, awareness of difference and up to a point acceptance of difference. The smell of burning in the play does not come from the desire to inflict pain, but from the realization of how much pain exists between them. Words become skylights on inner worlds, and on the interaction between those solitary worlds. Tough, often humorous, without sentiment, David Hare's dialogue enabled Michael Gambon and Lia Williams to create that inner play of controlled silence in which all that was not being said was being entered into by the audience. Dramatic writing of this range has been evolved out of the politicization of theatre in the last fifty years; but the achievement is subtler and more profound than much which has preceded it. When *Skylight* is revived in five or fifty years with different actors, it will require the same degree of technique and control; and will inevitably be altered by their appearance, their movements, their gestures and reactions in a way that only the living theatre makes possible. *Skylight* on film, however effective, would be fixed; on the stage it requires the intuitive spontaneity, recreated at every performance, which acting is all about.

Dialogue in Hare's play, for all its intuitive probing, works within a well-established tradition: its surprises, except in the introduction of Tom's son at the beginning, and his return with great effectiveness at the end, are surprises of character and situation. Brian Friel's *Translations* (1981) conceives a wholly new way of thinking about words in a play. It is set in an Irish-speaking community in County Donegal in 1833, at a time when the English are remapping and renaming Ireland for the purposes of colonial rule. The audience hears the characters speaking English while knowing they are speaking Gaelic. In addition, Jimmy or Jack Cassie, a bachelor in his sixties is more content quoting in Greek or Latin than speaking any modern language. Hugh, who speaks Irish and English, can interpret one community to the other. But while he recognizes the practical advantages of learning English, he knows 'English . . . couldn't really express us.' The substitution of English names for their Irish originals attempts to change the landscape of fact for political ends: that Ireland may be better ruled. But this invasion violates the human identity which comes from a shared language, and community of feeling. 'Words are signals, counters. They are not immortal. And it can happen – to use an image you'll understand – it can happen that a civilisation can be imprisoned in a linguistic contour which no longer matches the landscape of . . . fact.' (This profound remark defines the relevance of this play to all other parts of the world where, for whatever reason, English has been adopted.) The one Englishman, Lieutenant Yolland, who attempts to cross the boundary betwen these linguistic contours through falling in love with Maire invokes the retribution which comes from ancient hatreds and separations. Like Brecht in *The Caucasian Chalk Circle* and Timberlake Wertenbaker in *Our Country's Good* Friel succeds in writing a potent love-scene, where each speaks in a language the other does not understand. What they want to tell each other remains a mystery, until Maire catches a single word.

> YOLLAND: I would tell you I want to be here – to live here
> – always – with you – always, always.
> MAIRE: 'Always'? What is that word – 'always'.
>
> (Act II, scene 2)

They don't understand, and yet each knows what the other is saying. In dramatic terms, this becomes a new way of expressing the secrecy of love.

What remains possible between two individuals, even without a shared language, remains impossible between two communities or nations even with a shared language, where one is imposing and imprinting itself on the other by force of arms. Natural intuitive acceptance, a reciprocity of trust stabilizes *le milieu intérieur,* but cannot be absorbed into *le milieu extérieur* where these predispositions do not exist. Lieutenant Yolland goes missing, presumed murdered by the Donnelly twins, and the English army exacts a terrible vengeance for his disappearance.

The play ends with a speech which invokes the power of language to summon up a past culture:

> *Urbs antiqua fuit* – there was an ancient city which, 'tis said, Juno loved above all the lands. And it was the goddess's aim and cherished hope that here should be the capital of all nations – should the fates perchance allow that. Yet in truth she discovered that a race was springing from Trojan blood to overthrow some realms and proud in war who would come forth for Lybia's downfall
>
> (Act III)

At the same time it invokes the ghosts of the past as a warning to the present: dramatic language working with superb precision to express a person, and through him to express us.

At the first performance of *Translations* in Londonderry, people of both communities, politicians from London, Dublin and Belfast, Church dignitaries, critics and novelists rose to applaud what they had witnessed. 'Theatre only exists,' Peter Brook has written, 'at the precise moment when the two worlds of the actors and the audience meet: a society in miniature, a microcosm brought together every evening within a space' (*SP*, p. 236).

Words, whether between nations, cultures or individuals, translate and are mistranslated; language itself is the bearer of disease. It attempts to control what is made uncontrollable by its own subversive effect. Moses at the end of Schoenberg's *Moses and Aaron*, after the orgy of worshipping before the golden calf, can only exclaim in despair: 'O Word, Word that I lack!'

Ionesco at one time recorded in his Journal: 'There are no words for the deepest experience. The more I try to explain myself, the less I understand myself. Of course, not everything is unsayable in words, only the living truth.'

In beginning this chapter on 'words' with silence, and with its special role in theatre, I recalled what Wittgenstein said: 'what we cannot speak about, we must pass over in silence'. This is true not only of, or for, philosophers; but in a general sense for us all. Theatre and music are the only two arts which enact this truth. Theatre does so in a way that is more specific than music, because it shows silence in or between *people*: what they cannot articulate because there are no words to express their feelings, or their feelings are so complex that any attempt to express them would be a violation of what is true. As Pascal wrote, 'there is someting eloquent in silence, which is more persuasive than words'.

At the end of *Uncle Vanya* (1899), when everyone has left except Dr Astrov, we know that this is the last moment at which he could ask Sonya to marry him, if he wanted to do so.

Sonya and Astrov know this too; and know as we do that he won't. He walks to the back-wall, examines a map of Africa, and says: 'The heat must be terrible down there now!' All our attention is focused on that terrible intensity, and emptiness. The words do not fill the silence between them. They enlarge it. Theatre in using language on the threshold of silence takes the audience to a certain point, and then abandons them to their imagining.

Whatever the nature of the play, whether by Shakespeare or David Hare, theatre in this act of abandonment confronts us with what is held in abeyance, and with what cannot be expressed in words. Only theatre can do this in the living present which exists between actors and audience; and in doing so fulfils a function which is unique and irreplaceable. The French actor, Jean-Louis Barrault has described it as a 'collective cleansing, a smoothing out of all the wrong creases, a readjustment of balance: an act of Justice' (Barrault, p. 123). At the same time as the theatre holds a mirror up to nature, it also – to quote Shakespeare – 'halloos a name to the reverberate hills.' These 'reverberations' constitute the special nature of its genius. Actors who are aware of words in all their potentiality and their limitations confront us with human fallibility, with society's ills and with the healing powers of laughter. They do so by a living presence shared with the audience.

Peter Brook expresses it like this: 'Theatre's role is to give this microcosm a burning and fleeting taste of another, in which our present world is integrated and transformed'(*SP* p. 236). Such metamorphic moments may come rarely but, when they do, they bite deep. For the present writer, one such moment occurred when Edwige Feuillière and Jean-Louis Barrault played the final scene of Claudel's *Partage de Midi* in the World Theatre season of 1967. It ends with the words, 'l'esprit vainqueur dans la transfiguration de Midi!' And so it was.

3
Vision

The visible
Is not produced without light. In the going down
Of the light vision half-opens
(Andres Sanchez Robayna, translated by Charles Tomlinson)

When I studied the text of *Love's Labours Lost*, I was struck by something that seemed to me to be self-evident, but which at the time seemed to be unheard of: that when, at the very end of the last scene, a new unexpected character called Mercade came on, the whole play changed its tone entirely. He came into an artifical world to announce a piece of news that was real. He came on bringing death. And it was through this that I brought Mercade over a rise at the back of the stage – it was evening, the lights were going down and suddenly there appeared a man in black. The man in black came onto a very pretty summery stage, with everybody in pale pastel Watteau and Lancret costumes, and golden lights dying. It was very disturbing, and at once the whole audience felt that the world had been transformed.

(*SP*, pp. 11–12)

'It was evening, the lights were going down. . . .' As in 'Once upon a time', all theatre magic begins like this. But Peter Brook's poetic description of his 1950 production of *Love's Labour's Lost* highlights a particular moment in which a metaphorical interpretation of the whole play crystallizes. The solitary figure in black entering over a rise at the back of the stage to a peopled space changes the tone of a carefree play, with an old device: *Et in Arcadia ego* – 'I, death, am also in Arcadia.'

A revival of a well-known play paints it in new colours, and gives it fresh meaning: a vision and revision. Here, this comes for Peter Brook as much from a perception about the eighteenth-century paintings of Watteau as from Shakespeare, an awareness in them of an 'incredible melancholy' associated with a 'dark figure somewhere, standing with his back to you' who some people [...]

[handwritten note:] Taken £10 for stuff for dinner £4·55 change

Watteau himself. This still [...]ion, transposing the play [...]comes from the world of [...] Shakespeare's court of [...]rate in time, and instant[...] what matters most is the [...]ecause a performance is [...] the ear.

[...]stage – what is seen and [...]magining it sees – deter[...]ction. Scenery, costume, [...]nships, and, as here, the [...]e vision of a script, and its

[...]people in their relation[...]:, only some of which are [...]amatic meaning. Objects [...] of feeling, and not sim[...]cape in which an action [...]ays, the only object, apart [...]*Not I* is a 'sixteen-minute [...] which Billie Whitelaw [...]wards into hell'. Beckett's genius signals two things: first, that all drama conjures with objects in space and works upon the audience to interpret them. As in physics, the uncertainty of their relationship to one another, and of our relationship to them is central to the enactment. Second, that in drama the simplest things work best. Whether part of the script, or of a directorial vision, drama involves a reduction and an abstraction from experience, enabling the 'narrative' to achieve a symbolic force. This is true of acting and production alike. A cluttered stage, like any space with too many perspectives, diminishes the possibility of imaginative concentration: that intense focusing on something taken to be significant, even though simply interpretable. Beckett's 'mouth' shares with Wagner's 'ring' this simplicity of explosive power. As Samuel Beckett has put it, 'a theatre should have the maximum of verbal presence, and the maximum of corporal presence.' Perhaps one difference between the late nineteenth and late twentieth centuries is that the maximum which can be said, or represented, has shrunk, that we no longer have the certainty about objects in space, including ourselves, enabling us to invest them with the authority of an absolute presence: a change prefigured in Wagner's Wotan whose spear is broken. The maximum has been reduced to the minimal; the god has become a mouth!

A play occurs in four-dimensional space. In time, the two or three hours traffic of the stage, becomes an instantaneous event. Once we are out of the theatre, the action as a whole is what we consider. In space, the realistic acquires a symbolic power. Ralph Koltai, in his design for Hochhuth's *The Representative* (1963) – a play about the silence of the Catholic Church in the face of the extermination of the Jews – recreated a gas-chamber. In the centre of it stood a single object: the papal throne. A play, whether old or new, which does not make the audience ask what is the significance of this action for us and create a transaction between stage and audience, has failed. Director, designer and lighting designer explore the space of the stage, individually and together; the actors people it. The play and its production are not finally separable; but they originate in different arts: writing, and its 'physical' interpretation.

What we see on the stage is fixed within varying limits by what the dramatist has written. A play is concerned with people and objects within an envelope of space. *Waiting for Godot* needs a tree which is bare in the first act, and has leaves in the second, as well as a boot, a carrot, a hat. *Mother Courage* needs a cart; *Othello* a handkerchief. Objects act as catalysts within the dramatic action; and embody the dramatist's vision. Even on the page, a play is a visual and physical thing in which 'they move apart' and 'they move closer' can mean as much anything spoken.

The realization of the play becomes the problem for a director and the design team who have to explore the stage-space they have been given to work in. The director has a vision of what he needs; and the designer who is exploring space in a very different way has to meet those needs. The success of the production will depend on how well their two visions work together, and fuse. Until the nineteen-fifties, stage design was created mainly out of painted scenery; now the stage has become a sculptured space in which the effect of the design will be created by the materials of its construction: wood, glass, aluminium, steel, hessian, plastic, polystyrene, leather, as well as paint. Materials determine lightness, heaviness, transparency, occlusion, and produce in the audience a tactile response. They give the stage texture which is heightened by colour and light.

Costume, like everything else, has become more eclectic. Two forces which pull in opposite directions have both gained in strength. On the one hand, knowledge of costume, of materials, of how clothes are put together, of hair-styles, of jewellery and ornaments, and other accessories from canes to rapiers have become more detailed and precise, through the work of professionals like Lucy Barton and Janet Arnold. Distinctions in terms of class, age, gender, occupation and nationality have been researched and chronicled in precise drawings. On the other hand, authenticity has come to be recognized as only one aspect of dressing a play. A production has to create a psycholgical aura, which reflects both the dramatist's and the director's feeling for the play, which must be cohesive. This may be created from a mix of the historical and the modern, the formal and the casual, the exotic and the everyday, but the one thing it must not be is random. At an instinctive level, it has to be imagined.

Clothes in any period are the outward signs of particular

individuals; and are as distinctive as the people wearing them. They must be right for the actors playing those individuals. A splendid costume can make an actress, as Judi Dench has said, feel that she is Queen Elizabeth I; the wrong costume can inhibit the actor's ability to play the part at all, just as off the stage wearing the wrong clothes can embarrass and humiliate, or enlarge and liberate. The right costumes determine not just what the audience sees, but what the actors and audience feel. The overall effect lies close to the harmonies, and disharmonies, felt in music.

The fashion for updating the setting of 'classical' plays proves, when it works, a fertile way of seeing them with fresh eyes. This has more to do with an audience's visual response to the colours and atmosphere of a production than any important relationship with a changed historical period. *Othello* set in the First World War, does not become a play about it. The 'noble' Moor may seem less noble, or more ironically so, because of subsequent attitudes to generals in that war, and Iago's scheming be coloured by attitudes to class conflict in the twentieth century. More importantly, substituting khaki for Venetian robes will modify the audience's tactile reponse to the play as a whole. When, as often happens, it is asked what is gained or lost by changing a setting, the answer lies less in any intellectual justification, than in whether the changed visualization paints the play in fresh colours and tones so that we *feel* it as though through new eyes.

Stage-space has become sculptured by light as well as design. The coming of light at the start of the play makes visible, and then highlights, shadows, darkens, brightens, colours, mutes; lighting paints with colours which move; lighting is a 'living, tactile thing', a visual music creating its own rhythms, and noiselessly shaping its own transitions. The fading of the light at the end of the performance returns to darkness a completed image which lives only in memory.

All that has been conceived is set in motion by the actors who bring heat and life to what was cold. Their performance, and all that has gone into its making, cannot be separated from changing style, or styles, which themselves reflect the changing cultural context. The theatre has become more physical as we increasingly live in a time when we express ourselves more often physically, less often with the refinement of words. The writing of plays has nonetheless always drawn a great deal of its life from the visual and concrete. What Oedipus says will always be remembered less often than the image of Oedipus who has put out his eyes to atone for the plague he has brought upon Thebes.

The first part of this chapter is about the physical nature of plays; the later part about their staging when vision and visualization become one: theatre in the present, catching something on the wing and creating a transaction between stage and audience. The theatre of the last fifty years has been kept alive not only by the range of its acting talents but by the fertility of its experiment and innovation in the arts of direction, stage design and lighting.

★

The stage direction for Act I of Chekhov's *The Cherry Orchard* reads like this:

> *It is early morning; the sun is just coming up. The windows of the room are shut, but through them the cherry trees can be seen in blossom. It is May, but in the orchard there is morning frost.*

Here is an image of incandescent beauty, and stillness: an image made all the more poignant by the knowledge that at the play's end the axe will fall on the trunks of those trees. But should we see those blossoms, whether at the start, or a little later in the act, when the shutters are flung open, and the old house with its newly returned family comes once more to life? *The Cherry Orchard* is filled with a sense of joyful returning, and inevitable parting. It is only illusion to pretend that the room still referred to as the nursery can be a nursery anymore; and yet it still carries with it the signs, the objects of its original purpose. Objects in this play have a symbolic value conferred by our seeing them at the moment just before they disappear for ever.

As stage design has become less naturalistic in the last thirty years, so the cherry orchard is less often seen. In the Royal Shakespeare Company's 1997 production, directed by Adrian Noble, and designed by Richard Hudson, the set had no windows to open on other worlds: the cherry orchard could only be imagined. This may partly have been a decision brought about by the stage-space for which the production was designed at the Swan Theatre in Stratford; but it also reflects a basic decision about the interpretation of the play. Here, the house coming to life with the arrival of all the luggage, and its death with the removal of all the trunks and hat-boxes at the end, gave the play a material heaviness to which the invisible cherry orchard offered no relief. The objects we carry with us are the stuff of our lives; and what exists beyond the freight of our daily existence which weighs us down, remains only a transcendent possibility, always invisible and always remote. The house with its bare wooden floors, staircase and corridors, resounded with the sound of human feet, walking and dancing to the playing of the Jewish band. The enclosure of the set suggested not dancing as liberation, but as a futile distraction, while the cherry orchard was being sold, and an intensification of the family's inability to face the reality of what was happening to them.

Every play, as written, contains images, verbal, visual and physical which define what the play is about. They may be realized in different ways; but they cannot be excluded. *The Cherry Orchard* is about the cherry orchard, whether or not we see it. Michael Kustow recalled how twenty years later 'the form and pressure' of a production by Giorgio Strehler lived in the mind:

> He created a distilled world of fine white cloth. Above our heads, bellying from the stage out into the auditorium, hung a great white sail, which rose and fell. As it did so, autumn leaves drifted over its edge, and you realised it was

the cherry orchard that haunts everyone in the play: a presence more than a depiction. (Michael Kustow, Programme Note to Carlo Goldoni's *The Chioggian Quarrels*)

What matters is that we feel its presence. This part of a play – the objects in the script – come from the dramatic imagination of the playwright, and to a greater or lesser degree structure the action.

William Blake once wrote that 'the body is that part of the soul which perceives through the five senses.' The inner synthesis implied by this, as though the soul processes the disparate impressions and sensations of the senses, creating a single vision from them suggests the reciprocal relation between audience and stage. A performance creates a 'visual and audible poetry', capable of arousing intuitions beyond the normal reach of the audience. A director who tries to find a metaphor for a work is seeking to realize it in such a way that the intuitive or subliminal consciousness of the audience will be worked on. The theatre is in this sense like a musical instrument intended to create a 'swift movement from a world of action to inner impressions', to which everything which happens on the stage contributes.

In Ibsen's *Hedda Gabler*, Act II opens with Hedda, standing by the open French windows, loading a revolver. '*The pair to it is lying in an open pistol-case on the writing-table*'. She fires at Judge Brack, narrowly missing him as he approaches. At the end of the play she will kill herself with it. The pistols create a fierce and foreboding physical presence throughout the play; they are also essential to its inner action: what we are imagining Hedda's 'situation' to be.

The source of Hedda's fascination for actresses, and audiences comes from the fact that she cannot be known; the heart of her mystery cannot be plucked out. She is driven by demons of power and destructiveness, which the pistols symbolize. Her fear of being dominated, her loathing of trivial domesticity, her disgust at the thought of being disfigured by pregnancy, her refusal to be trapped in a relationship by Judge

Brack – all these offer insights into Hedda's 'daemon'; but she herself remains 'unreadable'. The pistols give the play its psychological focus, and its dramatic climax. Without the pistols, the play would lack its structural and figurative cohesion. Hedda is a woman spiralling downwards, and the pistols are there waiting at the end. Judge Brack's comment that 'people don't do those sort of things' shows the hollowness which cannot discourse with the demons within. Hedda's demons can only be brought into focus by a performance; but the performance will not throw light on the black hole which lies at their centre. At the end of Act III, Hedda sits feeding the pages of Eilert Lovborg's masterpiece into the flames. She is also having her revenge on Thea Elvsted who gave Eilert Lovborg what she, in her repression, could not.

> HEDDA (*throws one of the pages into the stove and whispers to herself*). I'm burning your child, Thea! You with your beautiful, wavy hair! (*She throws a few more pages into the stove.*) The child Eilert Lovborg gave you. (*Throws the rest of the manuscript in.*) I'm burning it! I'm burning your child!

Ibsen places the stove downstage right against the wall. When Peggy Ashcroft played Hedda, the stove was, as it were, in the position of the prompter's box. The flames cast a hellish glow on her face; and we saw them as an inner fire. The lighting, the body posture, the physical act itself fused in an image of Hedda's inner disintegration. Peggy Ashcroft saw Hedda as 'like an iceberg with a fire underneath'; and at this moment she crystallized the complexity of that conception.

The text of a play before actors or directors start to work on realizing it contains both an outward and inward action. The outward action is conceived in terms of stage directions, of the dialogue and its silences, of exits and entrances, of setting and costume, and the moments in time at which scenes or acts begin and end. The rise and fall of the curtain is like a guillotine-knife which shapes the size of a piece of paper, and the action is shaped by the precision with which it is used. The inward action is created out of what the audience is compelled to imagine; but which is not necessarily seen.

Waiting for Godot (or as it might be translated 'While Waiting for Godot') compels the audience to imagine who or what Mr Godot might be, if he ever came. The play could not, of course, exist without him; and he is entirely Beckett's invention. There is nothing for actors or directors to do with him, since he never appears, and is not described in the same way twice. But he remains as much a presence in the play as any of the characters who do appear. He is not God, but Godot; like God, and not like god, he becomes the focus of hope (his coming would fulfil Vladimir's and Estragon's expectations in some way), and of the non-fulfilment of human expectation. Life remains a process of waiting for what does not occur. It requires courage and ingenuity; it is also absurd. These conflicting 'silhouettes', seen through the action are as important a part of the audience's visualization of the play as what is actually seen on the stage. In the Middle Ages, the stars were sometimes thought of as light shining through holes cut in the sky. The inner vision of a play is not unlike this.

In the original 1955 production by Peter Hall, in which both actors and director confessed they did not know what the play was about, the performances had to draw upon the deepest of all theatrical resources which Michael Redgrave has compared to a conjuring trick. A conjuring trick, he goes on to say, *tells* us nothing. We watch absorbed and mystified. Only when we have seen it done many times, as now with *Waiting for Godot* do we ask how it is done, and what it means.

What is seen, and how it is seen, modifies the feeling of what is imagined. Vladimir and Estragon exist on a road, with a single tree. In theatre-in-the round, the road can seem like an open space, constrained and unconstraining, where the characters of the play fill their days between waking and sleeping. Behind a proscenium arch, with the road dominated by a sloping bank behind it, as in the National Theatre Production

of 1987, directed by Michael Rudman and with a set designed
by William Dudley, the feeling of enclosure was intensified, as
though these beings were crushed and confined by their
environment, as though the sky was quite literally about to fall
on their heads. Godot becomes part of their obsession, and
their claustrophobia. The piece of road they exist on remains
their only domain.

At the time when *Waiting for Godot* was first performed at
the Criterion Theatre, I had just been conscripted into the
army for National Service. For the first time in my life I had
learnt what it meant to be imprisoned, not to be able to walk
outside a wall without being arrested. On wet afternoons on
the rifle range, I read *King Lear* under my poncho in a tiny
edition measuring three by three, while waiting for my turn
to be told to shoot! I was literally on a stretch of road with
nowhere else to go.

One Saturday when I was given a 36-hour pass, I went up
to London and saw *Waiting for Godot. Godot*, like *Lear*, questions the nature of human life, at that cross-roads between
being and existing. It questions the significance, if any, of
being, and shows how we exist, filling our days with repetitions and routines. Both plays stare into the abyss of nothing-
ness and absurdity; both plays in their 'obligation to express'
redeem meaning from the dark. Vladimir and Estragon
aroused that uneasy laughter, when we are not quite sure
whether it is appropriate to laugh. Then Peter Bull as Pozzo
strode on to the stage driving a pasty-faced Lucky before him,
and the play began to burn. Lucky broke out of his silence
into those mouthings of a man trying to climb a cliff without
any footholds, and the stage was filled with an exultation, and
a terrible despair; the exultation of language trying to make
sense of a world which made no sense, of one man trying with
almost unbearable courage to say how it was, while another
cracked a whip over him, deaf, uncomprehending, calling him
'pig', 'hog'. And finally came the voice of a child, saying 'Mr
Godot told me to tell you he won't come this evening but
surely tomorrow.' The actors on the stage were not so much

characters as presences, made visible by actors: ancestral voices on whom, at the end of each act the moon rises, spectral and permanent, asking the questions which cannot be answered, about the nature of being and non-being:

What are we doing here, *that* is the question?
Only one thing is clear in this immense confusion: 'We are waiting for Godot to come'

Lear, unlike Vladimir, is denied even that ironic humour:

Why should a dog, a horse, a rat have life,
And thou no breath at all?

As Peter Hall has said, the greatest art is characterized by clarity and simplicity; and these qualities are often to be found in conjunction with the most ordinary objects, given an extraordinary meaning.

In Oscar Wilde's farce *The Importance of Being Earnest*, Lady Bracknell's discovery that Jack has lost both his parents, which seems like carelessness, leads to his admission that he has been found in a handbag in the cloakroom at Victoria Station. The fact that it is the Brighton line remains, as she says, 'immaterial'; but the handbag itself is not. In fact, its production in the third act, before the terrified Miss Prism who has left the baby in the handbag, and placed her 'three-volume novel of more than usually revolting sentimentality' in the pram resolves the mystery of Jack's parentage, and the problem of his suitability for becoming engaged to Gwendolen. The production of the handbag makes possible the happy ending; and its physical presence on the stage both a moment of high comedy, and theatrical gratification. The handbag has become as much a presence in the play as the characters. But the handbag is only the most significant object in a play about a very material society, where unsurprisingly objects – 'things' – count for a great deal. But the ways they are used in *The Importance of Being Earnest* makes it a more dazzling and defter play than Wilde's other works, and not least because

they have an originality and vividness more potent than elsewhere. Letters and a fan in *Lady Windermere's Fan*, shares and
diamonds in *An Ideal Husband* are used to dramatic effect in
plays of brilliant conversation; but cucumber sandwiches, a
cigarette case, lumps of sugar, pieces of cake, funeral clothes –
as well as the handbag – in *The Importance of Being Earnest*
derive their effectiveness from a mundane simplicity. To fill
someone's tea with sugar when they say they don't take any,
just as to eat all the sandwiches before the principal guest
arrives remains fair ground for a quarrel, even now; and our
pleasure is heightened by seeing the enjoyment with which
the bad behaviour is practised. The objects characterize the
society in which their appearance is entirely natural so that
they do not seem to be there for the sake of the plot. The
ritual of tea served by Merriman and the footman in Act II of
The Importance of Being Earnest dramatizes a social ritual which
occurs in country-houses throughout England; but once
Cecily picks up the tongs to fill Gwendolen's cup with sugar,
we are aware of the intense dislike she feels for her. Sugar
becomes a metaphor for feelings which are the opposite of
sweetness! The rite has been ruined.

   The physical nature of dramatic action, and the crystallizing
power of objects in it, before any debate about staging and
performance begins, stands out in all of Shakespeare's plays.
The Prince of Words understood with an equal genius how
physical, visual and simple theatre was. In Act III of *A Midsummer Night's Dream*, Bottom exits from the rehearsal of
Pyramus and Thisbe only to return, unbeknown to himself,
with an ass's head on his shoulders. His fellow actors are terrified by his 'translation'. ('O monstrous! O strange! we are
haunted. Pray, masters! fly, masters! – Help!'). Their amazement is our delight. A delight which is heightened when
Titania, awaking in her bower, perceives in him her love.

> TITANIA: I pray thee, gentle mortal, sing again:
>   Mine ear is much enamour'd of thy note;
>   So is mine ear enthralled to thy shape;

And thy fair virtue's force, perforce, doth move
  me,
On the first view, to say, to swear, I love thee.

The wooing of Bottom in the guise of an ass by the Queen
of the Fairies never fails to be one of the play's great comic
and ironic scenes. As ass, Bottom achieves an innocence he
does not possess as weaver; and Titania, as Queen of the Fairies, promising to purge him of his 'mortal' grossnness, reveals
the limitations of even fairy grace.

Like all effective metaphors, the ass's head acts in a resonant
way, suggesting the complexities of feeling involved in love,
and the different levels at which human life goes on. On a
larger scale, the 'visionary' world of the dream needs interpretation for a modern audience. In the famous all-white production by Peter Brook, with designs by Sally Jacob, in 1962,
trapezes were used to suggest the relationship between the
human and the fairy world. 'By dwelling on the image
"fairy", it gradually becomes clear that the fairy world is a
manner of speaking in symbolic language of all that is lighter
and swifter than the human mind . . . A fairy is the capacity to
transcend natural laws and enter into the dance of particles of
energy moving with incredible speed. (*SP*, p. 96). Through her
stage-design and her use of trapezes, Sally Jacobs found a way
of reinterpreting the fairy world, so that the fairies became
part of the physical world we all inhabit, and at the same time
an expression of the power to transcend our normal apprehension of it. When Titania sees the translated Bottom as her
lover, she sees with the folly of human love, as he for a time is
able to dream of being loved by the Queen of the Fairies. The
transaction works both ways. But when both are returned to
their own ways of seeing and loving, they will have grown by
their immersion in another level of feeling. The production
succeeded in conveying the joy and the folly of love, as in 'the
sounds on a musical scale.' Both in text and production, fairy
grace and human earthiness complemented each other; and
did so through a performance which was acrobatic. Acrobatics

demand physical discipline of the body, and at the same time make bodies light as air. What we saw became in a true sense visionary.

The staging of *A Midsummmer Night's Dream*, like that of *The Tempest*, presents problems of particular visual complexity. But in essence we are seeing things which derive their power from their simplicity. In the court-room scene of *The Merchant of Venice*, Shylock comes to demand his bond: a pound of Antonio's flesh, to be cut from his breast nearest the heart. Portia asks:

> Are there balance here to weigh
>   the flesh?
> SHYLOCK: I have them ready.
> PORTIA: Have by some surgeon, Shylock, on your charge,
>   To stop his wounds, lest he do bleed to death.

Shylock rejects the suggestion as not being in the bond; and Portia orders him to proceed.

> PORTIA: And you must cut this flesh from off his breast:
>   The law allows it, and the court awards it.
> SHYLOCK: Most learned judge! A sentence! come, prepare!

With the knife poised above Antonio's breast, Portia drops her bombshell.

> Tarry a little: there is something else.
> This bond doth give thee here no jot of blood
>   (Act IV, scene 1)

The physicality of this scene is of the essence of theatre. A knife, a pair of scales, a bare breast: the scene never loses its terror. Is Antonio really going to have that pound of flesh cut from his breast by that wicked-looking knife? When I first saw the play at the age of ten, I did not know the answer; and the terror has never left me. Now, the knife of the pathological killer poised to strike has become a visual cliché of innumerable films; but by comparison they reveal little of states of mind, of inner impressions. In Shakespeare's play, the transforming object is the scales; not just because they suggest figuratively the scales of justice; but because they attempt to domesticate, and legitimize, an act of enormity. We look at the scales, and realise the impossibility of weighing one thing against the other; they focus our attention on, and enlarge the monstrosity of what Shylock intends to do. They make us realize he is free to choose, to weigh one course of action against the other; but that being Shylock he has abjured his freedom. Without them the scene would be little more than a public execution, revolting enough if enacted; with them, the whole balance of human motivation, of what makes these hard hearts (a question Shakspeare asks even more insistently in *King Lear*), of the value of life (what price a pound of flesh?), and the relationship between crime and legality is raised. As Portia has just reminded us, these are all questions prior to the feuds between Jews and Christians, to race relations and the authority of the State over them:

> The quality of mercy is not strain'd,
> It droppeth as the gentle rain from heaven
> Upon the place beneath: it is twice bless'd;
> It blesseth him that gives and him that takes.
>   (Act IV, scene 1)

As we are witnessing a ritual which invokes more than human law, so too we are witnessing a ritual which depends on more than ceremonial robes. Portia comes dressed as a Doctor of Laws; and on the stage her costume proclaims her role. We are confronted with the majesty of the Law, its learning, amid its sense of its own dignity. On a point of law, Portia catches Shylock out: the pound of flesh must be exact, not light or heavy in the substance, or the division of the twentieth part of one poor scruple, and taken without the shedding of one drop of blood. The scales in which life and death seem only a moment since to have hung have shrunk again into their natural domestic significance, absurdly inadequate, even ridiculous in the drama where they just seemed about to play so central a role. We no longer have any interest in them; but without them the scene would have lost much of its tension, and its metaphorical meaning.

Shakespeare's plays – especially at moments crucial to the action as a whole – work through his understanding of physical objects in space, of the attention they draw to themselves, bringing about a transference of feeling between audience and stage. Mark Antony's oration over Caesar's body intended to stir the citizens of Rome to 'such a sudden flood of mutiny' (however much he denies it !) achieves its potency through his production of Caesar's mantle. (Brutus in his defence of the murder used only words):

> You all do know this mantle: I remember
> The first time ever Caesar put it on:
> 'Twas on a summer's evening, in his tent,
> That day he overcame the Nervii.
> Look! in this place ran Cassius' dagger through:
> See what a rent the envious Casca made:
> Through this the well-beloved Brutus stabb'd;
> And as he pluck'd his cursed steel away,
> Mark how the blood of Caesar follow'd it

When Caesar perceives the 'most unkindest cut of all',

> then burst his mighty heart;
> And, in his mantle muffling up his face,
> Even at the base of Pompey's statua,
> Which all the while ran blood, great Caesar fell.
> (Act III, scene II)

The mantle, with its stab-wounds (no doubt dishonestly identified) and its blood-stains has all the numinous power of an exhibit in a trial for murder. Antony plays his audience, onstage and off, like a matador caping a bull, until he knows the game is won. Without the mantle, without the physical object on the stage, the voltage of the drama would be very much lower, its power to electrify an audience – both audiences – diminished.

In all Shakespeare's plays, it is possible to perceive a kind of fulcrum in the dramatic action, like the trial scene in *The Merchant of Venice* or the play scene in *Hamlet*, after which nothing will be the same again. And very frequently, if not always, it is conceived in terms of a physical and visual event, which occurs at a mid-point in the play. In Act III, scene 1 of *Romeo and Juliet*, the swords flash out, and within seconds Mercutio is dead:

> I am hurt.
> A plague o' both your houses! I am sped.

Shortly afterwards, Tybalt will return, and within moments Romeo will kill him.

> BENVOLIO: Romeo, away! be gone!

As the stage empties in the play scene of *Hamlet* with Claudius's cry for 'Lights', here it is filled with a crowd of citizens, and the Prince. A sudden glint of steel, a fall and a cry, a rush of people – these signal the start of the end.

In comedy, as much as tragedy, Shakespeare conjures with the visual to bring about the transformation of the action, not to the exclusion of words, but in ways inseparable from them. In *Twelfth Night* Malvolio is set up by Maria to appear to Olivia in a guise which will ruin him for ever in her eyes:

> He will come to her in yellow stockings, and 'tis a colour she abhors; and cross-gartered, a fashion she detests; and he will smile upon her, which will now be so unsuitable to her disposition, being addicted to a melancholy as she is, that it cannot but turn him into a notable contempt.

The appetite in the audience for this encounter waits to be satisfied; and Maria feeds this hunger by describing him to her companions. When he does appear, the play, as with Bottom's translation, achieves a visual comedy of immeasurable delight. Malvolio was one of Olivier's great roles. He affected a deliciously dainty walk, a superior nasal whine and a self-parodying speech defect ('Some have gweatness thwust upon them.'); and his grimacing, lisping, contorted appearance, resembled a man still rehearsing every move in front of a mirror. Few pleasures in the theatre equal that of watching a great actor imitating a character who is putting on an act he cannot do: the timing, the moves, the facial expressions are all off-beat, grotesque, absurd. He becomes a musician giving a concert on an instrument he cannot play, or appearing not to, while at the same time doing it superbly well.

The visual extravagance which Shakespeare demands reflects the *vanitas vanitatum* for which Malvolio will pay in the end, when he is locked up for being allegedly mad. Visual playfulness, the device of costume, turns into a very dark joke, justifying Malvolio's equally dark desire to be revenged on 'the whole pack of you'. As audience we are moved by Malvolio's plight, but also too by a recognition in ourselves of the dangers of acting out our fantasies, of overreaching the roles we are 'called' to play, and turning ourselves into absurd fantasticks whom our friends and colleagues will reject. All the time we risk making fools of ourselves, and paying heavily for it, as Malvolio does, in being cast out from a household where he once had a role. His desire for revenge speaks only of the depth to which he has been hurt. Without the yellow-stockings, and the cross-gartering, Shakespeare would not have been able to let us see this, because it touches so nearly on how we feel about dressing every day. Is it just possible, that I have misjudged, look absurd, or, as in the nightmare, have forgotten to put on my trousers, causing everyone to laugh? Whatever the reason, few of us are entirely happy with our clothes, because we know the degree to which they expose us to ridicule. For all its comedy, Shakespeare's visual sense enables him to play on the audience's sense of a painful unease. He also transforms the everyday into the strange.

The bareness of Shakespeare's stage also enabled him to write plays in which the simple object could absorb the audience's whole concentration. As with Malvolio's stockings or Desdemona's handkerchief, bewitchingly embroidered with strawberries – and suggesting to Othello's fevered imagination the drops of blood which will have to be shed – the simple object seen in isolation acts as a prompter. It prompts Olivia to think Malvolio is suffering from midsummer madness, and needs to be taken care of (which his words and his body language confirm); but it also prompts the audience to imagine Malvolio's inner state of mind, his feelings, what manner of man he is. The process of prompting, whether between actors, or actors and audience, is central to the dramatic imagination – not as in a novel or poem as a matter of reflection – but as an instantaneous effect, an ignition of what had previously been in the dark. The role of the prompter is peculiar to the theatre, and may seem only a technical support for actors who 'dry'; but his unseen presence suggests metaphorically what is occurring the whole time in the nature of theatre magic. We, the audience, are being prompted into what we did not think we knew or felt.

In a recent book, edited by Dr Murray Cox, entitled *Shakespeare Comes to Broadmoor*, actors in the Royal Shakespeare Company commented on the significance for them of performing for an audience to whom the more extreme events in Shakepare's plays – murder, rape, violence – had been lived experience. Holding a mirror up to Nature was actually ocurring in a potentially dangerous way, and in a relationship with the audience which had little in common with performances in Stratford or London. Gertrude's cry to Hamlet that he is turning his eyes into her very soul – a felt, not a thought experience – was actually occurring. And yet that is, or should be, the function of all theatre, whether by making us cry, or laugh at human folly. In this summer lightning or darkness visible, the transforming power of simple images – at crucial moments projected onto physical objects – determines the depth at which theatre works, or, one might say, to which it works.

King Lear is, amongt many other things, a play about descent into chaos. Lear himself was recently and memorably played by Ian Holm, like an ageing Phaeton who cannot control the chariot of the sun, and causes the rapid dissolution of all bonds, familial, political and geographic. The play shows what happens when these bonds are sundered; and the first part of it culminates in the storm scene. How this is actually staged absorbs the ingenuity of the director, scene, sound and lighting designers. But whatever the effects, the words spoken by Lear – 'Blow, winds, and crack your cheeks' leave no doubt that the chaos is in his mind. In one sense, this is unactable and unstageable. The play is on the edge of an abyss, in which all germens are about to be spilled at once, leaving no action to be performed. Shakespeare restores the balance in this action of transcendent metaphor by his most terrible piece of physical theatre, and his most cruelly memorable use of 'objects' on the stage: the putting out of Gloucester's eyes. This is a scene which, like Dr Johnson, most of us do not want to live through again. When it was performed in Broadmoor, the prison for the criminally insane, and Regan castrated a servant as part of the action, the response was dead silence, apart from a stifled gasp, 'Jesus Christ' (Cox, p. 68). The blinding of Gloucester strips away the last defence of the audience before the image of horror, which is chaos. We are forced to look into the heart of darkness, and see an image of ourselves, when all the restraints of humanity have been fractured. Such things cannot be spoken of, but they can be experienced, and have been, in Auschwitz, Cambodia, Bosnia.

Through these objects – Gloucester's eyes so idly cast on the stage – Shakespeare makes us do just that. In any other play, it would have seemed excessive, and even here nearly does so, except through its power to make us look inward at what can result from a descent into chaos. The storm and the eyes are an inseparable part of the same figurative action. Theatre requires that the inward be made actual, if we are to experience an action, not merely watch it.

★

The vision of a play – all that we see on the stage – is created from a combination of what the dramatist has written, how the director and his design team interpret the text, and the resources of stage – space and money which are available. What matters is the effect on the audience.

When the screen fell down at the first performance of Sheridan's *The School for Scandal* the roar of the audience was heard all over London. The 'little French milliner' whom Sir Peter Teazle expects to discover in the house of the corrupt Sir Joseph Surface, turns out to be his wife. Ironically, he and Joseph's 'good-hearted' brother, Charles had hoped to discomfort Joseph by the disclosure; but the truth turns out to be more complex. As Charles Surface angrily remarks: 'Egad, you seem all to have been diverting yourselves here at hide and seek, and I don't see who is out of the secret.' *The School for Scandal*, as its title states, is a play about words (scandal does not consist of immoral acts but in the description of them as immoral by others). At the outset, Lady Sneerwell confides to Snake:

> Wounded myself, in the early part of my life, by the envenomed tongue of slander, I confess I have since known no pleasure equal to the reducing others to the level of my own injured reputation.
> SNAKE: Nothing can be more natural.

The envenomed tongue gives birth to plot and wit; but the play is made, and made memorable, by the falling down of the screen. What is disclosed will depend a great deal on the body language of everyone on stage, as on the way the Teazles have been visualized and played throughout: the degree to which Sir Peter has been presented as an old man married to a young wife in a match doomed to failure, or alternatively, as a marriage of affection, suddenly confronted with its own weaknesses.

Michael Billington, writing about the 1972 National Theatre production by Jonathan Miller described the effect like this:

> The screen scene is brilliantly handled, a marriage lying momentarily in ruins as Lady Teazle cowers in a corner like a frightened rabbit caught in a car's headlights and a stricken Sir Peter pulls his wig over his eyebrows.
>
> (*ONS*, p. 16)

The mirror which is turned on their marriage and relationship at this moment works, on the audience too, as a sudden and complex probe: a moment of confrontation in which the truth cannot be avoided. Such moments come to us all; but more often not through something said, but as here through some chance misadventure. The simplicity of the event is in inverse proportion to the complexity of the effect.

In Act III of Chekhov's *Uncle Vanya*, a play described as 'Scenes from Country Life', Vanya, finally driven crazy by Yeliena's rejection of him, and Serebriakov's inability to understand his rage at the proposal to sell the estate, rushes off. A shot is fired off-stage; and Serebriakov runs in, terrified, followed by Vanya. He fires the revolver again, misses and flings the revolver on the floor with a curse, before sinking into a chair exhausted. Chekhov combines a moment of potential tragedy with a farcical outcome. But in these few moments of frenzied action, Chekhov reveals the intensity of hidden feelings, the hatred and incomprehension which cannot be expressed, and the dangers of confronting them when they are suddenly released. As audience, we laugh, we are horrified at the sudden turn of events, and are amazed. Serebriakov is struggling for his life; Yeliena is struggling to prevent Vanya from committing murder; and for these few moments of physical action on the stage, the audience acts like the analyst on to whom Vanya's pent-up fury and frustration is transferred. We feel the burden of what he cannot deal with; and it arouses in us the anxiety of our buried frustration and anger. Chekhov succeeded in not ending his act with the conventional sock on the jaw; but in turning dramatic convention upside down, he produced an effect of a more deeply undermining kind – and one of his most memorable moments of theatre.

In Peter Stein's production at the Edinburgh Festival for the Teatro di Roma and Teatro Stabile di Parma in 1996, he began the next act with Vanya curled up on the bed in the corner of study, foetus-like, as though he had suffered a complete nervous breakdown, which the subsequent playing of the scene between him and Dr Astrov confirmed. This seemed the natural outcome of what Vanya had suffered. It darkened the tone of the last act, making the Sonya's final vigil with him the more terrible, lonely and relentless. As the lighting on the stage was slowly reduced to that of a single candle, Elizabetta Pozzi's voice rang out, while Vanya worked on at his accounts: 'Reposeremo . . . Reposeremo (We shall rest . . . We shall rest)'.

In this production it expressed not so much a hope as an elegiac comment on what could not be changed, and had to be endured. When, as is more usual, Vanya's eruption in Act III is played as a temporary aberration, Sonya's final words in the face of a relentless destiny can sound like a transcendent vision, as happened when Anna Calder-Marshall played Sonya to Paul Scofield's Vanya in Anthony Page's 1970 production:

> We shall hear the angels; we shall see the sky all dressed in diamonds; we shall see all this world's evil and all our sufferings drown in the mercy that will fill the earth

And we believed her.

However a director sees a play – whatever he or she feels its atmosphere, tone, and 'smell' to be – its effectiveness in performance will depend on a sense of timing. A play no less than piece of music has a pulse; it can be played faster or slower; but how it is played will determine its effect. In the playing of farce, timing and physical activity become central to its visualization. A mis-timed farce will be flat as an unrisen Yorkshire pudding. Exits and entrances, encounters, misadventures, confusions, mistakes, recognitions succeed each other in precisely controlled chaos. In the farces of Georges Feydeau, the performers need to be 'middle-aged, out of condition, Olympic athletes'. His women 'breathe virtue and are forthwith out of breath' (Mortimer). As one of his greatest interpreters, the actor Jacques Charon has said, Feydeau invented a new form of comedy which foreshadowed the crazy gags of the silent screen. Among his frenzied creations: rooms twirling on pivots, eiderdowns that walk by themsleves and hallucinated people who turn as required into visions of the Angel Gabriel . . . . Feydeau's nimble dialogue skips along with the action, keeping pace with its perilous leaps and gambols. It's like an acrobat's tights, lightweight and supple, which fit his muscles like a second skin'. In *A Flea in Her Ear*, the breathlessness of the action involves a man with a cleft palate who consequently cannot be understood, a German with a Lolita complex, and a hotel porter, Poche, who is the double (played by the same actor) of Chandebise, a husband, suspected of infidelity. In *A Little Hotel on the Side*, Matthieu suffers from a stutter which only comes on when it starts to rain.

For all the miraculous precision of their plotting and subplotting, Feydeau himself said 'my plays are entirely improvised'. And it is this sense of spontaneous inventiveness and ingenuity which the timing has to preserve. Our pleasure derives from seeing these apparently conventional people caught in the glare of their own indiscretions. Their panic generates the speed of the action. The director has to find a visual and physical equivalent for a kind of mania, mathematical in its precision: or 'total chaos in the grip of an iron vice'. As the characters have to perform physically (hiding, running, disguising themselves) and invent verbally, to save their bacon, so the set needs too to be a place for exuberant indiscretions: it has to accommodate their flight, and their concealment from one another. In *A Flea in Her Ear*, the stage-action requires a fast revolve. '*The right side of the stage is taken up by a small bedroom, with a bathroom door and a bed on a small raised platform. This bed is on a revolve which can turn to reveal a similar bed in the room behind it.*' The button beside the bed which controls the revolve enables the bed, and its occupant, to be switched, without the character on the front part of the stage having noticed, so that when he attempts to resume his advances, he finds his partner has changed from a woman into a man!

When Jacques Charon directed *A Flea in Her Ear* at the National Theatre in 1966, he succeeded in establishing his characters as being *vraies personages*. Feydeau's characters are in their right mind; they simply find themselves in situations where they act as though they are out of it. The director's sense of timing, keeping dialogue and action in relentless counterpoint made the whole action a jest, but never a joke. Farce enacts a simple law of Nature that, as John Mortimer has said, 'at a certain speed things disintegrate'. Sustaining the right momentum requires also an appropriate visual sense. In the 1989 production at the Old Vic, directed by Richard Jones with a set designed by the Brothers Quay, the Hôtel Coq d'Or became a grey place of morbid repressions, which no one would want to visit for a bit of fun on the side, except in a nightmare. The set which conveyed depression destroyed the relation between lightness and speed. This delicate balance has to be preserved too in the performances which must never deteriorate into mere jokiness, or an attempt to get laughs. No one who saw Alec Guinness in the 1956 production of *Hotel Paradiso* will forget the moment when he began to revolve on the end of a bit and brace, as the hall porter bored a hole in the opposite side of the wall to spy on what was happening inside the bedroom, or Robert Hirsch as the pigeon-breasted man of letters, Bouzin, in the Comédie Française's production of *Un Fil à la Patte*. In each the actor's control of his body, and the director's control of timing in the scene as whole (in other words no exaggeration for the sake of laughs) creates the visual effect.

The end of Noel Coward's one farce, *Hay Fever*, depends on a double action, in which the timing and the visualization must fuse precisely. While the Bliss family shout at each other as loudly as possible, their week-end guests, and lovers, ignored and disregarded, have to make their escape. The stage direction reads:

> *During this scene, Myra, Jackie, Richard and Sandy creep downstairs with their bags, unperceived by the family. They make for the front door.*

Well performed, this scene is both very funny, and a devastating criticism of a family's preoccupation with its immediate affairs. It will send the audience away, laughing and uneasy.

★

In the visualization of some plays, the director may decide to have a palpable design upon us, and add a great deal to what exists in the text. When successful this can give new life to a play, and make us see what seemed familiar with fresh eyes. In his production of J.B. Priestley's *An Inspector Calls* (1946), Stephen Daldry has done just this. Using stage technology to create a tremendous *coup de théâtre*, he has created a production which has run for years in England and been successful around the world, while a conventional revival at the Westminster Theatre in London a couple of years previously lasted a few weeks only.

The house in which the wealthy Edwardian industrial family live becomes quite literally a doll's house, standing in a desolate emptiness of rain-swept cobble-stones, looked down on by a lowering sky. Writing in 1946, Priestley intended his play as a warning to a country which had gone through two world wars, of the need to find some new sense of community if it was not to continue its progress towards self-destruction. The inspector, possessed of metaphysical canniness acts as a probe of the family's conscience, or lack of it, of people's desire to think well of themselves, without regard to the effect of their acts on others, or the communities in which they live. In Daldry's production, the doll's house (a solid-looking structure) collapses dramatically forward at one point, on its supports, and is later restored, when the family's self-image finds a way of rebuilding itself.. The metaphor is blatant; and its effectiveness derives from a combination of this blatancy, and the sheer surprise of what happens to the set.

Past time tugs at us all from behind, the future tugs us towards it. In the present moment these forces converge. Priestley's characters in their evening dress and ball gowns, belong to the past; their actions and attitudes gesture towards an increasingly ominous future, blasted, unpeopled as the spaces surrounding the doll's house suggest. In the present (and a stage-action is always in the present) where these forces intersect, the audience watches discomforted, and at the same time amazed, by what this piece of theatrical legerdemain can suggest. As visual theatre, and as theatre with vision, this production deserves its success.

In the last fifteen years vision in the theatre has become associated as much with companies, working together over long periods of time, as with the imprint of individual directors and design teams. Companies such as Shared Experience, Cheek by Jowl and, above all, Théâtre de Complicité have created new styles of visualizing a dramatic action, and a style of performing, inspired by a physical and often violent simplicity, in which the inventiveness of the actors counts for as much as that of writer and director.

Everything Complicité actors do is rooted in what they have heard and seen. This is a theatre of bodily functions and impulses, of class-defences and universal desires. Its logic is merciless, its techniques virtuoso, its energy without bounds. It is rude and funny and fearful, for inside the vortex of frenzy the individual is always alone.

(Michael Ratcliffe, Programme Note for
The Street of Crocodiles (1992).

Complicité, as a collective, devises its own shows, sometimes from a text as in the case of Dürrenmatt's *The Visit*, and sometimes from a theme or idea, developed through months of argument, rehearsal and research. Their work is created from vitality, invention, rhythm, humour and, in combination, a sense of texture on the stage which conjures with what the audience can be made to imagine. In *The Three Lives of Lucie Cabrol*, based on a story by John Berger in *Pig Earth*, Complicité created and explored the peasant life of Europe, now on the point of being extinguished by farming policies, devised by bureaucrats, and the gravitational pull of urban life.

Seven actors play children, chickens, cows lowing in their stalls, even the earth of the ploughed field as the ploughshare rolls it over. Outstretched fingers suggest the fruit and mushrooms Lucie is gathering; chairs and buckets become a path, planks a wall separating the cow-stall from the house, and the actors holding them the cows. This is a form of theatre in which the inventiveness of the actors, and the power of suggestion compels the audience to cross the boundary into the lives of the peasants, to see how they have lived, suffered and survived at a moment in time when their way of life is threatened with extinction, and in doing so makes the audience question whether the alternative being offered in the name of 'modernization' is better. The third life of Lucie Chabrol takes place after her death (felled by the axe of an unnamed intruder in her lonely chalet). In this other world of *la terre et les morts*, the peasants continue to work because they have nothing else to remember. Justice will only come about in such a world when the living come to know what the dead have suffered.

Mime, physical activity and suggestion become a means of exploring what had previously been invisible.

This theatre smuggles the public into places which are normally considered closed. And they smuggle out of those distant places the daily routines and the triumph and the pain of being alive, all of it stuff which, carried on their shoulders, in their voices and under their arms, is immediately recognisable and intimately familiar. Contraband nevertheless. Contraband because it's about what is habitually marginalised, dismissed, belittled, made voiceless. Maybe the essential contraband today is hope. Hope which is inseparable from life, like the violent theatre these gentle artists make.'

(John Berger, Programme Note to *The Three Lives of Lucie Chabrol* 1994)

In their production of Brecht's *The Caucasian Chalk Circle* at the National Theatre (1997), the Olivier auditorium was rearranged to create a theatre in the round. As in Chile and Brazil, where crowds have gathered to watch Complicité performing in the street, so here some of the intimacy, and proximity of 'folk' theatre was reinvented. As Brecht himself said, 'You can achieve every shade of seriousness by means of ease, and none of them without it.' Improvisation and informality, the simplest of props, create this sense of ease, leading naturally to the image which gives the play its title: Asdak's drawing of the chalk circle. Asked as judge to give the child to its true mother, Asdak makes the two contending women pull it out of the circle. As in the Judgement of Solomon, he awards the child not to the stronger woman who pulls the child out of the circle, but to the woman who in order not to hurt it, pulls least hard. In a play concerned with right judgement, with what is appropriate, natural and humanly best, the chalk circle is like the magic ring, the arena in which we succeed or fail in our lives. As a piece of theatre, and as a visual device, it could not be simpler, but it has the power to conjure from airy nothing a way of suggesting a test which applies not just to Grusha and the Governor's wife, but to us all. Where do we draw the limits of our own chalk circles? At what point do we think it right to let go to avoid the destructiveness of hanging on?

Simon McBurney's production of Ionesco's *The Chairs* for Théâtre de Complicité (1997) used a set, designed by Quay Brothers, in which multiple doors, and cupboards piled on top of one another, and painted a ghostly grey created a room which was surreal. The non-realism of the stage reflected the unreality of Ionesco's view of the world: 'At certain moments the world seems to me devoid of significance, devoid of reality: unreal.' And yet as the Old Man and the Old Woman ushered in their non-existent guests to hear the Orator deliver the lecture which would articulate the Old Man's 'message', filling the stage with empty chairs, the stage was filled not with the unreal, but with the presence of their loneliness, their need for each other, their anguish in trying to make sense of their lives, their desire to feel wanted and fulfilled – and finally in the presence of a non-existent God not to be judged harshly, to be treated with mercy. When the moment came for them to die, separated by the whole space of the stage, and stretching out their hands towards each other, 'as in love of a further shore', they discovered a kind of exultation which overcame space before death overtook them. When the Orator wrote on the door, 'Angel sweep', (or was it 'Angels weep?') and 'God is agone', enough reality had been lived through to make the angels weep. Here was no self-pity, or coldness of heart, but a yearning for explanation, for plenitude, and the discovery of 'nowhere without the no'. In every movement and gesture, as they ushered in the absent guests, Richard Briers and Geraldine McEwan discovered a grotesque and bathetic comedy, the comedy of the undefeated, grappling with the infirmity of age and language at the moment before night comes, when all must sit in 'doom-session' on their souls. The skills and inventiveness of acting were matched in these performances to a production where the rhythms and musicality reached always towards a meaning which existence could not supply, where theatre and life fused to reveal the face of the unreal to each other.

Peter Brook in his day-long (or night-long!) production of *The Mahabharata*, which toured the world, used the talents of a company drawn from many different countries and cultures. Peter Brook has related how, in 1975, he and Jean-Claude Carrière, who was to write the script, met a French Professor of Sanskrit who began telling them the stories of *The*

Mahabharata. They fell under their spell, determining at once to share these stories with audiences in the West. Together, they travelled widely in India to gain images of dance, film, marionette theatre, village celebrations and plays. They came back, knowing that what they had to do was not to imitate but to suggest. What was eventually created was a production of immense visual splendour and beauty, also of great simplicity, with ochre-coloured earth which covered the acting area suggesting the heat-baked soil of India. Red light was used to stand for fire, a piece of cloth a river running through ancient plains; boots stood for a dead person; a single wheel suggested a war-chariot, a stick became a sheaf of magic arrows. The play started from the oldest of all devices: an old man telling a young boy a story.

BOY: What's your name?
VYASA: Vyasa.
BOY: What's your poem about?
VYASA: It's about you.
BOY: Me?
YASA: Yes, it's the story of your race, how your ancestors were born, how they grew up, how a vast war arose. It's the poetical history of mankind. If you listen carefully, at the end you'll be someone else.

The musical-instrument on which Vyasa plays will in time be used to suggest 'a bow, a sword, a mace, a river, an army and a monkey's tail'. A stick can be either a weapon or a flute; a piece of cloth held by two performers suggest the barrier between the everyday and the magical worlds. And in the battle scenes, mime, orchestrated with sound and light, suggests the shooting of ten thousand arrows.

Chloe Obolensky, who designed costumes as well as properties and scenic elements has described her aims.

It was a question not of undertaking some sort of archaeological reconstruction of the costumes of ancient India, but of finding what could both evoke India and best lend itself to our purpose and subject matter. My only guiding principle: suggestion and evocation rather than illustration. . . . One thing that is truly beautiful to see in India is the way in which certain items of clothing are used constantly: the big rectangular scarves (*schotti*) they wash at the water's edge in the day are used as covers when they go to sleep at night. Now that's just what we are looking for: a rigorous economy, and incredibly strong and stark simplicity.

(*Mahabharata*, p. 74)

The vision of this epic was created from a 'poetic minimalism', in which the colours of India, red, white, saffron complemented its elemental life in earth, water and fire. Garlands of flowers, bowls of rice, spices, floating candles, the fabrics from India, and the cut of the wide-skirted *kurtas*, the masks of demons and Gods, the multiple use of bamboos, as biers and weapons, the low-footed tables at which people sat to play dice, the drums and the *nagaswaram*, all evoked an India, ancient, epic and continuing which was always suggestive because seen in the space of an uncluttered stage where the simple became the translucent. Unmistakably an act of Western theatre, and described by one Indian writer as a 'transcreation', the *Mahabharata* succeeded in asking a universal question: 'we live in a time of destruction – everything points in the same direction. Can this destruction be avoided?'

★

When I first started going to the theatre, naturalism (the fourth wall of the room removed so that we can look into it) still predominated as the visual style, for what was then known as the straight play, whether by Noel Coward, Terence Rattigan or N.C.Hunter. In the last fifty years, visual style, whether in clothes or cars, has been constantly changing; visual style in the theatre has been no more static. It has become more varied and eclectic, partly as a result of what has become technically possible – for example, the trucks on electrically operated air-castors which enable large pieces of scenery to be moved around the stage swifly and silently without interrupting the action; partly, from changing conventions about the nature of stage illusion, deriving from the influence of Brecht; and partly from an increasing rejection of naturalism, as an adequate, or even interesting, representation of the real. Fantasy, the surreal, dream and the subconscious have become ever more deeply embedded in our conception of how things are. In the late twentieth century what used to be called 'a slice of life' has broader and subtler dimensions; and visual perception in the theatre has been modified by this change. Visually, the theatre is both an interpretation of, and comment on, how we take things to be. Its inventiveness in relation to both derives from a constant scrutiny of its own conventions. Visual style in the theatre depends upon the space to be filled (the 'envelope' within which the designer has to work), the resources available, financial and technological, and changes occurring outside the theatre, which affect our visual perception of the world. When the Moscow Art Theatre first came to London in the nineteen-fifties, the interior life of the acting contrasted with the old-fashioned sets, and the 'tatty painted scenery'.

Stage designers, and lighting designers have increasingly developed their own arts, and work in creative collaboration with the director, but also independently, and in isolation. Each has to solve their own problems in their own way; but the conceptions of the design team and the director need to coincide with each other. The solutions to problems of design and lighting must give the director what he or she wants. They must also succeed in interpreting the play. The greater the play, the more essential it becomes for the visualization not to be intrusive, distracting the audience from the play's inner action. In 1983, John Gunter designed the sets for Sheridan's *The Rivals*, in the Olivier Theatre, and 'put the whole of Bath on the stage, with all the characters having their own houses.' The effect for all its visual elegance added little to the play, and detracted from the human interest of the plot.

While theatre directors are well known and often contro-versial figures, the names of designers, whether of scene or lighting, are much less familiar outside the theatre; and their work often unrecorded and undescribed in books. Jocelyn Herbert's *A Theatre Workbook* (1993) is an invaluable account of the process of creative collaboration, between designer and directors. She begins with a résumé of what is required for each production (for example, '*Purgatory*: Yeats calls for a ruined house and a bare tree in the background'), eventually commenting on what has succeeded, or failed. Held still, the stage has the appearance of a sculptured space; released into motion, it becomes a musical composition in which what is seen and what is heard create a rhythm of their own.

What works depends on the space to be filled. Intimate theatre, as Strindberg observed at the start of the century, has one particular advantage over plays performed in larger spaces. When Shakespeare wrote, 'the lunatic, the lover and the poet are of imagination all compact', he knew that what they saw was reflected in their eyes. The eyes are the mirrors and win-dows of the soul. One mark of the great actor is the degree to which he or she can open these windows. In creating a role, an actor develops a technique for using this form of self-revelation. In the greatest performances it becomes wholly instinctive and inseparable from the role: an essential part of its visualization. The degree to which the audience can respond to this part of the performance (in spite of all that can be done with modern lighting techniques) depends to some extent on proximity. Deborah Warner, writing about the experience of bringing the Royal Shakespeare Company production of *King Lear* to Broadmoor, commented:

> It is always an exciting experience when a production moves from a large space to a smaller one. There is no question that it brings out the best in everyone. Actors enjoy playing intimate spaces. Any company who has never had that experience is going to be tremendously inspired

by the freshness of the result. . . . The actors were very aware of the audience. Many spoke afterwards of playing lines quite differently because of this. The members of the audience were, as they should be, active contributors to the event. (Cox, p. 94)

The loss of eye-contact between stage and audience is an absolute loss for which nothing compensates. The photo of Laurence Olivier as Archie Rice ('dead behind the eyeballs') in John Osborne's *The Entertainer* has become a classic, not just as a photo, but because it reveals a great deal about the art of acting. The close relation between stage and audience in the Royal Court Theatre, particularly in Archie Rice's music-hall turns played by Olivier at the front of the stage, made this 'interrogation' of Archie possible. The Other Place in Stratford, the Donmar Warehouse, the Cottesloe at the National Theatre, the Almeida Theatre, as well as many other less formal spaces all over the country, preserve this form of communication without which audiences become passive observers, and cease to be active participators, interpreting all that they see.

In 1997, Trevor Nunn directed Ibsen's *An Enemy of the People* on the Olivier stage at the National Theatre in London. The settings were by John Napier, and the lighting by David Hersey. Ian McKellen played Dr Stockmann. The Olivier stage and its revolve were used to create the ambience of a coastal town in southern Norway, with its market-traders, bands, sky-scapes and the cries of gulls. Three out of the five acts take place in the Stockmanns' house; the action is domestic, and concerns the effect on family life of public pressures – a theme of obvious contemporary relevance. The spaces of the Olivier stage distanced this action, making the play seem more like an opera without music than a domestic drama. Only in the fourth act, where Dr Stockmann addresses the townspeople – some of whom were found in the audience – did the elaborateness of the staging, and its visual spaciousness enhance the action, and not diminish its intensity through the need for exaggeration of gesture, and of reaction.

Any acting-space, whether large or small, whether its stage-design is simple or complex, only comes to life when there are actors within it. The style has to create a space or spaces in which the actors feel at ease. When the performances begin, they are alone with the audience and, without this ease – a sense that the space is appropriate for the action – they cannot be expected to discover that naturalness on which all good acting (and all art) depends.

No one can enjoy playing, being playful, if they feel cramped in relation to the other actors on the stage, confined in terms of the movement expected of them, or within a stage ambiance which creates the wrong tone, atmosphere – at worst, where they are wondering if they will be killed getting on or off the stage. Disasters do occur, as, for example, when in a performance of Handel's *Samson*, Samson pushed the temple down not just on the Philistines, but into the orchestra pit as well.

★

Modern theatre has drawn life and strength from a variety, and a changing variety, of visual styles – painterly, architectural, constructivist, symbolic, minimalist – which themselves reflect changing perspectives outside the theatre. In 1944 when Tyrone Guthrie directed Ralph Richardson in *Peer Gynt* the sets designed by Reece Pemberton were painterly in style, but succeeded in reflecting the inner battles of Peer's consciousness. The mysterious Boyg which tells Peer to 'go round about', determining the future course of his life as an evasion of self, was seen as the branch of a vast tree in a misty wood. As I was later to realize, it had the force of those psychological blocks to which we cannot put a name, and which obstruct our self-understanding. It introduced me to the idea that the stage was not only capable of being a magical place (here, the enchanted wood of fairy-tale), but a place with its own poetic power. Whatever the visual style – and whatever the play – theatre is diminished when it loses poetic power. As in poetry itself, economy and compression determine intensity and depth.

Stage design of the forties and fifties was dominated – at least for being enduringly memorable – by Oliver Messel. His sets combined beauty with space, the fantastic with the real, and had a feeling for the play's world, whether in the detailed mediaevalism of Christopher Fry's *The Lady's Not for Burning* or in *Ring Round the Moon*, translated by Christopher Fry from Jean Anouilh's *L'Invitation au Château*, set in a rococo winter-garden in spring. In style, the play owes much to *commedia dell' arte*. Peter Brook, who directed the London production wrote of the play.

> His [Anouilh's] literary quality is that of theatre literature, the elegance of his dialogue appears when it is spoken by comedians in the rhythm of a comic scene. His plays are recorded improvisations. Like Chopin, he preconceives the acccidental and calls it an impromptu. He is a poet, but not a poet of words: he is poet of words–acted, of scenes set, of players performing. Messel created out of wrought iron, green plants and chinese lanterns a setting which reflected the improvised lives of those characters; decorative, stylised, witty and heartless.'
>
> (*Ring*, p. 7)

Unlike most designers before him, he realized the importance of materials in building the set, insisting that the winter-garden be built out of steel, not wood, which created an effect so light that, as Christopher Fry remarked, it would have taken off if not fixed to the ground. The rococo style offers no vision, its blandishment is to charm and amuse.

In the play, Paul Scofield played the part of two identical twins, one good without depth, the other scheming without kindness. The atmosphere of the play is ironic and comic, not farcical or tragic. The artificiality of Messel's stage decoration reflected the improvisation of the characters' lives, dominated by whim, impulse and desire. Like the charade which is only played for the pleasure and inventiveness of the game – and has no significance once it is over – the playing is all. Through his decorative style of scene-design, Messel created an equally playful set, making no reference outside of itself, and arousing delight as a *jeu d'esprit*.

Although stage design as decoration has become unfashionable, and can be deadly, Messel's influence can still be felt. Philip Prowse in his production of Oscar Wilde's *A Woman of No Importance* (1991) used visual richness in an equally appropriate and comparable way. Wilde's play is about a world where class and money count for everything, and goodness of heart for little at all. Few plays have a more ironic title: a woman whom society rejects and demeans turns out to be the only woman of any importance at all. A society which, like a luxurious and decaying *nature morte*, lavished its rewards on those whose shallowness was matched by their hardness of heart was reflected in a décor equally plush and dead. An exorbitant period sense – the massive chandelier, the red velvet banquettes, the gilt decoration – suggested the lack of any real worth: dingy, claustrophobic and heavy with the heaviness which comes from displays of opulence for their own sake. Unlike many productions of Wilde's plays which seek to flatter the audience by appealing to a nostalgia for a style now lost, Philip Prowse's production used visual style as a sign of inner corruption, of grandeur without human feeling, and an extravagant materialism which said as much about the 1980s as the 1890s.

Since the 1950s, the rejection of the decorative style of scene design has been inspired by the desire, as the director, John Dexter, has put it, to provoke 'the audience to think for themselves, and use their imagination.' This has taken many forms, and always been most productive when the design becomes inseparable from the interpretation of the play, not an excuse for showmanship on the part of the designer. Peter Hall on being shown a stage design is reported to have remarked on one occasion: 'It's very nice – but is it necessary?' Low budgets and the stripping-away of the unnecessary have often proved good medicine.

In Stratford in 1951, Shakespeare's tetralogy of history plays, *Richard II, Henry IV, Parts One and Two, Henry V*, was performed for the first time as a cycle. Tanya Moiseiwitsch designed a permanent set of rough wooden beams which included a balcony, and an inner recess, or acting area, as in the Elizabethan theatre. This structure could be transformed to indicate change of location by the simple and fast use of drapes and curtains. Banners and flags told us which army we were with, whether in Wales or France. The set gave continuity to the action. These plays were both about individual lives (with Michael Redgrave as the moist-eyed poet king unfitted for his role) and about the relentless tide of historical events which carry some upwards as others are swept away. The simple indications of change of location compelled the audience to imagine what was suggested by a brush-stroke or two, while at the same time allowing the drama an unimpeded flow. In addition, by concentrating colour in the costumes and emblems of power, national and heraldic, it presented the four plays as about kingship, and the nature of personal authority which the legitimate King Richard lacked, and the conscience-stricken usurper Bolinbroke, played by Harry Andrews, possessed. Richard Burton as Hal and Henry V blazed upon the scene as a brooding presence whose gaze was always fixed on the fulfilment of ambition, indifferent to the feelings and advice of others. The new-found comet was to blaze its trail across the skies, but disappointingly in lesser Agincourts.

If Tanya Moiseiwitsch's set-structure now seems too dominating and assertive, this is because its strengths – speed of change in locality, flexibility in the use of stage-space and imaginative involvement on the part of the audience – have been built upon and developed, as the technological resources of the stage have increasingly allowed. What used to be called the transformation scene in pantomime, when a tap on the wall revealed to the astonished audience the 'cloud-capped towers' behind, has now become a modern convention. The scene is transformed in time and space without any break in the action. The device may be as simple as getting the actors to create a new space by moving the objects within it, so that we see them in altered spatial relatonsips, and in a new light indicating a time change, which creates a new tone and atmosphere.

In Christopher Hampton's *Tales from Hollywood* (1983) the story-teller, Ödön von Horvath, killed in a thunder storm on the Champs-Elysées by the falling branch of a tree, shifts the audience's perpective from Paris to Hollywood as the locality of the stage changes behind him. Summoning up people and things from his imagination – Garbo, the Marx Brothers – he can show us around his 'brave new world'. As in the novel, he can appear to us as a reliable and unreliable narrator, since we know him to have died before any of this happened. Stage-time and stage-space become supple, allowing the power of visual suggestion to take the place of verbal explanation.

ACT II

Light-show: garish neon. Franz Waxman's music for Sunset Boulevard. *Projections: Hollywood landmarks of the forties. Horvath steps into this, grinning.*

HORVATH: Ah, Hollywood! The kitsch! The désespoir!

This suppleness and speed may be achieved with technical sophistication, as here, or with the utmost simplicity. In Deborah Warner's production of *King John*, at The Other Place in Stratford (1988) the scenes before, and on, the walls of Angiers were suggested by placing ladders against a stage-balcony, creating the idea of siege ('Our cannon shall be bent Against the brows of this resisting town'). Because the playing had urgency, and conveyed a feeling of real threat, the siege was more effective than in many film sequences costing millions of dollars, which leave nothing for the audience to imagine, except that nothing ever happened like this except in a Hollywood movie!

Chekhov's early play, *Platonov*, has long been regarded as an over-long, wordy attempt at a form of comedy about the irresistible boredom of country life, of interest only as a precursor of his later great plays. In Michael Frayn's version, called *Wild Honey*, performed at the National Theatre in 1984 in a production by Christopher Morahan, with settings by John Gunter, an inventive piece of staging, and a memorable performance by Ian McKellen gave it new life. In this production, a steam train roared to the front of the stage, looking as though it was about to plunge into the stalls. The effect was comic and theatrical. But the point was not mere ornamentation. Platonov, the local schoolmaster suffers from a lack of energy and boredom, alleviated only by sexual attraction (hence the title) and booze. In contrast to the human world of late nineteenth-century society, the train exudes steam, power, energy and the determination to get somewhere! The visual contrast between the train, and the laid-back, despairing quality of Platonov's existence commented humorously and without over-emphasis on the conflicting forces in Chekhov's world.

The effective solution of problems of staging can also determine what productions it is possible to mount. In a recent season of plays by the Peter Hall Company at the Old Vic Theatre, a simple but flexible box set was desgined by John Gunter to allow performances of plays by Shakespeare, Vanbrugh, Granvillle Barker, Chekhov, Beckett as well as new work by contemporary dramatists to be set up quickly – with two productions a day. In Vanbrugh's *The Provok'd Wife* the lowering of topiaried trees in the shape of gallants and beaux indicated the setting of St James's Park, and the atmosphere of lecherous assignation, of eavesdropping and revelation, associated with it. The obtrusive artificiality of the visual design reflected a social world where outward appearance and the intention to deceive went hand in glove. Settings like this derive their effectiveness from a simplicity which is both literal and metaphoric.

In scene design, the use of varied materials has also
increased the range of visual responses. Heavy leather costumes in Peter Brook's production of *King Lear* (1962) intensified the feeling of a relentless world, without gentleness or
pity. As in all aspects of stage design, radical experimentation
has renewed visual language. Jocelyn Herbert, designing *The
Seagull* for the Royal Court Theatre in 1964 described her
approach like this:

> The garden was just a tree and a painted backcloth of
> birch trees and the lake – birch trees are somehow the
> symbol of Russia. When I was working on the tree I first
> made it by cutting folded paper and making holes, then I
> found some material and experimented with it, and it
> really looked quite like a silver birch. There was an awful
> problem about fire-proofing the leaves – there always was
> in those days with trees – now it's easy because you just
> dunk the material in fire-proofing liquid. The backcloth
> was filled with gauze so that as the moon came up you
> saw it rising above the lake until it reached an unpainted
> space in the gauze where it shone through. (Herbert,
> p. 62)

Change, however never occurs without meeting resistance.

> When I introduced the idea to the workshops at The
> Court they were upset and wanted to use wood. In 1960
> when I used metal for *Antigone* the carpenters and painters
> would't touch it and I had to do the whole thing myself.
> Workshops are often wary of new materials and feel threat-
> ened; it's their whole way of life and you can't blame them.
> (Herbert, p. 41)

By bringing the originality of her ideas to stage design,
Jocelyn Herbert has contributed a great deal to keeping the
poetry of the stage alive; and her involvement extends, as that
of the true artist always does, to concern for every detail.

When Peggy Ashcroft was rehearsing the dual role of Shen Te/Shui Ta in Brecht's *The Good Woman of Setzuan* she was against wearing a mask to begin with, but wanted to move from one sex to the other without changing costume. Jocelyn Herbert designed a half-mask of leather which was light and supple; and Peggy Ashcroft recorded its effect upon her:

> I remember the horrible process of having it made – my face was covered with plaster. The mask was very light and it thrilled me to see its effect on me. It was very, very exciting. I think my idea of a mask had been something much less plastic, much harder and more confining, but this little affair was the reverse of that. (Herbert, p. 19).

Many years later when Rex Harrison was rehearsing the part of Captain Shotover in Shaw's *Heartbreak House* and driving the director, John Dexter, to despair, because he couldn't get the part, Jocelyn Herbert again invented a solution.

> He wanted to wear the proper reefer jacket from Watts, the yachting place, and a navy blue sweater and black boots. I thought it was completely wrong, but I got him what he asked for. I also got a very old donkey jacket from Porto-bello Road, and I made some old dhotis – those baggy Indian trousers made from cheese-cloth – and collected an Indian type shirt and waistcoat, an old cap and some espa-drilles. . . . One day he [Rex Harrison] said he didn't know about the costume, that it didn't seem to give him anything. I suggested he tried the old clothes I'd collected. He put them on and suddenly saw he could play the part. The trousers were shapeless and hung on him – I explained they were things he had picked up on his travels, and that he didn't mind any more about clothes, it was part of his eccentricity. I put the espadrilles out and he was very suspi-cious of those but they helped him to shuffle about like an old man. From the moment he put the costume on his performance took off and it was fascinating to watch it

develop. The old clothes gave Rex a way of doing the part; you can't impose that sort of thing, you just have to wait for it to happen. (Herbert, p. 161)

This was a problem which Stanislvasky had discovered when trying to play Othello dressed as an Arab. As with other aspects of stage design, much of the hard work which goes into the final effect, and its artistry, involves a process of discarding the unnecessary, or inappropriate. What remains from this process of stripping down is the essential which reveals rather than adds.

Jocelyn Herbert's designs – especially associated with the Royal Court Theatre, a space which she particularly loves with its 'beautifully proportioned stage' and close relationship with the audience – have always discovered the appropriate and the beautiful in the simple. As with the plays of Beckett with which she has been closely associated, everything on her stage tells, and has its place in the dramatic telling; nothing is overstated, and nothing which matters can fail to be observed by the audience. In designing Brecht's *The Life of Galileo* for John Dexter's production at the National Theatre in 1980, she created a space which was free, and flexible, incorporating the use of stage-trucks and projections, and allowing the expository nature of the action to be conveyed with poignancy and force. The space of the Olivier stage seemed right for a play about the movement of the stars, and at the same time right for a scene like the first where Galileo gives a lesson to the son of his housekeeper, about the difference between a universe of which the earth is the centre, and one where the earth moves round the sun. To do this Galileo carries the boy on a chair, asking him what he sees as the chair swings round; and whether the sun is on his left or his right. He makes the boy see the sun does not move; but the chair on which the boy sits gives the impression of movement. The boy realizes with a sudden rush of excitement how his perception of the world has been transformed by this simple demonstration. And the audience feels it too. With this visual device, Brecht creates the intellectual excitement, and dramatic energy on which the rest of the play depends. Jocelyn Herbert's design for that first scene combined both the domestic and the cosmic, by designing a stage in which spatial relations were very close, and at the same time suggestive of immense distance. We could feel the fear that comes from the silence of space (*le silence éternel de ces espaces infinis*)and at the same relate to the human drama which everday is played out within it. The success of this production which brought Brecht for the first time to a very large audience came from the fusion of language and visualization: a vision of the play.

Stage design as an exploration of space and what can be done with it has created a new language on the stage since the days of painted scenery; and in some productions achieves a power equal to anything said. Peter Shaffer's *The Royal Hunt of the Sun*, produced by John Dexter, with scenery and costumes by Michael Annals in 1964, about the Spanish conquest of Peru, achieved its great success not so much through its verbal debate between two ideologies and cultures, but through the splendour of its visualisation in which, as Simon Callow has pointed out gesture, voice and movement, a linear movement, count for more than depth. (Callow, p. 115).

Peter Shaffer, while noting that all that is required is a bare stage and an upper level, has paid tribute to the way in which Annals succeeded in solving the visual problems of the play.

Basically this design consisted of a huge aluminium ring, twelve feet in diameter, hung in the centre of a plain wooden back-wall. Around its circumference were hinged twelve petals. When closed, these interlocked to form a great medallion on which was incised the emblem of the Conquistadors; when opened, they formed the rays of a giant golden sun, emblem of the Incas. Each petal had an inlay of gold magnetized to it; when these inlays were pulled out (in Act II, scene 6) the great black frame remaining symbolized magnificently the desecration of Peru. The centre of this sun formed an acting area above the stage, which was used in Act I to show Atahuallpa in majesty, and in Act II served for his prison and subsequently for the treasure chamber.

   This simple but amazing set was for me totally satisfying on all levels; scenically, aesthetically and symbolically. (Shaffer, pp. 7–8)

When skilfully used as here, stage technology becomes a means of clarifying and deepening meaning. *The Royal Hunt of the Sun* concerns two countries 'gorged with gold', both of which die different deaths of their avarice; the set was able to dazzle with its lure, and warn of the doom it engenders.

Stage technology has been equally effective in creating fantasy worlds, as, for example, in Mark Thomson's staging of *The Wind in the Willows* (1990), dramatized by Alan Bennett, which filled the National Theatre for many months and several Christmas seasons. Standing outside the auditorium just before the performance began, with an audience in which many children were present, you could be aware of an immense sense of excited anticipation which reaches back to the origins of all performance at the moment when something is on the point of being created before our eyes, and which the young give back to the theatre. Mark Thomson used the drum revolve of the Olivier stage to create beneath the Wild Wood the homes of Badger, Moley and Mr Toad. The simultaneous use of the revolve with the lowering and raising of stage made possible a flow of visual images which prevented our sense of being in an enchanted fantasy world from being fractured, as inevitably happens with the lowering and raising of a curtain. Almost paradoxically, the technology of the stage becomes part of the magic of the fantasy and, in its arts to enchant, a form of modern wizardry.

   The habits of Badger, Moley and Toad had been observed in their natural habitats, and the actors, under Nicholas Hytner's direction, brought to them that mixture of animal sense and human eccentricity which creates the imaginative genius of the book Kenneth Grahame started to write for his five year-old son. Mr Toad's red car was driven furiously round the revolve, and went 'Poop-poop' at anything real or imagined which got in its way, while under the vast cyclorama, and the lighting of Paul Pyant, the Wild Wood endured winter and wild weather. This was theatre magic conjured out of all the arts of a National Theatre, and the technology of its stage. More recently, the cluttered and crude (in design and colour) set of the Never Never Land in J.M. Barrie's *Peter Pan*, (1991), on the same stage, lacked visual magic of any kind.

Neither money nor technology create it. Often it occurs in circumstances with little of either. In 1978 Richard Blackford wrote an opera based on the fourteenth-century poem *Gawain and the Green Knight* for the village of Blewbury in Berkshire. The orchestration included tuned wine-glasses and a home-made bamboo organ, as well as recorders, guitars and strings, brass, wood-wind and percussion so that a huge variety of musical talents, both young and old, could be included. The opera was conceived as a work for children and adults performing together. A hundred and fifty members of the community made the props and costumes, creating out of the simplest of resources a work about the journey from innocence to experience, involving both the supernatural and the human. In the dark January days when it was performed, *Gawain and the Green Knight* created its vision out of music, colour, light and movement; and without any of the resources with which Harrison Birtwistle a few years later was to create a costly bore on the same subject for the Royal Opera House. Stage technology has become part of the language of theatre (the best thing in Birtwistle's opera was the head of the Green Knight which continued to sing after it had been cut off); but the power to conjure with our imaginations is not dependent upon it.

*

Colour – indispensable for the Green Knight! – plays an essential role in interpreting the text, and shaping our response to it. As with light, from which it is not separable,

colour determines tone. In Nicholas Lehnhoff's production of
Janáček's *Jenůfa* at Glyndebourne in 1989, with sets designed
by Tobias Hoheisel, Act 1, set in a lonely mill, revealed an
orange-red barn stage left, and the mill house, with slowly
turning wheel, stage right. Between them running across the
stage was a high green bank cutting out any view except of
distant mountain tops. The set with its sacks of corn and its
turning water-wheel created a picture of rural life in Czecho-
slovakia, but the colours conveyed the emotion: the acid green
bank, and the oppressive red buildings evoked a feeling of
hatred, jealousy and enclosure, acting as a tonal reflection of
the impassioned score, and its narrative of insoluble emotions
in a place from which there is no escape.

Nuria Espert in her production of Lorca's *House of Bernarda
Alba*, with designs by Ernesto Frigerio (1988) used absence of
colour in an equally emotive way. Bernarda Alba keeps her
five daughters as 'prisoners' inside their Spanish home. Her
love of power, memorably suggested by Joan Plowright in her
voice and her use of an ebony walking-stick which seemed
like a rod to beat their backs, is directed at preserving their
virginity, so that they do not bring shame on the family 'honour'. The high white walls, with barred windows, of the set
reflected the domestic architecture of Southern Spain; it also
created a space within which the family was imprisoned, and
repressed. As the sun scorches in Andalucía, so these lives were
scorched by the dryness of their virginity. The whiteness of
the set was realistic and symbolic.

As this production suggests, perhaps no single factor is
more important in the visualization of a play than how it is lit.
None has seen more radical changes in the last fifty years, and
none by its very nature is more difficult to analyse and
describe.

In 1957 Richard Pilbrow founded Theatre Projects, a
company which developed computerized lighting systems,
and promoted the training of 'lighting designers' — a role
which had previously been part of the function of the director, and in many cases still is. But the centralized control of

lighting together with computerised memory enables one person to control many hundreds of dimmers. Multiple banks of spotlights (which can be motorized at a price) above and at the side of the stage, as well as within the auditorium allow intensity and colour to be mixed throughout a performance to create changes of mood and atmosphere, as well as to sculpture the performers in three-dimensional space. The theatrical effects of new lighting techniques are seen most blatantly in pop concerts, where light, colour and rhythm are orchestrated together. Within the theatre itself, the removal of footlights except as a historical device, where they can still be used effectively to recreate an earlier stage style, has helped to break down the barrier of the proscenium arch between actors and audience. The thrust-stage and theatre in the round have meant the mounting of lights, usually visible, which enable performers to appear within the audience, and to use the same gangways to approach and leave the stage. At the same time lighting design has made make-up less and less necessary, except for special effects, and reduced the reliance on greasepaint (once a symbol of the theatre) to create the effect of legerdemain on which acting depends.

Technology can only act as an aid, however, to light's elemental relationship with theatre. Artifice which loses its contact with central human feelings thins into emptiness, provoking the response, 'amazing but so what?' Theatrical ritual, whether at Stonehenge or Epidaurus, was responsive to the rising and setting of the sun, to the seasons and solstice. Light and darkness shape the human world. The dark theatre, like the tomb, is a place without life; and the illumination of the spot on a single figure a conjuring into life of what was previously concealed. Light is a shaping power, which has qualities in itself, and a border where shadows and darkness begin. Light allows us to see, but does not allow us to forget that we only see what it shows. Light is in this sense always gesturing towards the invisible. Tiepolo, the most theatrical of all artists, many of whose paintings, especially *The Banquet of Antony and Cleopatra*, looks like a stupendous stage-design, thought that 'light was divine'. Glancing, shifting with infinite gradations of tone, colour and atmosphere, light controls our psychological responses with varying degrees of intensity, inside and outside the theatre. When God said, 'let there be light', he made visible the separation of heaven from earth, and illumination from shadow.

In the performances of 'Cirque du Soleil", whose name invokes the ritual and elemental nature of theatre, light fixes our gaze on figures whose daring and precision of timing enables them to fly through the air, passing and meeting, locked as a matter of life and death into their solitary worlds, describing their swift parabolas, plunging in and out of the darkness, like the notes in a musical composition. In their silence they write in air what light enables us to see as both equilibrium and liberation.

As scenery has become less painterly, light has become more so. When Beckett writes in his stage direction for *Act without Words II*, 'Desert. Dazzling Light', he describes what painters over the centuries have done, capturing the quality of light in a particular place, whether in Venice or Essex. Light sculptures actors in three dimensions, but also captures them in the particularity of the fourth, as when Romeo says to Juliet,

> It was the lark, the herald of the morn,
> No nightingale; look, love, what envious streaks
> Do lace the severing clouds in yonder east.
>> (Act III, scene 5)

Richard Pilbrow in *Stage Lighting Design* (1997) quotes a remarkable passage from Robert Edward Jones's *The Dramatic Imagination* (1941) on the creative effect of working with light:

'At rare moments, in the long quiet hours of light rehearsals, a strange thing happens. We are overcome by the livingness of light. As we gradually bring a scene out of the shadows, sending long rays slanting across a column, touching an outline with colour, animating the scene moment by moment until it seems to breathe, our work becomes an incantation. We feel the presence of elemental energies.

There is hardly a designer who has not experienced at some time or another this overwhelming sense of the livingness of light.'

Jones goes on to describe the first duty of the lighting design to the actors, to make them and their environment 'clearly and fully visible'. But in a very special way.

'Lighting a scene consists not only of throwing light upon objects but in throwing light upon a subject. We have a choice of lighting a drama from the outside, as a spectator, or from the inside, as part of the drama's experience. We reveal the drama. We use light as we use words, to elucidate ideas and emotions. Light becomes a tool, an instrument of expression, like a paintbrush, or a sculptor's chisel, or a phrase of music.' He sees light on the stage as being like Wordsworth's visionary light that 'never was on land or sea': its aim to achieve 'lucidity, penetration, awareness, discovery, inwardness, wonder'. (Pilbrow, p. 114)

But shadow too is as important as light.

'How shall I explain to you the meaning of shadow in the theatre – the primitive dread, the sense of brooding, the blackness, the descent into endless night?' (Pilbrow, pp. 114–15).

Othello understands this better than anyone:

> Put out the light, and then put out the light.
> If I quench thee, thou flaming minister,
> I can again thy former light restore,
> Should I repent me; but once put out thy light,

Thou cunning'st pattern of excelling nature,
I know not where is that Promethean heat
That can thy light relume.

(Act V, scene 2)

The effectiveness of the lighting design in Act V of *Othello*
remains crucial to its dramatic effectiveness. Light, just as
much as Desdemona in this scene, is a 'tactile thing'.

Light and colour create a tone, an atmosphere, feeling. How
they relate to the action determines the tactile style of the
play, and becomes an interpretation of it. Luchino Visconti in
directing John Ford's *'Tis Pity She's a Whore* (called rather
coyly in French *Dommage qu'elle soit p. . . .*) in Paris in 1961
drew upon a very simple fact about an Italian setting. In the
piazza seen through the arches of the room, the sun shines
down brilliantly on unpeopled spaces. Everything is clear,
bright, hard and empty. Inside the room which occupies most
of the stage, salvers heaped with fruit, shadowy embrasures
create an atmosphere of a claustrophobic luxury, where private emotions will fester in a play about the incestuous love
betwen brother and sister. The scene heightens a simple
observation about an Italian setting; the contrast between the
simple sunlit beauty of the public world, and the shadowed
inwardness of the private. Light and shadow were used to
create an atmosphere, and a context in which the tragedy was
played.

The problems of lighting have to be solved in relation to
the flow and feeling of the whole production. Ralph Koltai
once designed *Love's Labour's Lost* for the Royal Shakespeare
Company with all the colours and shades of Autumn, and a
lighting scheme appropriate for it. The desire to create feeling
or atmosphere, though, must never be allowed to make it hard
for the audience to understand what is happening. Lucidity as
in all aspects of production is what counts most in the end.
Act IV of Mozart's *The Marriage of Figaro* always presents a
particular problem. Set in a garden at night it depends on
assignations and encounters between characters in disguise;

and yet we need to be sure exactly whom we are looking at, and to perceive the mistakes they are making, so that we can also appreciate their eventual embarrassment, when their true identities are revealed.

The first and third scenes in *Hamlet*, when the Ghost appears on Elsinore's battlements, need bright illumination and obscurity at the same time. An audience cannot be involved with an action which cannot be seen; and the irritation of trying to see will distract from the words. The storm scenes in *King Lear* need the right balance between what we hear of the storm, what we see of it and what see of Lear's face. When Paul Rogers played King Lear at the Old Vic in 1962, he seemed almost to be standing under the lights of a boxing-ring so that the lightning became a form of self-examination, accentuating to great effect the inner nature of this scene.

In Ibsen's later plays light becomes both a presence and absence on the stage. What his characters search for within, and cannot find, is reflected in the weather outside. *Rosmersholm* is set entirely indoors. The country house of the title stands in a grey landscape where the rain pours down. We do not see the landscape, but the weather outside suggests and confirms that struggle with unidentified inhibitions which will in the end send Rosmer and Rebecca into the mill-chase, as Beata has gone there before them. The lighting needs to suggest that Rosmersholm is not just a gloomy country house, but a spectral place, where the appearance of the 'white horses' presages death. In the last scene of *John Gabriel Borkman*, when John Gabriel goes out alone on the mountain, the lighting, even more than the snow, will convey the cold which having entered his heart, will kill him. Perhaps most momentously of all, light and dark as symbols of inner life become presences on the stage in Oswald's 'dying' words in *Ghosts*: 'Give me the sun, Mother ! Give me the sun!' The effect of that line will be determined as much by how it is lit as how it is spoken.

In any play, pace, variation of rhythm, acceleration towards climax and retardation (all qualities of musical composition) are essential in the writing, and in the playing. Light-changes control rhythm too by indicating movements in time and location. In Alan Ayckbourn's *A Small Family Business* (1987), a single set served as the rooms in various houses of a single family. The setting remained the same, but the location was different: a change made perfectly clear by the attitudes and behaviour of those in the house. Changes of light advanced the action through the autumn week in which the whole play takes place, as, for instance, in the following stage direction: '*The location changes again. It is evening now, a couple of days later. A rumble of thunder and rain.*' As always in effective theatre, the point is not just a matter of technique. The various houses in which the families live are the same house: an ordinary modern house, '*perhaps on an executive estate*'. The life-styles in each are the same, involving corruption, lies, dishonesty, betrayal, and ripping each other off. The single set becomes an accumulating revelation of rottenness in a society of competitive materialism and self-gratification, even though its plot contains a great deal of farce, to which the set is also well – suited. At the end of the play, the 16-year-old Samantha, unable to face the family party downstairs, will be left sitting in the darkened bathroom, drugged and blankly staring ahead. The contrast between the 'adults' gathering below, toasting 'the family business', and Samantha's despair is suggested by light and its absence.

As light can be used to create flow and continuity in the action, so too through the use of 'black-out' it can be used for an action which is fractured and episodic, conceived as a series of scenes which are associative, rather than linear. Harold Pinter constructs a play like *No Man's Land* in this way, using 'black-outs' to allow a fresh start to the action between Spooner (originally played by Gielgud) and Hirst (played by Richardson) in which the opposites in their characters and ways of life are seen from different angles, and the struggle for domination between them never finally concluded.

As in many aspects of theatre, Samuel Beckett proves the

most radical in his use of lighting, especially in *Play*. Three characters, two women and a man, up to their neck in urns, speak only when 'their' spot shines on them. The spot illuminates the character on whom the audience's attention is directed: a simple theatrical device. The light also acts to interrogate each in turn, probing their memories, and their anxieties in the triangular relationship which they have shared. But since they never speak directly to one another, the light, like consciousness itself, is the pain of an inner light which only in darkness, whether of sleep or death, finds any peace.

The demands made by the staging, though not the performance, of Beckett's *Play* are minimal. The staging of Wagner's *Ring* demands immense resources. The relation between light and vision – not just what we see, but how we see it – is equally critical in both cases; and *The Ring* because of its scope and length, has provided the opportunity to incorporate new technologies of staging and light as means of reinterpretation.

As the longest and most complex work of theatre, taking more than twenty hours to perform, *The Ring* has attracted many of the major European talents in every aspect of production over the last fifty years, and has offered them the scope to experiment with new forms of design and lighting. Like the exploration of space, and whatever value is attached to the project, *The Ring* has helped to develop potentialities within the theatre, which have been influential and of lasting importance, for reasons which Wagner himself could not have foreseen, though he might in the end have approved. Ironically, *The Ring* having helped to develop these new technologies, now seems almost unstageable!

Wagner's own staging at Bayreuth was dominated by the pictorial scene-painting of the nineteenth-century theatre, in an opera house where the orchestra was concealed by a hood, so that nothing intervened between the audience, and the vision on the stage. Wagner was drawn to the idea of a grand 'show', but also frustrated by the inability of the stage to represent his visions. As he said on one occasion ' now that I have made the orchestra invisible, I should like to invent an invisible stage'. The revolutionary ideas for staging Wagner's operas came not from Wagner himself, but from Adolph Appia (1862–1928). Close in spirit to Edward Gordon Craig (who was to be equally influential on British designers and lighting designers), Appia believed that the staging of Wagner's operas should reflect the music with its power to reveal 'the hidden world of our inner life'. Appia thought of the stage as a three-dimensional space of sculptured or architectural forms in which the movement of the performers was conceived in terms of the rhythmic configurations of the music. Light, as for Edward Gordon Craig, was to be the key to unifying the stage-action.

> Light is to production what music is to the score: the expressive element in opposition to literal signs; and, like music, light can only express what belongs to the 'inner essence of all vision'. (Burian, p. 14)

The resistance of Wagner's widow, Cosima, to seeing Wagner's stage directions as anything other than the final word on Wagnerian production kept the operas in a time-warp, until the reopening of Bayreuth after the Second World War. Bayreuth needed a new style to shed the Nazi image which Hitler had created around it, and Wagner's music. Wieland Wagner, Wagner's grandson, had both the vision, and the understanding of the revolutionary ideas of Appia and Gordon Graig to create this new style. By conceiving the operas on an almost bare stage, which emphasized their elemental mythic nature, he did much to purge them of their nationalist consciousness, their anti-semitism, and their glorification of German art. But he was also putting into practice ideas about staging which neither Appia nor Gordon Craig, for various reasons, had had much opportunity to realize. Although the changes which Wieland Wagner initiated in Bayreuth from 1951 had much to do with the problems of Bayreuth itself, they can now be seen as part of a much larger movement in the theatre against naturalistic settings and production styles which failed to make use of the far-reaching changes in the technology of the theatre which were being developed and were radically altering the languages of theatre.

To anyone who had sat through the sheer ugliness of Nordic representations of Wagner, with heavily clad figures plodding about an unimaginative pictorial set, or a crudely symbolic one, the liberation of Wieland Wagner's staging was immense. Figures when they moved – and there are great distances to be moved on the Bayreuth stage – moved in a natural rhythmic configuration with the music. The stage became a place as Appia wanted it to be of 'rhythmic spaces', with a lighting design that picked out the simple beauty of the costumes.

The second of Wieland Wagner's *Ring* cycles which I saw in 1967 two years after it opened showed how his ideas had changed since the 1950s. He understood how swiftly visual language could become sterile, how an audience's response to visual effect changed, and recognized the need for vision in the theatre to be renewed. The 1965 cycle was more heavily symbolic than that of the fifties; some elements of 'scenery' had been reintroduced; and the production reflected the influence of Robert Donington's *Wagner's 'Ring'* (1963), which analysed *The Ring* in terms of Jungian archetypes. In the programme note to *Das Rheingold* Donington described the visual effect of the production:

> The large stage looks even larger for being left almost bare; the lighting is commonly subdued, often verging on darkness. But the figures who appear out of darkness are brilliantly lit. The colours of their costumes are pictorially beautiful; the light picks them out with all the concentrated vividness of a painting. The actors look like characters in a dream. And they act neither with the stiff exaggeration of the old operatic tradition, nor with the studied realism of the naturalistic stage. They may hold a long, quiet pose; but when they do make a gesture or a movement, the effect is all the greater because of the previous restraint.

Donington's account of the Bayreuth stage here brings out some of its memorable effects: a formalized and a-historical beauty created out of the colour of the costumes (itself a quality of the light in which they are seen), the lighting of the figures in spaces which shade away into darkness so as to give these figures the appearance of sculptured forms, and the restriction of movement to those which have a musical necessity.

Discovering a visual style for *The Ring* cycle remains an immense task, different in degree but not in nature to the problems of all theatre design, which involves a wide range of difficult choices. Götz Friedrich in his 1974 Covent Garden cycle, with sets designed by Josef Svoboda, mounted the whole action on a vast platform which revolved and could be tilted, angled, raised and lowered to create different stage spaces. The underneath side of the platform, which weighed three and a half tons and could be raised to an angle of forty-five degrees was mirrored, so that the underworld of Nibelheim where the ingots were being hammered by the Nibelungs was seen in a fiery half-light. The tilting of the platform at different angles (which was completely silent), combined with brilliant use of laser lighting, allowed the scene to move from one location in a seamless *verwandlung*. At the end of *Götterdämmerung*, Hagen fell into the Rhine from the tilted edge of the platform into the trap beneath, while the Rhine Maidens were seen on the top of the platform, as it reversed its tilt, in a flowing water projection on the surface.

This vast, shifting platform gave a visual coherence to the whole production; its technology suggesting the crushing weight and power of the forces at work in the contemporary world. 'The basic intention', according to Friedrich, 'was to present the *Ring* "as a parable of this world on the *stage*. The world as theater, the stage as world theater"' (Burian, p. 155).

By refusing to impose a single interpretation on *The Ring* and conceiving it as a piece of music theatre, they hoped to present Wagner's thought in its contradictions. The empty platform, the most basic and elemental of all stage spaces, became here an entirely flexible stage space, 'capable of interpreting everything we need . . . . Can we have a nineteenth century stage dragon and laser beams? The answer is yes if we're playing theatre – world theater. We have the right because the moment that we elected to have an ordinary stage, a platform, a stage floor, we created the right to play theater from antiquity onward, perhaps even Chinese theater.' (Burian, p. 57). The stage is what we take it as being.

In the introductory and transitional passages, Svoboda used laser lighting, creating moving patterns of light projected onto cycloramas or even parts of the set as an abstract, expressive accompaniment to the music and action:

> The intention . . .was to produce not a tight correspondence between the images and the musical score, but rather an impressionistic accompaniment . . . As the prelude of *Das Rheingold* began, a spark of red light was cast on to the dark cyclorama: the inception of life. The spark became a streak, then a swirl of ever-changing red and blue patterns as the platform silently rose, leveled and began to rotate slowly. Out of the void, creation and matter. Svoboda described the event; ' We have created a world, our world. The world of the *Ring*. We've given birth to a stage, bare boards, the plainest stage floor, the most simple reality.' (Burian, p. 59)

As the platform at the close of the cycle finally returned to its original 'almost level position' where we had first seen it, it stated once again that what we had witnessed was a piece of theatre. It made no concluding statement, but like the end of a ride at the fun-fair, invited you to 'roll up for another ride'. Whether the world, or the stage, next time round, will be different remains to be seen. Theatre is always a gesture towards something, not a statement about it. The *Ring* makes a gesture in two directions. The ring returned to the

Rhinemaidens by Brunnhilde stands for a world redeemed by Love, but it also stands for a world which has gone up in flames, been annihilated, where nothing remains except the possibility of a new beginning. As Götz Friedrich put it, 'Every ending conceals a new beginning, and only that could mean a step forward toward Utopia.'

Whether the world ever changes, is ever more than a cyclic wheel of fire, only the future will tell. In seeing the *Ring* as theatre, the Friedrich–Svoboda production brought together these two gestures which asks their questions about the nature of being, of recurrence and evolution.

Like Wieland Wagner, Friedrich and Svoboda put into practice the ideas which had first been advocated by Appia, and Gordon Craig, but used too ideas and technologies relating to their own time. Svoboda, like Wieland Wagner, believed that stage design must reflect 'contemporary sensibility', and not merely echo past traditions. Its function is always to convey a play's (or an opera's) meanings. This problem is not solved by accumulating meanings in an elaborate visual style, loaded with cultural references, as in the Jones–Lowery cycle at Covent Garden in 1996; nor can a 'strip-cartoon' style diminish the power of Wagner's music superbly played by more than a hundred people, or comment upon it. The function of effective stage design is not to puzzle the audience by making them ask what does this mean, or why this is here; but to clarify the meaning of the work as a whole. A ship that is over-loaded with freight inevitably sinks. Tom Sutcliffe in the *Classical Music Weekly*, commented with accuracy: 'Josef Svoboda's designs, wholly integrated with Friedrich's conceptions in their practicality, provide some of the most stunning images I have ever seen in the theatre. At last Gordon Craig's dreams of the visual impact of which a Wagner production should be capable are being matched. Yet each image, whether it follows or ignores Wagner's wishes, serves to underline clearly aspects of the total work: nothing is there for prettiness or convenience.' (Burian, p. 78). In a work as long and as complex as *The Ring*, the process of paring-down so that only the essential remains enables the vision to shine through. And so it is with all theatre.

★

The vision of a play, and the way we respond to its visualization, cannot be separated from the way in which it is cast. The light which sculptures an actor sculptures a presence: a physique, a vocal range and a deportment. A stage-space which only comes to life when there are actors within it is given its life by their individual and particular presences. The English stage has been fortunate in the last fifty years in the richness and variety of its memorable human talents.

When an actor seems to be miscast, it may be out of a failure to 'make out of the eating a fruit, or the folding of a letter, profound mirrors of character' (Callow, p. 230), but also because their stage presence jars with the rhythm and feeling of the production, like a piece of music scored for the wrong instrument. When we go to see a well-known actor or actress, they will always impress us with these unique physical and physiognomical attributes which are quite instinctively part of their presence, and which reflect in a profound way their underlying psychology whatever part they are playing. This power to be utterly different, and always the same remains an essential part of the magic with which theatre works. Companies, both old and new, have often tried to do away with the star system for good reasons. And yet, although we can and do respond to a performance by actors entirely unknown to us, a part of the potency of theatre depends on the relationship between the familiar and the strange. Theatre is always playing on, whether unconsciously or consciously as in Pirandello, our sense of the different identities within us, so that in seeing a familiar actor play a role we compare him in this role with previous performances in other plays. The presence of the familiar creates a sense of permanence in a shifting world; but the strangeness prompts an awareness of the actor as shape-shifter whose 'real' identity we never know. As Proust remarks, the actor in performance becomes so transparent that he is only a window opening upon a great work of art.

In the cinema we go to see an actor in a film which is the conception of the director. Even the language of the credits suggests this: 'A film by . . .' In the theatre we go to see the actor in a role, knowing that this is only one of many roles they might play. The type-casting of an actor not only limits his talents, but also restricts, or buries this other dimension of acting which the audience supplies. We are aware at every gesture, glance, movement, look, of how deep the transformation is. Only the living presence, felt along the blood, and in the veins, can give us this sense of illusion creating reality and of a reality which is also illusion.

Vision in theatre depends on the chemistry of this reaction and, however skilful the performance, it does not happen in quite the same way with actors entirely unknown to us. Shakespeare and Sheridan wrote parts for those they worked with; and who also were known to their audiences. Playwrights from Shaw to David Hare have continued to write parts for particular actors and actresses, who become familiar to those who go to the theatre with any frequency.

Not all actors possess this quality of stage-presence, itself a form of alchemy, which is part of their talent, and at the same time separate from it. We have been fortunate to live in a period rich and distinctive in its talents, as even the briefest of lists will recall: after the generation of Laurence Olivier, Ralph Richardson, Donald Wolfit, Sybil Thorndike, Edith Evans, and Alec Guinness, that of Paul Scofield, Ian McKellen, Albert Finney, John Wood, Judi Dench, Dorothy Tutin, Maggie Smith, Robert Stephens, Alec McCowan, Richard Pasco, Daniel Massey, Penelope Wilton, Alan Howard, Donald Sinden, Patricia Routledge, Anthony Hopkins. Michael Gambon, Frances de la Tour, Fiona Shaw. Everyone will have their own list, and it could be much longer.

Vision in the theatre is always a vision of particular people in particular places, made memorable by the coming together of the familiar and the magical which gives to aery nothing a local habitation, and another name.

4
Music

Music when soft voices die
Vibrates in the memory.
Percy Bysshe Shelley

Music has been inseparable from drama in performance since
the Pan-Athenaic Festivals. The orchestra or dancing-floor
separated the audience from the *scēnē*, or stage. The Choruses
in Greek drama were written in metres which differed from
the main action, and were chanted in strophes and antistro-
phes. The performance began with their offering a libation to
the gods. The dramatic ritual which followed composed of
words, music and movement, initiated a style which persists,
for all the changes in cultural context, to the present day in
West Side Story. In the tragedies of the House of Atreus, as in
the American musical, a 'curse written on the underside of
things' is being worked out; in each the expression is inseparable from its music. Opera, and the musical, among other
things make audible what is at work in the rhythms of all
drama and its performance.

Music in the ancient world was used as a means of
curing madness and soothing minds that were troubled.
Symphonia meant a harmony of sounds, inducing concord in
the listener. Many performances still perform a similar function for their audiences, and their performers. The poet
Orpheus plays his lyre to restrain the furies of the Underworld and, later, transcends his sorrow, by 'controlling it in
song'.

In many different kinds of play, music is indispensable to
the dramatic action. In *King Lear*, Shakespeare uses music to
restore the King to sanity:

DOCTOR: Please you, draw near. Louder the music there.
CORDELIA: O my dear Father! Restoration, hang
Thy medicine on my lips, and let this kiss
Repair those violent harms that my two sisters
Have in thy reverence made.

(Act IV, scene 7)

With music too, Hermione is returned to life and Leontes at the end of *The Winter's Tale*:

PAULINA: Music, awake her; strike! (*Music*)
Tis time; descend; be stone no more

(Act V, scene 2)

'A play of Shakespeare', T.S.Eliot once remarked, 'has a very complex musical structure': a structure which only performance brings out; and this is true of many plays other than those by Shakespeare, where music as an expression of harmony sets the seal on the forgiveness of human illusion. Peer Gynt's restoration to Solveig, at the end of his life's long search for the self is suggested by music, whether or not by Grieg.

As well as acting as a restorative, music in the classical world inspired frenzy. Bacchus (or Dionysus) drove his followers to wild dancing which induced a state of ecstasy or 'standing outside of oneself'. Pop concerts with the electronic sophistication of their amplified sound, and new forms of 'worship' still have the same effect. In a more implicit way the same thing happens when an audience is 'rapt'.

Drama, whether or not it actually uses music (to comment, heighten, cause echoes beyond the power of words) possesses a symphonic structure, moving from apparent order, through arousal of conflict to a climax, followed by a restoration of order, however temporary or insecure. An audience responds to this musical structure; and the success of a performance depends on the sensitivity of the cast to its notation. Richard Eyre has developed the comparison like this:

When I see a production, I think – as it were after a few bars – ah, the director has brought the actors in on the beat, and even if I'm not altogether having a wonderful time, even if every moment of the production is not illuminated by the vital spark, I think: It's not drifting, it's being 'directed'. (Eyre, p. 109)

In opera, the tempi of the conductor affect the length of the performance, amounting in some performances of Wagner's operas to a difference of half an hour for a single act; but these variations do not necessarily correspond to a listener's sense of whether the work is being taken fast or slow. All good theatre depends on a sense of ease, on establishing a natural rhythm between what is seen, and what is heard or sung.

A distinction, though not a very clear one, is often made between plays, musicals and opera. The relation between words and music differs in all forms of theatre but in other respects they are the same, requiring the skills of performance, of acting, direction, costumes, scenery, sound and lighting; and a space for the performance to take place. As with all forms of theatre, opera has come to be performed in spaces of many sorts: from floating stages on lakes, to Roman arenas, in tents, gardens and private houses. The opera house has long since been superseded as the only place in which performances of the highest standards can occur, though it may still be the place where singers and orchestras of the greatest talent are most often to be found. While opera is sometimes dismissed as being a minority interest for the wealthy (clearly untrue), musicals are equally looked down on as being mere popular entertainment, a view which is equally spurious, and ignorant. Each can be *mere* entertainment, or 'distraction from distraction by distraction'; each can be a form of art, which explores an aspect of truth. Whatever the style of music, and whatever the degree to which it shapes the work, drama remains a musical, rhythmical art, drawing upon ancient rituals, and absorbing the audience into its own world through the power with which those rhythms work upon them. Audiences, listening to a song in a musical, an aria in an opera or responding instinctively to the rhythm of a stage action, are engaged in the same activity. In all forms of theatre, the relation between words and music is inseparable from theatre's magic power. W.H. Auden summed up the situation in a memorable aphorism when he described *The Importance of Being Earnest* as 'the only pure verbal opera in English'. This final chapter is concerned both with the implicit musicality of all performance, and the explicit ways in which music becomes a living presence, as important as the actors, in many different forms of theatre, culminating in opera where it assumes the central role.

*

Music exists in individual lines of dialogue, as in the action as a whole. Harold Hobson, writing ten years after seeing Ralph Richardson as Dr Sloper in *The Heiress* (a dramatization of Henry James's *Washington Square*) of the moment when he was reminded that his wife had died a long time ago, said he could still see him

> a cruel, relentless figure whose cruelty and relentlessness were due to a great grief within; and I can hear his voice ring out, 'That is no consolation', every word spoken as if it were a note in music, resonant, reverberating, echoing down the corridors of interminable years of sorrow. The emphasis on the word 'that' was terrible; at one stroke it destroyed all the healing properties of time, and the 'consolation' lingered on the air like the distant and dying tolling of a bell.
>
> (Miller, pp. 133–4.)

When an actor cannot speak a line, it is not because no one would say such a thing, but because his sense of the inner ear of the dialogue is fractured. No emphasis, or lack of emphasis, can make it sound right to the inner ear, or form part of that inner action which involves every movement on the stage. Paul Scofield when playing with Ralph Richardson in Graham Greene's *The Complaisant Lover* recorded how this affected performance.

> Ralph was an actor of rhythm – he had a beat, a pulse inside him which dictated to him; and playing opposite to him one had to learn to respect that rhythm. I am inclined to syncopate a little, and coming in one night with a line a shade later than usual, Ralph clapped his hand behind his ear as if to say, 'What was that?' His rhythm had been broken – -I had let him down. It was the discipline of music.
>
> (Miller, p. 174)

Peter Brook, writing about Scofield, illustrates the same innate musicality working in a somewhat different way.

> Scofield, when I first knew him as a very young actor, had a strange characteristic: verse hampered him, but he would make unforgettable verse out of lines of prose. It was as though the act of speaking a word sent through him vibrations that echoed back meanings far more complex than his rational thinking could find: he would pronounce a word like 'night' and then he would be compelled to pause: listening with all his being to the amazing impulses stirring in some mysterious inner chamber, he would experience the wonder of discovery at the moment when it happened. Those breaks, those sallies in depth, gave his acting its absolutely personal structure of rhythms, its own instinctive meanings: to rehearse a part, he let his whole nature – a milliard of super-sensitive scanners – pass to and fro across the words. In performance the same process makes everything that he has apparently fixed come back again each night the same and absolutely different. (*ES* p. 111)

Simon Callow in *Being an Actor* reveals the importance of music in preparing a part.

The various approaches are perforce idiosyncratic, because everything you do in a the play must be completely grounded in your own personal sensations. For me, music is the most immediately acccessible point of reference. Since childhood, I have been immersed in classical music. My first question for myself is what is this character's – and for that matter, this play's – music. (Callow, p. 170)

The musical action of a play as a whole, like music itself, expresses feeling which is complex. The complexity lies both in the characters, and in our reponse to the action as a whole. Watching Othello murder Desdemona or commit suicide does not make us feel murderous or suicidal; we continue to be aware of the nobility in Othello's soul. Even as he destroys the most 'precious pearl in all his tribe', he is aware of the 'pity' of it. His tenderness is not exclusive of his rage, or his jealousy of tenderness, just as in listening to a piece of music we can be aware of sadness and joy.

Every performance of a play has to discover this inner musical structure, and communicate it to the audience. As in a piece of music, striking the wrong note will jar. As Richard Eyre has written,

> I don't know a good actor who is not intelligent, but this intelligence is like a musician's, to do with timing, rhythm, hearing, sensibility, physical coordination, rather than with cleverness and the ability to express ideas. (Eyre, p. 87).

The actor who plays to the audience by ad-libbing, or deliberately upstaging others on the stage whether by ham or 'great acting' breaks this internal rhythm. An actor who is miscast will not fail only because of an inability to imitate the part, but because his performance will sound out of tune with the rest. The physical expression, and speaking of the lines, have to fuse as in a symphony with all other players in the performance. This becomes more possible when a company play together for a season or more, and the players become increasingly well-attuned to each other: a vision which inspired Peter Hall and Peggy Aschcroft in the founding of the Royal Shakespeare Company, as it had inspired the companies in the Elizabethan theatres of London, the Moscow Art, and the touring companies in England and elsewhere today. The idea of the troupe or company does not differ from that of the chamber group or symphony orchestra whose work together over a period of time enables them to respond to the mutual interaction of feeling and rhythm between them: in a true sense, philharmonic.

When Hamlet rebukes Guildenstern for his disloyalty, he reminds him of an important difference between the solo player and the member of the company:

> You would play upon me; you would seem to know my stops; you would pluck out the heart of my mystery; you would sound me from my lowest note to the top of my compass; and there is much music, excellent voice, in this little organ, yet cannot you make it speak. (Act III, scene 2)

The heart of the mystery in an actor can only be played upon by other actors who can make it speak, and who can hear at the same time the echoes which return from the audience. Ensemble playing, the absence of a star system – even the interchangeablility of roles which Stanislavsky introduced in the Moscow Art Theatre – are all aimed at this same end. But a company, for all the desirable things it embodies, cannot be held together too long. It needs the fresh air of new ideas, or it dies.

Musicality in performance reflects what the greater dramatists have always made part of their words, and their stage action: the poetry of life, which comes from its suggestiveness and all that remains inexplicit. Because of its brevity, a stage action requires the associative strength of what has been deeply felt; and what in poetry itself creates lyrics. The term 'lyric theatre', sometimes used of opera, makes a false distinction, as all theatre is lyric.

Samuel Beckett, rehearsing his own plays, insisted on their being performed exactly as he had written them. This could involve conflict, even if unspoken, with the actor trying to find a way into a part, as this account of the rehearsals of Peggy Ashcroft in *Happy Days* shows.

> Her approach to a role is one of steady digging towards psychological truth via *tonal* [my italic] accuracy: Beckett regards his texts almost as scores in which words and gestures amount to a tonal notation. . . . Peggy is far too diplomatic and admiring of Beckett to admit that the first two weeks of rehearsal were pretty hellish as he gave her every gesture in fine, meticulous detail. What is revealing is her observation that, even with a role as exactly orchestrated as a piece of music, the actress still has to find her own personal route into the character. (*Ashcroft*, p. 238)

To do this, Peggy Ashcroft had to discover how Winnie should sound, borrowing in the end a great deal from Beckett himself.

> Peggy allowed his gentle incantatory reading of the text to creep into her own. She realized instinctively what scholars have confirmed: that Beckett is a profoundly Irish writer. . . . The result was a performance gaily flecked with the *music* [my italic] of Irish speech. (*Ashcroft*, p. 239)

Some directors prefer not to bring out Beckett's Irishness because this ties the action to a specific location, but in some way an internal rhythm needs to be discovered and sustained, as Natasha Parry succeeded in doing in Peter Brook's production of *Happy Days* (1997), through playing Winnie with the self-mockery of the demi-mondaine.

Shaw's plays, though sometimes thought of as being plays of argument and debate, work on the stage because they are nourished by the musicality of Shaw's Irishness, and an ear which made him, among other things, the finest music critic of his time. After watching Ralph Richardson make his first entrance as the 'Chocolate Soldier' in *Arms and the Man* Shaw took him aside and said.

> When you come in you're very upset, you spend a long time with your gasps and your pauses and your lack of breath and your dizzinness and your tiredness; it's very well done, it's very well done indeed, but it doesn't suit my play. It's no good for me, it's no good for Bernard Shaw. You've got to go from line to line, quickly and swiftly, never stop the flow of the lines, never stop. It's one joke after another, it's a firecracker. Always reserve the acting for underneath the spoken word. It's a musical play, a knockabout musical comedy. (Miller, p. 41)

Act Three of *Man and Superman*, in which the characters of the two previous acts take on the roles of the characters in Mozart's *Don Giovanni*, represents his most extraordinary and daring exploration of ideas, sustained by his inner ear for the rhythms of speech. We listen – and one of Tanners/Giovanni's speeches lasts at least fifteen minutes – not just because of the intelligence of the ideas, but because of a sensuous rhythmic ebb and flow in their expression. The ear, as well as the mind, is seduced by the pulse, not just of what is being said, but of how it is being said.

Shaw's Prefaces have this quality to a much less marked degree because they do not need the rhythmic variation of a dramatic action, nor do they have to catch in their net the dissonances and conflicts of opposing points of view and feelings, or resound with the complexities of which all human speech is made up. In his Prefaces, Shaw always tries to persuade his reader of his point of view; in his plays he knows that he has to draw the audience into the action by the internal rhythms of speech, in which a word or a phrase accentuated or paused over can bring back echoes from the deep.

Heartbreak House is notable, in dramatic literature, for the number of times in which characters fall asleep. (Not, it might seem, the most theatrical of activities, but of course, a rhythmic one!) The play even begins with Ellie Dunn falling asleep when no one takes any notice of her, on her arrival in Captain Shotover's house. At the start of Act III, almost everyone is asleep under the stars. The lull in talking is only the silence before the storm of the bombs which will start to fall; and sleep an image of the day-dreaming which prevents these 'idle, futile' creatures from seeing the rocks on to which they and their society are drifting. Heartbreak House is described by Ellie in the final act as 'this silly house, this strangely happy house, this agonizing house, this house without foundations'. Heartbreak House is to be wept over, and loved: loved not least because of the presence of Captain Shotover, who in his old age can still remember what it is like to be the Captain on the bridge in the eye of the storm, and now still hopes to achieve the seventh degree of concentration.

> I sit here working out my old ideas as a means of destroying my fellow-creatures. I see my daughters and their men living foolish lives of romance and sentiment and snobbery. I see you, the younger generation, turning from their romance and sentiment and snobbery to money and comfort and hard common sense. I was ten times happier on the bridge in the typhoon, or frozen into Arctic ice for months in darkness, than you or they have ever been. You are looking for a rich husband. At your age I looked for hardship, danger, horror, and death, that I might feel the life in me more intensely. I did not let the fear of death govern my life; and my reward was, I had my life. You are going to let the fear of poverty govern your life; and your reward will be that you will eat, but you will not live.
>
> (Act II)

Anger, turbulence, irritation but never quite despair, or the longing for rest, impel the rhythms of Shotover's speech: a part which has been memorably played in recent years by

Roger Livesey, and Paul Scofield, but which seemed inappropriate for Rex Harrison, an actor fired by irritation at human silliness, in conflict with his own ego, but never capable of suggesting that he wasn't entirely satisfied with being himself. Shotover has never ceased to be an explorer, for whom arriving matters very much less than never coming to journey's end. The musicality of the play comes from the conflict between resistance and inertia, between rest and exploration, between sleep and defiance: inner rhythms to which the audience responds all the time instinctively, while consciously thinking of the cleverness of what is being said.

In verse drama, unlike Shaw's prose, we are aware of the design which the music has upon us in the varying rhythms with which characters speak. In T.S. Eliot's fragments of *Sweeney Agonistes*, the rhythms of the jazz age are audible in the rhythms of the words:

> Under the bam
> Under the boo
> Under the bamboo tree.

In *The Ascent of F.6*, by W.H. Auden and Christopher Isherwood (1937), Mr and Mrs Smith respond to each other, and the world, as though programmed by a computer (proving themselves prophetic!) and speak in rhythms wholly distinct from other characters.

> MR. A.: No, nothing that matters will ever happen;
> Nothing you'd want to put in a book;
> Nothing to tell to impress your friends –
> The old old story that never ends:
> The eight o'clock train, the customary place,
> Holding the paper in front of your face.

The other characters speak in prose, except at moments of visionary intensity. As T.S. Eliot said in 'The Use of Poetry', 'Poetry may make us from time to time a little more aware of the deeper unnamed feelings which form the substratum of our being, to which we rarely penetrate.' It can also be used as in the lines above to express our failure to do so. Both become part of the rhythmic variation of the play.

In T.S. Eliot's plays, *Murder in the Cathedral, The Family Reunion, The Cocktail Party* – all of which prove their continuing dramatic life in revivals – music and form are fused in a more subtle way. In writing *Murder in the Cathedral* for a religious drama festival at Canterbury, Eliot became aware that he would need another kind of verse for a contemporary play. In his later plays he achieved this, though not without being criticized for writing verse which could not be distinguished from prose. This overlooks how Eliot's plays draw a response from the audience by rhythms and repetitions which flow like currents through what is being said. In *Murder in the Cathedral* (1935), the Choruses of the Women of Canterbury express, at the start, anxiety and fear at the thought of Becket's return to England. They are 'living and partly living', not wanting to be disturbed, or to have to bear witness. They speak in questions, their minds full of an unknown fear, obsessed with danger, the heavy throb of the verse creating a feeling of uneasy anticipation.

> CHORUS: Why should the summer bring consolation
> For autumn fires and winter fogs?
> What shall we do in the heat of summer
> But wait in barren orchards for another October?
> Some malady is coming upon us. We wait, we
> wait,
> And the saints and martyrs wait, for those who
> shall be martyrs and saints.

But at the play's end, when Becket has been murdered, the Knights have made their excuses and given their explanations in prose (which, as Eliot noted, had been influenced by Shaw's *Saint Joan*), the Chorus have moved, or been moved to a new tone of acceptance, even of praise.

For wherever a saint has dwelt, wherever a martyr has given
   his blood for the blood of Christ,
There is holy ground, and the sanctity shall not depart from it
Though armies trample over it, though sightseers come with
   guide books looking over it

The significance of Becket's martyrdom is expressed in this
change from a minor to a major key which works below the
level of questions of belief raised by the play. Music is in this
sense irresistible; and its rhythms cannot be misinterpreted.

   In *The Family Reunion* (1939), Eliot develops a more elaborate musical structure, though now in the secular setting of a
country house in the north of England. Like the Women of
Canterbury, the uncles and aunts, gathered at Wishwood for a
family reunion, are forced to bear witness to things they do
not understand, and would prefer to avoid. They are 'embar-
rassed, fretful, ill at ease', like actors who have been assembled
and not assigned their parts. They neither see nor understand,
in contrast to Amy who owns the house and does not wish to
see or understand; and Harry, her son, Agatha, her sister and
Mary, a cousin who in the course of the action come both to
see *and* understand the meaning of their experience. When
Harry arrives home, haunted by guilt (pursued by the Furies),
and by the fear that he may have murdered his wife, seeing,
and not seeing obsess him. He sees the Furies, but knows that
others do not see them, and so they can bear to be stared at 'by
eyes through a window'. Michael Elliott in his 1979 production at the Round House in London solved the problem of
how to stage this part of the play by using a non-proscenium
stage. 'The mysterious up-stage, and its evocation of other
worlds, is not locked away beyond French windows. We have
reversed the polarity so that the audience are closest, not to
the tea-cups, but to the Eumenides' (Michael Elliott's Programme note to *The Family Reunion*). Harry entered through
the audience, and the Furies in their black and malign form
intervened between him and the illuminated figures on the
stage, before Harry joined them.

A little later Harry comes to understand the special nature of his seeing:

> Now I see
> I have been wounded in a war of phantoms.
> Not by human beings – they have no more power than I
> The things I thought were real are shadows, and the real
> Are what I thought were private shadows
>
> (Part Two, scene 2)

The contrast between those characters to whom nothing has ever happened, and those who live in a tormented privacy ('the awful privacy of the insane mind') is sustained again by rhythms and repetitions of varying kinds: words which invoke the power to see, or express the desire to remain unaware. As Professor Katharine Worth has pointed out, the two most moving and effective scenes of the play take the form of 'lyrical duets' between Harry and Mary, and Mary and Agatha. Harry's final decision to leave his mother's house and follow 'the bright angels' reduces his previous contortions of syntax to a simple statement and a single image, which Paul Scofield made to resonate with all the echoes from submerged being that had not yet come to light, and Edward Fox to burn with the conviction of a new illumination.

The Cocktail Party (1950), like the two earlier plays, develops out of a conviction that 'all things are but simple when they are known'; and involves the audience in the solution of a mystery or mysteries, which centre around the disappearance of a succesful barrister's wife, and the appearance of an enigmatic psychiatrist, Henry Harcourt Reilly, in his apartment. What sounds from its title like another West End drawing-room comedy becomes an anatomy of souls, forced to choose a pathway through life, and accept the consequences wherever they lead. The rituals of social life – food, drinks, cooking, telephoning, going to parties – have been absorbed into another ritual: that of understanding. Edward cannot understand why his wife has left him, Celia cannot

understand why she feels 'a sense of sin' at the life she is
leading in London. Reilly's role, as a healer of souls, is to help
them understand for themselves. Once again, this inner pil-
grimage is mediated through the interrogations of the verse.
Characters echo each other, picking up on each other's
words, creating patterns of meaning and sound, which press
towards a solution.

> ALEX
> . . . . I'm afraid you can't have Celia.
> PETER
> Oh. . . . . Is she married?
> ALEX
> Not married, but dead.
> LAVINIA
> Celia?
> ALEX
> Dead.
> PETER
> Dead. That knocks the bottom out of it.
> EDWARD
> Celia dead.
> JULIA
> You had better tell them, Alex,
> The news that you bring back from Kinkanja.
> (Act III)

Reilly, with his taste for drinking gin and water, and his
strange song about 'One-eyed Riley'(with its refrain 'Too-ri–
oo–ley, Too–ri–i–ley, What's the matter with One-eyed
Riley') requires the talent of an actor whose presence depends
on an Oriental inscrutability, wholly in command of the situation because he has the power to understand more, even
though he never intimates the source of this power, and the
grounds on which he knows he is right. The part seemed
made for the style of Alec Guinness's acting in which there
always remains a secrecy, a slyly humorous unwillingness to

divulge what exactly is going on. But Reilly was also played with equal skill by Alec McCowan in 1986, whose air of puzzlement tempered with authority humanized the role. In this production by John Dexter, with designs by Brian Vahey, Edward and Lavinia's London flat was given a 1930s décor which reflected the style of a play, set in 1949, but whose tone belongs to the pre-war period.

In his essay on 'The Music of Poetry', Eliot claimed that 'the properties in which music concerns the poet most nearly are the sense of rhythm, and the sense of structure'. It is these properties which he brings to the writing of his plays whose strength lies in what remains unsayable, what characters do not understand about themselves or their behaviour, which the rhythms of the verse catch on to, as reeds are caught by the flow of a stream.

In the plays of the other verse dramatist of the post-war period, Christoper Fry, whose work attracted many of the major talents of the English stage from Richard Burton to John Gielgud, Laurence Olivier and Edith Evans, in productions by Peter Brook, and with designs by Oliver Messel, the verse was driven not so much by the inner rhythms of character, as by a witty evaluation of the world. In a blithe way their problem was existential; their conflict was not so much with each other as with existence, with 'the hard heart of the world', amounting at times to an indifference at being in it. 'Where', asks one of the characters in Act II of *The Lady's Not for Burning* (1949), 'in this small-talking world can I find / A longitude with no platitude?' Nonetheless, when Edith Evans played Rosmarin in *The Dark is Light Enough* (1954), she brought to the role a pained authority which at times discovered a music beneath the surface of the verse, as, for instance when she asked of Colonel Janik,

> Only
> Tell me what is in this war you fight
> Worth all your dead and suffering men ?
> (Act II)

Christopher Fry's characters were often a source of wit, and always interesting to listen to, but their music too often belonged to the surface; its flow was elegant, swift but lacked a dark undertow, or that feeling of danger which comes from what is not spoken, and to which an audience who watches and listens responds. Recent revivals of *The Lady's Not for Burning*, and *Venus Observed* at the Chichester Festival Theatre with Donald Sinden have revealed the pleasure to be derived from hearing Fry's dialogue spoken with such relish for its polished surface, but have also shown its lack of an inner music which words do not touch.

Memory has been used in a number of prose plays, including Wilder's *Our Town*, (1938) Tennessee Williams's *The Glass Menagerie* (1944), Pinter's *Landscape* (1969) and Friel's *Dancing at Lughnasa* (1990) to create a music of this sort. Memory is by its nature a kind of inner music, working with feelings, associations, images, words, experiences only half recaptured and questioned. In a memory play the audience is confronted with a present which it watches being woven from the past: watching people who have already become ghosts, but who still exist as though alive in the memory of the narrator or, as in Pinter's case, the two separate memories of Beth and Duff. In the memory play we are asked to accept as 'present and living' (a dramatic performance is *de facto* in the present) a way of life which the narrator knows to exist no more. He has to recreate it for us and, in this act of conjuring, he will cast upon the audience the spell of a time gone by, of people who can no longer speak for themselves, and whose lives were passed in rooms, and circumstances, now utterly changed. Memory, though it may contain nostalgic feelings, is not nostalgia; it is a re-creative act. What we hear and see is not just the figure on the stage, but the figure on the stage succumbing to the spell of his own memory and casting it on us. Tennessee Williams in his first major play, *The Glass Menagerie*, creates Tom, a narrator close to himself, who recalls his own mother, Amanda, and sister, Laura in their lives of depressed gentility in an apartment in St Louis where the Williams family had lived. Amanda, who had once been a Southern belle, deserted by her husband – 'a telephone man who fell in love with long distances' – lives in her own memories, and in her over-protective love for her daughter, who walks with a limp, has no 'gentleman callers' (except one as the action develops), and the isolation of whose life is mirrored in her collection of glass animals. What Tennessee Williams catches through the rhythms of Tom's memory combines a Southern tolerance with a neurotic tension, drawling and wounded, susceptible of being hurt, and capable of causing pain: a stability as threatened and fragile as that of the glass animals themselves, but also enclosing somewhere a heroic toughness. Tom alone is destined to escape.

> I left St Louis. I descended the steps of this fire-escape for a last time and followed, from then on, in my father's footsteps, attempting to find in motion what was lost in space. I traveled around a great deal. The cities swept around me like dead leaves.
>
> (Act II)

The cities which sweep around him like dead leaves have swept around us too, turning themselves into the figures of his family, and their shattered, continuing lives. The candles which Laura blows out to close the play bring to an end Tom's memories of those days, until as he says somewhere else Laura touches him on the shoulder. As she touches us too: an effect which only the theatre in the intensity of its present and its brief lightning before darkness can bring about.

In Friel's play, *Dancing at Lughnasa*, memory and music are associated even more closely, becoming the source of the play's whole action. In the closing words of the play, Michael sums up what we have entered into through him. His memory of Lughnasa is composed of a

> dream music, both heard and imagined; that seems to be both itself and its own echo; a sound so alluring and so

mesmeric that the afternoon is bewitched, maybe haunted
by it. And what is so strange about that memory is that
everybody seems to be floating on those sweet sounds,
moving rhythmically, languorously, in complete isolation;
responding more to the mood of the music than to its beat.
When I remember it, I think of it as dancing. Dancing with
eyes half closed because to open them would break the
spell. Dancing as if language had surrendered to movement
– as if this ritual, this wordless ceremony, was now the way
to speak, to whisper private and sacred things, to be in
touch with some otherness. Dancing as if the very heart of
life and all its hopes might be found in those assuaging
notes and those hushed rhythms and in those silent and
hypnotic movements. Dancing as if language no longer
existed because words were no longer necessary . . . (*Slowly
bring up the music. Slowly bring down the lights.*)

(Act II)

In these words, about the limitations of words, Michael
defines much that is true not just of the memory play, but
about the inner action of all drama, which brings us into
touch with 'private and sacred things', which puts us in touch
with 'some otherness', the otherness those on the stage are
living, so that we may feel at times they have forgotten they
are acting, possesed by the actual and the illusory. Acting at
this level can only be instinctive, performed out of the
rhythms of an inner invisible life.

In Pinter's much more laconic play, *Landscape*, Duff and
Beth, created by David Waller and Peggy Ashcroft, are divided
by a cleft running across the floor and along the wall behind
them, suggestive of two identities joined in marriage, divided
by time and memory. (The set for the first production was
designed by John Bury.) For Duff, life is to talk of beer, and
walk his dog; for Beth to recall an ecstasy of love, now past for
ever, summed up at the close in a single line, 'Oh, my true
love, I said.'

As with the set, the life between them is fractured, whether because they do not hear each other, or because Beth dreams of another man, is never clear. What matters is that the dialogue creates a broken music between them, in the same room together, and distant as people on different planets in their feelings. The love which in John Donne's poem makes a little room an everywhere makes a little room here a desert in which two voices are heard, out of all contact with each other. Not knowing this, they cannot talk about it, or to each other; only the rhythms of their contrasted voices, their pauses for reflection, their silence can suggest it to the audience: a suggestiveness which goes on expanding through the presence of those two words, 'I said', which fade away into interstellar space, carrying with them a memory of what has been unspeakable and remains unsayable.

*

The whole performance of a play has an innate musicality. In plays of many sorts this sense of rhythm breaks through the surface. Song, and dance are used to heighten the inner action, to intensify and ritualize a particular moment, or to comment upon the action as a whole.

Songs, dances, solemn music, drums, fifes, trumpets are all used by Shakespeare as instruments of dramatic action; they are never separate from the dramatic action, but a way of conceiving it. The mask'd dance at which Romeo meets Juliet in the house of the Capulets surrounds them with danger, while providing the opportunity for the first private conversation between them, stolen, secretive and passionate.

Songs in Shakespeare's plays – and the way they are performed which differs from production to production – crystallize aspects of their feeling, and give the audience a pause to reflect upon it. Feste's song at the end of *Twelfth Night*:

> When that I was and a little tiny boy
>   With hey, ho, the wind and the rain;
> A foolish thing was but a toy,
>   For the rain it raineth every day

dismisses the audience from the sunlight of Illyria, with its wedding feasts and true loves knotted, to the wind and rain of London streets. It can be sung in many different ways; but what it must preserve is the magic of performance (all our attention is concentrated on Feste in his skills as entertainer), and an awareness that even spells have an ending.

> The best rendering of that song that I have heard not vocally, but dramatically, was in Peter Hall's production at the Playhouse a few years back. The Feste used his tambourine as if raindrops were beginning to fall, starting with a few slow, heavy drops, such as we often experience at the end of summer, and then increasing in intensity with the feel of winter. You almost turned up your coat-collar for protection. The actor was only drumming with his fingers under the tambourine, but it was magic. (Guinness, *My Name* p. 80)

The actor was Robert Eddison; and Guinness describes precisely the effect of what happened.

The song and dance at the end of *A Midsummer Night's Dream* create magic of another kind. Oberon and Titania enter with their train, invoking 'beings of another sort', to bless the house, and the issue of its marriages:

> Now until the break of day,
> Through this house each fairy stray.
> To the best bride-bed will we,
> Which by us shall blessed be;
> And the issue there create
> Ever shall be fortunate.
> So shall all the couples three
> Ever true in loving be
> (Act V, scene 2)

Through the power of music, the fairies cast a spell of heavenly grace, capable of preventing disfigurements in birth, and quarrels in marriage. Music as in the later Saint Cecilia's Ode is inspired with the power to raise a mortal to the skies, and call an angel down. Blessing, grace and harmony are the gifts of song; the gifts of the fairy world to the human world; and the audience are touched by them too when they have dreamed this dream. The song at the end of the earlier *Love's Labour's Lost*, a play for, and about, courtiers ends with an earthier and no less effective reminder that 'greasy Joan must keel the pot'. At close of play, music can set the seal, and turn the knife. How the songs are performed becomes a commentary on the action as a whole.

Shakespeare's songs intervene in the action, as well as concluding it, and matter as much in tragedy as in comedy. The mad Ophelia torments Gertrude, and Claudius, with her song, 'He is dead and gone, lady' reminding the audience of the finality of death, a prelude to the numerous deaths about to occur, including her own by suicide, and the frailty of the mind before unbearable grief. (Her own ex-lover has violently murdered her doting father.) Desdemona's willow-song expresses grief of a different, but no less desperate kind: Desdemona's loneliness, her distress and incomprehension at the frenzy of which she has so suddenly become the object:

> The poor soul sat sighing by a sycamore tree
> 　Sing all a green willow;
> Her hand on her bosom, her head on her knee,
> 　Sing willow, willow, willow
> 　　　　　　　　　　　　(Act IV, scene Two)

Shakespeare's infinite variety means that not all tragedies or plays contain songs; and their positioning, like their effect, surprises. In *Measure for Measure*, a bawdy, lustful play (ultimately concerned with judgement, human and divine), there is only one song, given to a boy who sings to Mariana in her moated grange at the start of Act IV:

Take, O take those lips away
That so sweetly were forsworn;
And those eyes, the break of day,
Lights that do mislead the morn;
But my kisses bring again,
      bring again,
Seals of love, but seal'd in vain,
      seal'd in vain.

The song is broken off by the appearance of the Duke, disguised as a friar. She apologises for being found so musical:

Let me excuse me, and believe me so!
My mirth it much displeas'd, but pleased my woe.
DUKE: 'Tis good; though music oft hath such a charm
To make bad good, and good provoke to harm.
                    (Act IV, scene 1)

Mariana, already contracted to Angelo, is about to be per-
suaded to take Isabella's place in his bed, in order to save
the life of Isabella's brother, Claudio. Angelo has demanded
Isabella's body as the price of reprieving him. (The bed-trick,
however implausible, becomes the means of preventing the
play from becoming a tragedy.) In this play, dominated by lust,
and partly set in the brothels of Vienna, the song reminds us of
another kind of sex: sex as desire, as bodies given, however
temporarily, as 'seals of love', of eyes which shine so brightly
they make dawn think the night is over, and of desire to make
love again. This is the sex of reciprocated pleasure, of an
exchange, as opposed to an exaction, a rape – the price which
Lord Angelo who is 'very snow-broth' demands of Isabella.
Just for a moment, the song reminds us that even in faithless
love, there can be pleasure as well as pain. When John Neville
played Angelo in 1962 he conveyed precisely the coldness of
his desire for self-gratification, arising out of a nature purit-
anical and power-loving to which the song presents a tender,
even if almost despairing alternative.

Feste's earlier song in *Twelfth Night* also invokes light loves and passing amusements but in a way appropriate to Illyria, and not disfigured by the money-making or power-breaking exchanges of Vienna:

> What is love? 'tis not hereafter;
> Present mirth hath present laughter;
> What's to come is still unsure;
> In delay there lies no plenty;
> Then come kiss me, sweet and twenty,
> Youth's a stuff will not endure.
>
> (Act II, scene 3)

But, coming where it does, it also sustains the dramatic action of *Twelfth Night* at another level. Toby Belch and Andrew Aguecheek, devoted to cakes and ale, have asked for a love song; and the love song they get does not reflect their own boisterous and jaded appetites, but the appetites of young lovers to whom in the end this play belongs: those of Sebastian and Viola. In another play where they were not brother and sister, they would be intended for each other. Here in Illyria, they are both destined for older and more sophisticated partners, Viola for Orsino (whose appetite for love has to be fed with music) and Sebastian for Olivia, whose life would otherwise be confined to 'watering her chamber round with eye-offending brine'. Neither has the vigour of a Beatrice or a Benedict, or the mad intoxication of a Romeo and Juliet. Autumnal stagings of this play suggest this love on the brink of maturity, while Feste's song warns of the danger of forgetting that youth's a stuff will not endure. In *Twelfth Night* Shakespeare writes his farewell to young love, until at the end he returns to it not so much for its own unfettered joy, but as part of the pattern of 'great creating Nature'.

In Shakespeare's last play, *The Tempest*, the songs of Ariel become the instruments of that island music which as Caliban knows 'give delight and hurt not'. Ariel alone can articulate the sounds and sweet airs of which the isle is full, and turn them into the exactness of a song. As in *A Midsummer Night's Dream* this involves magic, but not just fairy magic: Ariel draws down the powers which exist in Nature, and invokes their help to prevent murder and restore harmony. Alan Badel who played Ariel at Stratford in 1952 brought to the part a speaking voice both musical and other-worldly, so that in his songs he seemed to be drawing down powers just out of human reach. At the banquet offered to the conspirators and whisked away before they can enjoy it, Ariel acts as Master of Ceremonies. Solemn and strange music accompanies its appearance; Ariel in the shape of a harpy claps his wings and causes the feast to disappear, before he too vanishes in thunder. '*Then, to soft music, enter the Shapes again, and dance with mocks and mows, and carry out the table.*' Over against Stephano's and Caliban's drunken songs, Ariel offers the music of transformation:

> Come unto these yellow sands
> And then take hands:
> Curtsied when you have, and kiss'd
> The wild waves whist. . .
> Full fathom five thy father lies;
> Of his bones are coral made:
> Those are pearls that were his eyes:
> Nothing of him that doth fade,
> But doth suffer a sea-change
> Into something rich and strange.
>
> (Act I, scene 2)

When Prospero releases him from his tasks, Ariel will be found 'under the blossoms that hangs on the bough'. Ariel's songs come closest in the play to expressing the powers which Prospero, as white magus, has learned from his books, drawing upon the resources of Nature of which Ariel, as spirit, always remains a part. Song becomes another kind of harmony – not the music of the spheres, as in *The Merchant of Venice* – but music unheard by those whose senses are deadened by the 'muddy vesture of decay'.

In drama, since Shakespeare, music has continued to be used as a means of intensifying the dramatic action. In Ibsen's *A Doll's House*, Nora dances for Torvald to prevent him looking in the letter-box where she knows he will find the letter from Krogstad, betraying her forgery of her father's signature. The rhythms of the tarantella express her increasing desperation; and at the same time heighten the audience's anxiety about what is going to happen. In Strindberg's *The Dance of Death* (1901), the Captain dances himself apparently to death as yet another way of tormenting his wife. In a lonely marriage, on an island fortress, their relationship is sustained (or their days are passed) in a series of games and black jokes, of which this dance becomes the most deadly example. The Captain's fiendish glee on reviving, which Laurence Olivier played with all the relish of a man possessed, expresses his pleasure in surviving to torment her further: life is quite literally a dance of death.

In Chekhov's plays, music is used to suggest things which are not spoken of. Prozorov in *Three Sisters* has had ambitions to become a university professor in Moscow; but he knows that his time has passed, and he will never become more than a member of the local council. Chekhov, unlike Ibsen, does not write about what causes the failure of hopes and dreams; but he does write about the consequences of their failing. Prozorov finds refuge from his unhappy marriage and failed hopes in his playing the violin, which we hear off-stage. Played unaccompanied, the violin's plaintiveness expresses, more succinctly than any words could, his isolation, and his will – close to despair – which makes him go on. Prozorov does not complain (except, ironically to the deaf porter Ferapont); but his violin expresses the yearning of an unfulfilled soul, and an unhappy man: a part to which Anthony Hopkins brought a grim fortitude.

Prozorov's solitary playing stands in contrast to the use which Chekhov makes of the military band in the last moments of the play. Vershinin, like Prozorov trapped in an unhappy marriage, has fallen deeply in love with Masha, and

Masha with him. But when his regiment is posted away from the town he has no choice except to go with them, in company with a wife who revenges herself on him by her attempts to kill herself. Masha is left, equally unhappy in her marriage to the worthy but boring schoolmaster, Koolyghin. Almost unable to bear the future, Masha listens with her sisters to the sound of the band's receding music. As it fades way into the distance, the sisters talk once more of their longing for Moscow, and of their uncertainty of what the future holds for them. 'If only we knew. If only we knew.' The playing of the band becoming more and more distant accentuates that fading hope, even as it carries away Masha's one hope of love. As this happens, Chebutykin, the doctor who has given up on caring, and has done nothing to prevent the Baron being killed in a duel sits humming to himself the song associated with him:

Tarara–boom–di–ay . . . I'm sitting on a tomb-di–ay.

This fragment of song, expressing an awareness of mortality which nurtures indifference, recalls another totally diffferent fragment of music earlier in the play for which there can now be no reprise, expressing the intensity of Masha and Vershinin's love for each other.

MASHA (*sings*): To Love all ages are in fee,
　　　　　　　The passion's good for you and me . . .
　　　　　　　(*Laughs.*)
MASHA (*sings*): Tara–tara–tara . . .
VERSHININ: Tum–tum . . .
MASHA: Tara–tara . . .
VERSHININ: Tum-tum, tum-tum . . . (*Laughs.*)

Masha's and Vershinin's inner life is conveyed here with a clarity and intensity which explicit statement could never match.

The three sisters are left isolated from each other, and from

what they believe would give them a new way of life. In
Moscow, they would find refuge from this terrible isolation,
and from a suffering they can neither understand nor over-
come. Music fading into silence matches the fading of their
lives into silence: a balance rendered with almost unbearable
anguish in the National Theatre production by Laurence
Olivier in 1967, with sets of great beauty and simplicity, by
Josef Svoboda, who used silver rods to suggest the enclosure of
their lives, and the birch trees which Chekhov so much loved.
In that production, Robert Stephens brought to the part of
Vershinin a mixture of disillusion and passion, matched by
Joan Plowright's Masha whose yearning existed on the very
edge of total breakdown.

Music in Chekhov's plays brings to the surface currents of
feeling which are always flowing underneath, whether of
temporary communion, or more frequently of isolation. The
originality and genius of his dramatic technique comes from
holding together an action in which every character follows
(they have no choice) their own path through life, separated
from, and independent of those with whom they are associated by kinship or location. Houses bring people under the
same roof; they derive from them their identity; and within
them they play their roles as husbands, lovers, mothers, sons,
uncles and so on. But these *liens* matter far less than the inner
life which every character carries within the enclosure of the
self, and which the dramatic action enables us to imagine. *The
Cherry Orchard* combines the unifying force of the image
which gives it its title and the explosive, disintegrating force of
its characters' incompatible lives. The luggage which is carried on in Act I, when they return to the house, and taken
away again when they leave in Act IV suggests their arbitrary
and transient togetherness, like the cast of the play, and like all
our lives.

As with everything Chekhov wrote it is done with a lightness of touch, and an indirectness of expression which makes
us see the more clearly what is going on underneath. In Act
III, when Lopakhin is off making his bid for the orchard,

Madame Ranevskaya (Liuba) is giving a dance, for which she lacks the money to pay. Everyone knows what news is awaited; and the orchard bobs in and out of the conversation like a cork on the sea. While the Jewish orchestra play, the German governess, Charlotta entertains the guests with her tricks, and Liuba cares only about the telegram from her worthless lover in Paris.

Everything that happens is 'a fashion of forsaking', until Lophakhin, the former peasant, enters to tell them all that he has been the one to buy the orchard. In the embarrassment which ensues, only the music again can cover up feelings which no one knows how to express, as Lopakhin whips up the band to more fenzied tempi, in keeping with his mood of crass self-approbation.

> 'Hi, you musicians, come on now, play something. I want some music. Now then, all of you, just you wait and see Yermolai Lopakhin take an axe to the cherry orchard, just you see the trees come crashing down. . . . Come on there, let's have some music! (*The band plays.*)

The music cannot conceal that Liuba is crying. The cherry orchard, it is true, has been sold; and somewhere else it will have to be planted in some form again, if her life is to be renewed. We all know that for her the dance is over; and the dance-band continues to play.

Chekhov has used the dance to structure the Act. Once again it repeats what the two previous Acts have shown: Liuba's recklessness in the face of disaster, her unwillingness even to notice it coming; but it also suggests a continuing normality to which Lopakhin belongs, and which remains indifferent to the ways human beings ruin their lives.

Music performs a different function here to that of Telyegin's guitar playing in *Uncle Vanya*, signalling his withdrawal into a private world, which no one can share because they already exist in their own.

YELIENA: What a lovely day! . . . Not too hot either . . .

VANYA: It would be even pleasant to hang oneself on a day
      like this . . .

(*Telyeghin tunes his guitar. Marina walks to and fro near the house,
calling the chickens.*)

MARINA: Chook, chook, chook.

SONIA: Nanny, what did the peasants come for?

MARINA: The same as before – they are all still going on
      about the waste land. Chook, chook, chook . . .

SONIA: Which is it you're calling?

MARINA: The speckled one. She's gone somewhere with
      her chicks. The crows might get them . . . (*Walks
      away.*)

(*Telyeghin plays a polka; all listen in silence.*)

(translated by Elizaveta Fen)

Each character has his or her own music. Each is lost in
solitude.

The recurrence of music in Chekhov's plays articulates his
awareness of the rhythms of people's lives which life orchestrates in its own arbitrary ways. What is offered today will not
be offered tomorrow. The trajectories of individual lives cross
but do not meet. The unique effect of his drama comes from
the randomness of its inner music, and his control over form.
Acts in his plays are structured around an event: a performance of another play, a name-day party, a duel, a fire, an
announcement, a declaration, a return, a departure – techniques which he learnt from his enjoyment of popular
vaudevilles, in his youth. But unlike *The Bear* and *The Proposal*
(1888) – two of the funniest short plays ever written – his
major plays depend not on a single accelerating rhythm, but
on the discovery of a pulse in the play – sometimes slower,
sometimes faster – which holds together the varied and individual pulses of the cast as a whole. Mannered playing by one
or more actors which has the effect of retarding the action
can wholly destroy this. Each member of the cast has to be in
tune with all the others, and all responsive to the particular

tone of the play's production. This is in every nuance a musical activity.

Apart from Shakespeare, Chekhov's plays have probably been more frequently revived with more distinguished casts than those of any other dramatist in the last fifty years; and performances of all his major plays remain in the memory: Gielgud as Ivanov, and Gayev, Michael Redgrave and Laurence Olivier, as Vanya and Astrov, Vanessa Redgrave and Jonathan Pryce in *The Seagull*, Robert Stephens as Vershinin, Tom Courtenay as Trofimov, Peggy Ashcroft, Dorothy Tutin, Lil Kedrova, and Judi Dench as Liuba, Anna Calder-Marshall as Sonya, Albert Finney as Lopakhin, Michael Gambon and Ian McKellen as Vanya; Alec McCowan as Gayev; Ralph Fiennes as Ivanov; the visits of the Moscow Art Theatre itself. Everyone who has been to Chekhov will have their own list of memorable performances and productions. They are bound together by a love for the author, shared by audiences and actors, and by the author's love for most of his characters. (Although they are plays which require ensemble playing, paradoxically, they are also memorable for interpretations of particular roles; and in this too they resemble life.) When played by a company attuned to each other, Chekhov's plays, as well as using music from squeaking boots to guitars and military bands, create another kind of music which is of individual souls, not at one with each other (we are all alone) but transiently brought together. It is this which we hear all the time in listening to Chekhov's plays: a harmony which remains discordant because one can never be attuned to another, or anyone to life; and an action in which harmony is sought for, whether in 'rest' or in Moscow, or in death. The musicality of Chekhov's plays results in 'something understood': a contact between the imaginative subconscious of the performer and the audience: symbolized by the distant breaking of a string which is heard in Act II of *The Cherry Orchard*, and again at the play's end. Chekhov's plays work with the deepest resources of theatrical art; and at the same time only once refer to it directly.

★

It is a pity we do not have live orchestras any more. In the old days, if the play was not very successful, or was rather thin such orchestral interludes brightened things up a little, although it was often somewhat grim, with an awful chamber orchestra sawing away under a lot of imitation palm leaves, playing tea-shop music between the acts. (Gielgud, p. 172)

Brightening things up a little between the acts does still occur, though usually on tape, and with the advantage of professional recording and stereophonic sound, as the scene is changed. Such music – like other off-stage sound effects – adds to the suggestiveness of a production, and helps to confirm the mood at which the director is aiming. It provides a link or bridge between scenes or acts, not broken by an interval, amplifying feelings which run as an underground stream through any production. The selection or composition of this music sustains a tone, atmosphere, feeling which might otherwise be lost. As with lighting, the technology of sound in some theatres has become very sophisticated and expensive, though no amount of money can substitute for the imagination which integrates every aspect of a production.

In some plays, the dramatist prescribes the music which needs to be used, as at the start of *Death of a Salesman*.

ACT I

A melody is heard, played upon a flute. It small and fine, telling of grass and trees and the horizon. The curtain rises.

Before us is the Salesman's house. We are aware of towering, angular shapes behind it, surrounding it on all side. . . . From the right, Wily Loman, the salesman enters, carrying two large sample cases. The flute plays on.

This flute music, recurring throughout the action, becomes Willy's theme. Elegiac and dream-like, it expresses the unfulfilled aspirations of the salesman to whom society no longer 'pays attention'. After his suicide, and at his requiem it is heard as Linda begins to speak, '*not far away, playing behind her speech*'. When the stage is left empty, '*only the music of the flute is left on the darkening stage as over the house the hard towers of the apartment buildings rise into sharp focus.*' Willy's music is always reaching for feelings which words cannot express, and so lies close to that relationship between music and drama, associated with musicals and opera. At other moments in the play, Miller specifies different kinds of music to create other kinds of tone.

Act II begins with music which is '*gay and bright*'. Howard, Willy's boss, who is only interested in showing off his new wire recording machine, makes Willy listen to his daughter whistling 'Roll out the barrel' on it, while Willy waits to ask him for a job in New York (which will be refused). The brash, cheerful song ('Roll out the barrel, we'll have a barrel of fun') acts as a counterpoint to the anguish of Willy's last desperate attempt to get work he can cope with; his life has passed beyond all fun. Raw, sensuous music accompanies the scene in which Willy is caught by his son Biff in a Boston Hotel with another woman, accentuating the gap between what Willy wants to feel, and what Biff's unexpected arrival has made him feel.

At the end of *Our Country's Good* Timberlake Wertenbaker uses music to celebrate and confirm. The convicts in the Australian penal colony have overcome the disadvantages of lack of education and present suffering to learn and rehearse the first performance of Farquhar's *The Recruiting Officer* (1706) in Australia. As the curtain is about to go up on this triumph of civilization over barbarism which theatre has made possible, we (and they) hear the opening bars of Beethoven's Fifth symphony with its famous 'morse-code' chords for Victory. The play has opened with a very different music; the sound of the lashes being counted out as a convict's punishment. The trajectory of the dramatic action moves from violence and

negation to triumphant affirmation, sealed by Beethoven's
music. As was discovered in the Second World War, when this
symphony of Beethoven was used to disconcert the Germans,
no one can listen to its opening without responding to its
feeling of an unassailable confidence won over despair.

In Peter Shaffer's *Amadeus* (1979) Mozart, and his music,
become the centre of the action. Many films have been based
on the lives of composers (Liszt, Wagner, Mahler, Elgar); they
provide, among other things, a sound track, which can be used
to half-conceal the defects of the screen play. On the stage,
however, the music needs far more subtle treament, if it is not
to bring the dramatic action to a standstill. Peter Hall who
believed in the importance of *Amadeus* from his first reading,
recognized from the start its central problem on the stage.

> All day working on Mozart and *Amadeus* selecting little bits
> of music for the production. Music, like colour, is the most
> dangerous thing to put in the straight theatre. It generalises
> emotion, generates it easily, and ends by dissipating it. And,
> my God, when it's Mozart. . . . You can't easily let him into
> a play.

The problem was solved with the help of the composer,
Harrison Birtwistle.

> It must be distant, under speech; Mozart's music, of course,
> but as if through a slightly distorting glass. If we inject
> Mozart's music into the play, to then follow with speech is
> impossible. (Hall, p. 462)

Shaffer's play is concerned with the enmity between
Salieri, the court composer blessed with talent but no genius,
who realises that Mozart – as his name and the title of the play
suggests – is beloved of God, inspired with a divine gift, oddly
accompanied by a love of scatological humour and farting.
Salieri knows that whatever the defects of Mozart's character,
his own compositions will never approach Mozart's inspired

art; and jealousy of this 'child of God' turns to the need to have him murdered. As Salieri is telling his story, the distortion of Mozart's music reflects its emotional impact on him. As in many post-modern novels, the narrator's viewpoint is perceived to be a distortion, which the audience is left to interpret, at times through hearing Mozart's music briefly as it really is. As Peter Hall said, 'there must be tension between what the audience sees and what Salieri describes. A difficult balance to achieve' (Hall, p. 465).

The solution of the technical problems of Shaffer's play turned it from being a play with music (most films about composers are only films with music) into a play which questioned the origin of music. The 'heaven' of Mozart's music is contrasted with the 'hell' of Salieri's hatred: music of another sort. Both humanly and metaphysically, the savagest sorrow arises from the feeling of love to which we are exiles. As a young man Salieri has made a contract with God – or thinks he has that in return for leading a virtuous life he will be inspired with music which is 'God's Art'. God chooses to inspire Mozart instead. Ironically, Salieri has the talent to realize, as few of his contemporaries do, that Mozart's music is immortal; and that his music, although acclaimed for a time, will soon cease to be played. His one chance of immortal fame lies in spreading the rumour that he has murdered Mozart. In the original production the part of Salieri was played by Paul Scofield with the half-concealed menace of a rabid dog; in its 1998 revival David Suchet brought to the part a rhetorical circumspection which demanded the audience consider its mediocrity, as he was compelled to confront his own.

Words in Shaffer's play matter very much less (Mozart's scatological humour exemplifies this) than feelings. The dialogue, apart from Salieri's rhetoric, is unmemorable and repetitive, throwing no light upon the nature of Mozart's genius. The originality of his play comes from the difference between the feelings aroused in the audience by Mozart's music, and its effect on Salieri. Music becomes the instrument for suggesting the difference between talent and genius, and the inexplicable nature of inspiration. Ironically, and perhaps consciously, Mozart's music comments too on the limitations of Shaffer as a dramatistist.

★

Music, and musicality in plays is absorbed, sometimes more, sometimes less obtrusively, within the action as a whole. In two dramatic forms, the musical and opera, words and music have a more specific, though very different, relationship. Opera is dismissed by low-brows as élitist; musicals are dismissed by high-brows as mere entertainment. No one buys a ticket for any form of theatre without the desire of being entertained; and any form of theatre which does not entertain deserves to fail at the box-office, the sole arbiter of what continues to be performed.

The power of the musical to entertain needs no arguing beyond its success at the box office, which may also feed on the impossibility of buying a ticket! But the success of a musical is secured by the number of arts which go into its making and the skill with which the languages of theatre are used. When Ira Gershwin wrote:

> I got rhythm
> I got music
> Who could ask for anything more?

he asked a very good question.

The words in a musical are always waiting to burst into song. In the second scene of Rodgers and Hammerstein's *Carousel* (1945), Julie and Billy are left alone. Billy has lost his job for putting his arm round her on the carousel; Julie has lost hers for refusing to return to the mill-owner's lodging-house before the doors are closed. After a short conversation between them, the musical accompaniment begins in the background (creating a sense of expectation in the audience), building to the moment when Julie will break into song:

If I loved you
Time and again I would try to say
All I would want you
To know

Once she starts to sing, her words and its melody takes over from the orchestra. As in any good song, every word has to be audible, and the feeling behind the words has to communicate itself immediately and directly. Through the melody we enter into, and share, the feelings of Julie and Billy as they imagine what they would say if they loved each other (which as yet they don't!). Simplicity is essential to this effect: in a musical, however complex, there is no indirect action; everything belongs to the immediate present of what we are looking at, and listening to. The orchestra exists to provide a rhythmical accompaniment, harmonise the melody, and improvise round it, with the tone being varied when the melody is taken up by different instruments. Nothing must distract from what happens on the stage; the orchestra never upstages the singer; the orchestra is seldom allowed to act.

Unlike opera, where overture or prelude initiates the dramatic action, the overture of the musical contains a medley of as yet wordless songs, to which the audience pays little attention, even if they are not still arriving. The big numbers are created only when they have been sung; and are inscribed on the memory by the reprise, which often occurs in changed circumstances.

When we hear the reprise of 'If I loved you' in Act II of *Carousel* Billy is dead; he has returned from Heaven as a spirit to comfort Julie; and he sings it on his own. As soon as the orchestra takes up the melody the audience can complete it with the words, and the melody itself becomes an instrument of dramatic irony, and nostalgia. The singer is quite literally the song, confirming what Julie has just been told in the show's other big number, 'You'll never walk alone'.

The formal reprise has no place in opera, though Verdi uses brief repetitions for intense dramatic effect in the final acts of

La Traviata and *Otello*, as Puccini does in the last act of *La Bohème*. The musical has another tradition inconceivable in the opera house of playing the audience out with a further repetition of the main numbers, which the audience carry away, with accretions of feeling, absent in the overture, and built up in the course of the dramatic action, through the addition of the words, and their repetition, in a changing situation. The melodies in a musical are memorable not just in themselves but for the particular feelings they arouse; and they are incomplete without the words as in Rodgers and Hammerstein's *Oklahoma* (1943):

> O what a beautiful mornin'
> O what a beautiful day
> I've got a glorious feelin'
> Everything's goin' my way

The words and the melody are infectious, and cannot be separated from each other.

In the 'operas' of Gilbert and Sullivan, made famous in their performances by the D'Oyly Carte Opera Company, W.S. Gilbert played ingeniously with rhyme schemes and rhythms in the verses which Sullivan set to music. But for all their tunefulness, these musical plays lack any deep feeling (perhaps reflecting an English embarrassment before it). There is fancy, sentiment, energy, humour (of the good clean fun sort); but the effect is of brightly painted screens, with nothing behind them. Only in *The Yeomen of the Guard* (1888) does the final reprise of 'I have a song to sing O' generate a resonance of effect like that in the reprise of later musicals.

The effectiveness of Gilbert's words depended on the absolute clarity with which they were heard, the comic skill with which they were performed, and the inventiveness of actors, like Martyn Green (famous for the Lord High Executioner in *The Mikado*), who knew how to vary the repetitions within the rhyme schemes of the lyrics, and the *da capo* form of the songs as a whole. The orchestra ornamented and emphasized, but could not be allowed to intervene between the words and the audience, or the point of such numbers as 'I am the very model of a modern Major-General' would have been entirely lost.

Verbal wit, and humour, have remained a vitalizing instrument in the lyrics of many twentieth-century musicals, a source of pleasure and energy derived from plays without music, and easy to remember in themselves. For example, Adelaide in Frank Loesser's *Guys and Dolls* (1950):

> Take back your mink
> Take back your poils
> What made you think
> That I was one of those goils?

Or Annie in *Annie Get Your Gun* (1947):

> My uncle out in Texas
> Can't even write his name
> He signs his checks with Xs,
> But they cash them just the same.
> He's as happy as can be
> Doing what comes naturally.

Cole Porter in *Kiss me Kate* (1951), his spoof of Shakespeare's *Taming of the Shrew*, rivalled Byron in the wit of his rhymes, brilliantly accentuated by their musical accompaniment, in songs such as

> Where is the life that late I led
> Where is it now
> Totally dead
> Where is the fun I used to find?
> Where is it gone?
> Gone with the wind.
>
> A married life may all be well
> But raising an heir

Can never compare
To raising a bit of hell.
★
In dear Milano
Where are you Momo?
Still selling those pictures
    Of the scriptures
    In the Duomo?
★
And sweet Lucrezia
So young and gaieii
What scandalous doin's
    In the ruins
    Of Pompeii?

I've often been told
Of nuptial bliss.
But what do you do
At quarter to two
With only a shrew to kiss?

and 'Brush up your Shakespeare':

Brush up your Shakespeare
Start quoting him now
Brush up your Shakespeare
And the women you will wow.
★
Just declaim a few lines from Othello
And they'll think you're a helluva fellow.
★
If she says your behaviour is heinous
Kick her right in the Coriolanus.
★
If your baby is pleading for pleasure
Let her sample your Measure for Measure

Brush up your Shakespeare
And they all kow tow.

Alan Jay Lerner's songs in *My Fair Lady* (1955) preserved a good deal of George Bernard Shaw's Irish acerbity in *Pygmalion* (1912):

> Why can't the English teach their children how to speak
> This verbal class distinction by now should be antique . . .
> If you use proper English you're regarded as a freak
> Why can't the English learn . . . to speak?

Stephen Sondheim's lyrics for Leonard Bernstein's *West Side Story* (1958) were sharp and inventive, in their rhymes as well as their rhythms, in a very different manner. Both need to be performed in such a way that the audience can pick up every syllable:

> Dear kindly Sergeant Krupki
> You've gotta understand
> It's just our bringing upki
> That gets us out of hand
> Our mothers all are junkies
> Our fathers all are drunks
> Golly! Moses!
> Naturally we're punks!
>
> Officer Krupki, we're down on our knees
> And none wants a fella
> With a social disease

But social 'dis-ease' had also been for a long time an important element in the musical, providing a counterbalance to the innocent sweetness of songs like 'Maria' and 'Make of our hands one hand', in *West Side Story*. Shakespeare in *A Midsummer Night's Dream* knew that his enchanted wood needed 'rude mechanicals' as well as fairies; the sentiment of the musical has been tempered by grit and raunchiness, drawing upon the anarchic energy of the underprivileged and the dispossessed. Brecht and Weill, with help from the *Barrack-Room Ballads* of Rudyard Kipling, achieved this modern balance in *Die Dreigroschenoper* or *The Threepenny Opera* (1928).

In this opera for, and about 'poor people', Brecht and Weill drew their lyricism from the dark underbelly of society. Their words, and their music expressed a zest for living, an energy which they found in those who were repressed or ignored by the existing social order, and were happy to make 'beef-steak tartare' out of their opponents. Brecht and Weill achieved an economy not characteristic of many later musicals, but they created a style which in the relation between words and music has remained central. In the other great 'folk-opera' of the period, George and Ira Gershwin's *Porgy and Bess* (1935), the blacks on Catfish Row in Charleston, South Carolina became the voices of a new direction in American society as well as American music. The crippled Porgy expresses it in his final song when he sets out in pursuit of Bess, tempted away to New York by Sportin' Life, with the words, 'I'm on my way'.

In very different ways, the central figures in the Amercan musical remain the dispossessed who become in musical terms the self-possessed, and provide it with the energy which comes from liberation: the cowboys in *Oklahoma*, the sailors in *South Pacific*, the crap-shooters in *Guys and Dolls*, the Jets and Sharks in *West Side Story*. The 'heroes and heroines', as well as the chorus, are also to be found among those excluded, or isolated from society: Billie and Julie in *Carousel*, Porgy and Bess, Sarah in *Guys and Dolls*, Anna in *The King and I*, Liza Doolittle in *My Fair Lady*, Maria and Tony in *West Side Story*.

The popularity of the American musicals which followed after the Theater Guild's success with *Oklahoma* was created out of a lack of complication, a directness of feeling, even a kind of innocence, which never let high spirits get depressed too far, or for too long; and sent audiences away feeling like a million dollars. This transformation of feeling is something more than entertainment.

The enormous success of Richard Eyre's production of *Guys and Dolls* at the National Theatre in 1982 and again in 1996, both repetitions of its original triumph in 1953, point to the truth in Kenneth Tynan's description of it as 'the second best American play' (after *Death of a Salesman!*). George Kaufman, the original director, wrongly insisted on calling it a play with musical numbers, and retired to the lobby for a cigarette when the singing began.

Guys and Dolls has two good stories, which intersect, and are finally brought together, one comic and the other romantic. Frank Loesser, who wrote the music and the lyrics, possessed a talent for 'romance', and a wit which captured the originality of Damon Runyon's style, on which the work is based. Like P.G. Wodehouse, Damon Runyon created characters, and a language for them, which was *sui generis*, and original as his own life in which he was a kind of Boswell to Al Capone, and other mobsters, who liked to have him around.

Adelaide, the 'well-known fiancee' has been engaged to the crap-shooter, Nathan Detroit for fourteen years; meanwhile she sings in the Hot-Box, and waits for her wedding day, while writing letters to her Mama about her husband and five children (with a sixth on the way). Adelaide, ever hopeful and eventually (of course) victorious embodies the feminine spirit of another age. In the romance plot, Nathan Detroit bets the gambler Sky Masterson a thousand bucks that he can't persuade the Salvation Army Girl, Sarah Brown, to fly with him to Havana for the day. Sky wins, and falls in love, which leads in the finale to his own marriage to Sarah, and Adelaide's to Nathan. On the way, Loesser writes a score of songs which combine innocence and knowingness, wit and pathos, and raw energy as in the mobsters' chorus:

> Sit down, sit down, sit down!
> Sit down, your're rocking the boat!

The moral of the tale that whatever a guy is doing, he's doing it for some doll derives its zest from seeing the battles of the sexes as comic in the case of Adelaide and Nathan Detroit, and romantic in the case of Sally and Sky. The intersection of the two inspired Loesser to write music of constantly shifting rhythms, incorporating the marches of the Salvation Army ('Follow the Fold '), the Crap Game ('Luck, be a lady tonight') and romantic yearning of 'I've never been in love before.'

The variation in rhythm and tone of plot and music were matched in Richard Eyre's production by John Gunter's set. Under the neon signs of the New York sky line for Wrigley's, Camel and Coca Cola the brilliantly lit signs by night transformed the seediness of the city by day, and created a changing environment which suggested not just the New York of Damon Runyon, but the composite and swiftly changing city of the late twentieth century in which we live. The literal and metaphoric languages of the theatre were fused.

Stephen Sondheim, in a style which reflects a more sophisticated New York, has continued to write musicals where lyrics, music and dramatic action nourish each other. A lyrical form needs its lyrics, and it needs them to have punch, as the oyster needs grit to secrete its pearl. The non-linear plot of *Company* (1970) brings together a group of New Yorkers, all of whose lives are in disarray. As Bobby, the unmarried 35-year-old for whose birthday party the company has assembled, puts it: afraid of commitment, afraid of being alone, afraid of life. In this post-modern world, Sondheim's musical is more self-absorbed than its predecessors, and has lost some of the exuberance which draws upon the resources of deep social feeling, of which wit, as the child of repression, is the natural outcome. As in the famous, 'Send in the Clowns' from *A Little Night Music* (1973) Sondheim's musicals reflect 'our sad lives' where his predecessors were set alight by an anarchic and positive force.

The musicals of Andrew Lloyd Webber are an altogether different case. The structure of the American musical with its strong story-line, its distinctive characters, its constantly changing melodic inventiveness, and its catchy words has been dissolved into a more operatic form where the music lacks grit at one extreme and sublimity at the other, inhabiting a middle land of over-orchestrated emotion, squeezed out of words of little intrinsic interest. This might not matter, as in many operas, if the music itself was not so meretricious.

Lloyd Webber's musicals succeed by making no demands on the audience, except to 'experience', and to say 'we have been'. In spite of their immense success, they diminish what musical theatre is capable of. The auditorium of the New London Theatre was rebuilt for *Cats*. ' "Scenery" disappeared and environment and machines took its place.' (*British Theatre Design*, p. 157). The words of T.S. Eliot's finest poem on 'The Naming of Cats' are lost in the company's singing, and only occasionally do the words of any of the poems make any impact. Bustopher Jones who wears white spats, and McCavity, the Napoleon of Crime have no more character than turns in a pantomime, while the dance-routines of the Jellicle Cats are repetitious. The role of the audience is only to watch and exclaim.

Alain Boublil and Claude-Michel Schonberg's *Les Misérables* is slightly more interesting. While it aspires to a political concern for the future, its message is emasculated by the complexity of plot, its inaudible words and its pre-occupation with technical sophistication. As its designer John Napier has written: 'My starting-point was the centre of the play's biggest moment, the barricade. Once that was solved everything else fell into place. The barricade could split, lift and revolve, and was a mass of *objets trouvés* which the actors picked up from time to time and used' (*British Theatre Design*, p. 151). It remains the production's most memorable feature. As Noel Coward once remarked of over-elaborate theatre, 'I came out humming the sets.'

In the British musical theatre of the last decade, technical virtuosity attempts to conceal the vacuousness of the 'show': earnestness has taken the place of wit, emotion of feeling, lugubriousness of joyfulness. All the languages of theatre have been diminished by making them serve the sensational effect. As the saying goes, 'we have had the experience, but missed the meaning', which is not surprising because there was very little. In the theatre technique is never all.

*

The central difference in the relation between words and music in opera as compared to the musical is indicated by the role of the conductor. The names of the conductors of musicals are scarcely mentioned, and remain unknown outside the profession. Performances of opera are often remembered by the name of the conductor: Klemperer's *Fidelio*, Böhm's *Tristan*, Giulini's *Falstaff*, Haitink's *Ring*. In all performances of opera, the orchestra is an actor, as important as any of the singers. The orchestra acts under the direction of the conductor, whose sense of the architecture of the opera, and its rhythmic flow, whose power to bring out the local subtleties of the orchestration and relate them to the drama controls the stage performance. But the singers have also to act with their voices, which a few great singers can inflect with the tones and atmosphere of the action (a gift which Angela Georghiu shares with Maria Callas) as well as their physical presence on the stage. Not all singers can suggest the physical embodiment of their roles; and, when this is so, the performance remains flat, no more than a speaking picture, as in non-musical theatre. But the operatic stage in the last fifty years in many countries of the world has been rich in talents where beauty of voice was combined with the power to become the part. Birgit Nilsson, Hans Hotter, Tito Gobbi, Boris Christoff, Anya Silja, Geraint Evans, Placido Domingo, John Tomlinson and Bryn Terfel are among those who like Callas and Georghiu at once come to mind.

The words of the libretto tell a story which music develops into a dramatic action expressing feelings and emotions which the words alone cannot express. The words on which the composer sets to work, whether their own (usually disastrous) or other people's (often lacking dramatic plausibility or even good sense) act as sounding-boards to liberate and explore, as theatre always should, what is often half-hidden or unsounded. In many nineteenth-century operas, the music becomes the means of expressing real feeling, for which neither the plot nor the words would be adequate on their own, as they are often melodramatic and lacking in resonance. The conductor's role in finding a balance between everything which happens on the stage, and in the orchestra pit needs above all to be well-judged.

Robert Schumann once wrote about the setting of poems to music: 'The poem must be crushed and have its juices expressed like an orange; it must wear the music like a wreath, or yield to it like a bride.' In opera it is the last which most often happens: the words yield to a union with the music which expresses what neither could express alone, and which can encompass changes of mood and feeling as swiftly as the wind changes the surface of the sea.

In the first great opera in English, Purcell's *Dido and Aeneas* (*1689*) (with words by Nahum Tate who also rewrote *King Lear* with a happy ending!), the sailor at the start of Act III, exhorts his mates to board their ships, and set sail from Carthage:

> Come away, fellow sailors, come away,
> Your anchors be weighing,
> Time and tide will admit no delaying.
> Take a boozy short leave
> Of your nymphs on the shore,
> And silence their mourning
> With vows of returning
> But never intending to visit them more.

Once the sails are unfurled, the witch can rejoice:

> Our plot has took
> The Queen's forsook
> Ho, ho! Ho, ho! ho, ho (etc.)

But within a few minutes, the action has moved to Dido's suicide, and her lament to her companion, Belinda:

Remember me! Remember me! but ah, forget my fate!

Here, the words inspire one of Purcell's most haunting and plangent melodies, which raises the action from a Gilbertian frivolity (in which deep feelings have no place) to a tragic elegy for loss, and betrayal, worthy of Book IV of Vergil's *Aeneid* on which it is based.

Music can encompass, and frequently does, these swift changes of mood from the playful to the solemn, from one level of being to another, from one kind of drama to another, through changes of rhythm and key signature. In later opera, feelings of different and conflicting kinds are expressed simultaneously in duets, trios, quartets, quintets, sextets, etc., while the chorus as a whole can comment, as in Greek drama, on the action which they are witnessing, whatever its mood. They identify for the audience a generalized response, while the principal singers continue to express and relate their own individual feelings. While opera is often criticized for its artificiality, it remains the only form of dramatic art in which the simultaneous expression of wholly different states of mind and feeling (by a group of people in a room) can be represented. The solitariness of the individual finds liberation in song, but song which remains at variance with the songs of others. In real life we can never be sure what other people are thinking or feeling; sorrow, rage, hope despondency exist in the same room together. In opera, music expresses that dramatic undercurrent, making audible what often remains a silent rhythm beneath the surface of plays.

As in all kinds of theatre, playfulness – in this case the skills of orchestra and singers in 'performing' together – remains central to the delight they give. Purcell's Frost Scene in *King Arthur* expresses musically what it is like to shiver and shake:

> I can scarcely move or draw my breath
> Can scarcely move or draw my breath.
> Let me, let me, let me
> Freeze again to death.

Soloist and a Chorus of cold people suffer from a spell cast by a wicked enchanter, which only love can thaw. The inventiveness and effectiveness of the scene depends on the skills of the director, designers of scene, costume *and* lighting (cold turns us blue!) as well as the performance by orchestra and singers; and the singers' ability to act with their voices as well as their bodies. Although the scene has a symbolic significance, its aesthetic pleasure derives as much from its play with all the languages of theatre.

In comic opera, music as well as words can become an instrument of humour, inseparable from the exuberant sense of fun on the stage. In Rossini's *Italian Girl in Algiers* (1813), the first act ends with a septet for the principal characters, who, by this time, are all suffering from the confusion of their situation, making them hear ringing, hammering, cawing and booming in their heads. After telling us how they are afflicted, they give up words for the onomatopoiea of what they are hearing, which the orchestra through its varied instruments joyfully reflects:

ALL: Ding, ding, ding, etc.
Caw, caw, caw, etc.
Boom, boom, boom, etc.
Bang, bang, bang, etc.

And so they continue to the end of the act, discussing their situation in utter perplexity, with musical exactness. Only in opera can such play be made with the confusion of human lives.

Once the orchestra becomes an actor in the drama, the balance between words and music assumes a subtlety and complexity wholly different to works in which the orchestra accompanies the singers, however inventively. Richard Strauss in *Capriccio* (1942), described by him as a conversation piece for music, creates an opera in which the relative significance of words and music are debated. 'First the words, and later the music; or first the music, and later the words?' At the end the

Countess is asked to choose between the poet and the composer. Is it the words, she asks herself, or the music which has the more powerful effect on her feelings? They are bound together, she replies, in a new harmony, the mystery of the moment, in which one art is reborn of the other.

The operas of Mozart, like the plays of Shakespeare, contain words which are beautiful to sing and to listen to, because they are about human feelings which are immediately understood. Like all the greatest art it is apparently very simple. When in *Die Zauberflöte* (1791), Tamino, looking at the portrait of Pamina, the daughter of the Queen of the Night, sings:

> Dies bildnis ist bezaubernd schön
> Wie noch kein Auge je geseh'n!
> Ich fühl es, ich fühl es
> Wie dieses Gotterbilt
> Mein Herz mit neuer Regung füllt . . .
>
> This picture is bewitchingly beautiful
> No eye has ever seen anything to equal it.
> I feel it, I feel it!
> This heavenly face
> Fills my heart with new feeling

we know at once the magic of falling in love with an image, which he is experiencing. Equally when Pamina, drawn to her lover by the sound of his flute-playing, is ignored by him because he is bound to an oath of silence, of which she is ignorant, we understand at once the pain of her rejection:

> Ach, ich fühl's, es ist geschwunden
> Ewig hin der Liebe Gluck!
> Nimmer kommt ihr, Wonnestunden,
> Meinem Herzen, mehr zurück!
>
> Ah, I feel it has vanished now
> For Ever ! The joy of love.

Never again will joyful hours return
Bringing gladness to my heart.

The Queen of the Night's desire for revenge when she feels her power is being challenged, the longing of Papageno for a wife, the mean vidictiveness of Monostatos because he is ugly and a slave, the determination of Sarastro to preserve a sacred place from violation – all these feelings are ones which we can at once recognize and respond to. As in all good lyric poetry, the feeling behind the words, even if complex, is clear. Mozart's melodies reflect and magnify this complexity which is at the same time very simple. But the words must be audible and understood.

In the part of the action concerned with Papageno, where the humour delights, Mozart's music has a profound seriousness. It is not possible for music alone to be moral or immoral; but in Mozart's operas, in conjunction with words, it becomes so. Papageno is punished first for his lies, and later for his cowardice; Tamino however much he loves must prove his love through a rite of passage in which he overcomes his fear of death; and Pamina, helped by the playing of the flute to endure, must also be purified of human fear. At another level, the Queen of the Night's murderous desire for revenge ('Der holle Rache kocht in meinem Herzen') must be overcome by the wisdom of Sarastro. While verbally he may seem a figure of repressive authority, like Prospero in *The Tempest*, musically Sarastro's solemnity comes from harmony beyond the self. As it is impossible to listen to the Queen of the Night's music, without recognizing the self-destructive nature of rage, so Sarastro's music, and those of his initiates, is felt as an unshakeable self-assurance and faith. The music generalizes what the Temple of Isis and Osiris stands for; but the words give it a local habitation and a name. As the Countess says in *Capriccio*, one art is born of the other.

Depth [as Isaiah Berlin once observed] is an odd word. It's a metaphor, but you can't translate it into other terms.

Depth means penetrating into something very basic in one-self, and touching it, and feeling an electric shock.

Act II of Mozart's *Le Nozze di Figaro* (1786) stands out for its complexity of feeling – its depth in Isaiah Berlin's sense – within a dramatic action as complete and perfect as it is possible to imagine one to be. At the end, Marcellino, Basilio and Bartolo come to demand the fulfilment of the contract by which Figaro will marry Marcellina for failing to repay the money he owes her. Susanna and the Countess express their hope of having avoided disaster by enabling Cherubino to escape through the window without the Count discovering him in his wife's bedroom; the Count still deeply suspicious tries to reimpose his authority by demanding silence, and Figaro blames the devil for bringing everyone together at the same moment. Only in opera can this simultaneous action be performed, with the music driving towards its harmonic resolution, and binding together with absolute precision the dramatic differentiation of the characters' individual feelings. The effect combines expectation of what is going to happen in the next act (in other words an effective curtain) with an aesthetic joy at the completion of an act which has developed faultlessly with dramatic surprises and reversals, from the Countess's heart-broken lament for the loss of the Count's love, to Cherubino's light and unstressed expression of desire (the contrast between the power of Love, and the prickings of Cupid) to the Count's sexual rage and hurt pride in suspecting his wife unfaithful, and the humour of the appearance of Antonio, the gardener, complaining of the flowers which have been trampled on, when Cherubino has jumped from the window. Cupboards, windows, doors, keys, disguises, love-letters, tools for forcing locks, a drawn sword and a bunch of crushed flowers all play an essential part in the drama. Da Ponte's libretto, based on Beaumarchais's play, provides an action which is tender, witty and acerbic. Mozart's music creates the shifting colours and flow of human feelings beneath the surface of spoken words. In all dramatic writing the goal towards which the action is moving must never be lost sight of (though not apparent to the audience till the end). In this act, this development is flawlessly matched to a musical action which begins slowly, elegiacally, in the highest style in the Countess's aria 'Porgi Amor' and ends with a septet of turbulent and uproarious confusion. The action on the stage needs a comic and dramatic timing as precise as the tempi of the music from the orchestra; and actors capable of styles which range from the coldy aristocratic to the grumpily rustic.

Throughout *Le Nozze di Figaro*, Mozart wrote music which embellishes the words, by widening and deepening the feeling. In the Countess's second aria, 'Dove sono i bei momenti', Mozart expresses both a sense that the only true paradises are the paradises which are lost, and a more personal regret for what the Count's lust has destroyed. Such feelings are musical, because by their very nature they are non-verbal, though we are always looking for ways of identifying their nature. In the first few bars of Act IV when Barberina is hunting in the darkened garden for the pin she has lost, Mozart writes music without words, expressing loss, anxiety close to despair, which have been born of deceit, unkindness, betrayal: a few brief bars as beautiful and haunting as anything he ever wrote.

The moral failings of all the characters will be fully revealed by the end of the Act, and call for atonement. The Count will kneel to ask pardon of the wife he has wronged. In that moment of confrontation, the words are necessary, they have to be spoken ('Contessa, perdono, perdono, perdono') before the festivities can begin. The musical transition is inevitably from minor to major; and only in music can mood and feeling be changed with such speed. The moral force of the need to forget and forgive if contentment is to be achieved is matched by the psychological force of an instantaneous musical change which is irresistible. No one can fail to respond to a sad tune, or resist a cheerful one. But no one also leaves at the end of *Le Nozze di Figaro* doubting what the cost of contentment must be.

Don Giovanni, or *Il dissoluto punito* (1787) penetrates even more deeply from its first D minor chord into what is basic in oneself, because it is concerned with damnation, a concept or feeling which may be theologically unfashionable but remains in spiritual terms wholly comprehensible. When Macbeth speaks of Duncan's murder as 'the deep damnation of his taking off', we know at once what he is feeling. Deborah Warner's production at Glyndebourne of *Don Giovanni*, in 1995, much criticized by some for its modern costume, brought out what is undoubtedly true that *Don Giovanni* tells a tale of rape, murder, lust, deceit, and self-gratification of the kind which makes newspaper headlines every day. What Mozart adds through his music, when the Commendatore comes to life in the graveyard, and as stone guest accepts the invitation to dinner carries with it the cold from 'thrilling regions of thick-ribbed ice'. The music expresses the spectral haunted nature of the guilty soul confronted with its crimes, and Mozart does so in music which chills the marrow, leading to the judgement which all must make of what they have witnessed: 'this is the end of the man who does evil'.

The moral force of music in Mozart's operas is reduced in many later operas to an intense personal feeling. To adapt Schumann's words, the poem, or the libretto must be crushed, and have its juices expressed like an orange. Quite literally, till the pips squeak. *La Bohème* (1896), a superlatively effective and moving piece of theatre, is about the discovery of love, and its loss, first through jealousy, and finally through death. The music's power to move comes in the first act from Rodolpho's and Mimi's voices finally joined in unison (an effect of total identification, difficult to achieve through words alone because people cannot speak simultaneously; and then at the end of *La Bohème* where the music (and death) strikes suddenly out the darkness in a single chord, to which Rodolpho's numbed reaction can only be: 'It can't happen like this.' But it does, and it has. Music acts here not as a revelation (what cannot be said in words) but as an intensification of a human situation, making us realize its pain, its fragility and briefness; it 'orchestrates' what we are watching.

The score of the second act of *Tosca* (1900) orchestrates a human situation of a very different kind, expressing the mounting lust of Baron Scarpia for the woman he is determined to make love to, and her controlled rage as she hears the cries of her lover whom Scarpia is torturing (a scene played with unforgettable precision by Maria Callas and Tito Gobbi, and preserved on film). The act reaches its climax in Scarpia's cries for help as she stabs him: 'Aiuto! Aiuto!', and her remorseless, 'Muori, muori, muori!' ('Die, die, die!'). The music expresses with great dramatic intensity the different emotions which they are simultaneously feeling.

Impassioned human feeling – often in circumstances which are doomed – inspires much of the music in the operas of Verdi and Puccini, as well as the *opera seria* of Donizetti, Bizet, Janáček and others. But at the end of Verdi's final opera, *Falstaff* (1893), the humanist balloon goes up. Mocked, and haunted by what he takes to be elves and fairies in Windsor Forest at night, Falstaff is paid back by his neighbours for his attempts to cuckold them. But unlike his previous opera, *Otello* (1887), where alleged adultery leads to murder, *Falstaff* ends with festive mockery: 'Tutto nel mondo e burla': 'All the world's a joke. . . . All are cheated. Everyone laughs at everyone else; but the best laugh is the last laugh'. This choric, and comic, rejection of taking the world too seriously points in a direction, which Verdi had not pursued, of a wholly different relation between words and music, and another kind of music-drama. In humanist opera, the music enlarges upon and intensifies ordinary human emotions – jealousy, love, hate, lust and so on; but in another kind of music-drama, the music transcends the words, suggests another level of reality, into which we are drawn; and of which music is the only possible expression. Music which is always intensely physical, producing through its rhythms an inner vibration (which in turn expresses itself in dance and song) becomes the instrument of a vision which is transcendental and metaphysical. When

Walter Pater remarked, 'all art aspires to the condition of music', he indicated what some operas, in which the words are only signposts, achieve through the languages of theatre. A difference exists between 'pure' music – let us say the arietta of Beethoven's Opus 111 – which when we listen to it leaves no doubt of an experience, unnameable, beyond normal human perception, and Beethoven's opera, *Fidelio* (1805), which identifies words with musical expression, while the music soars into orbit, beyond all language.

Here, the literal and metaphorical effectiveness of the staging matters a great deal. In Act I, we are in the gaoler Rocco's house, and in the courtyard of the prison where he allows the prisoners to enjoy fresh air and sunlight, until they are driven back inside on the orders of the evil Governor, Pizarro. Sunlight and darkness mirror good and evil. In Act II, we are in the dungeon, where a single prisoner, Florestan, is kept in isolation and is being starved to death, because he has spoken up about Pizarro's crimes against humanity.His wife, Leonora, has disguised herself in order to gain access to the prison and to try to discover where Florestan is being kept by Pizarro. As she and Rocco descend into the darkness of the dungeon, the music gives way to spoken dialogue. Leonora does not know if the man in solitary confinement is Florestan, and neither knows whether the man whose grave they have been ordered to dig is dead or sleeps. When he stirs, he asks first for a message to be sent to his wife in Seville, and then for something to drink. Leonora gives him the last drop of Rocco's wine: 'Da ist er! Da ist er!' And a crust of bread. Then the music begins: 'Euch werde Lohn in besser'n Welten! Der Himmel hat euch mir geschickt.' ('May you be rewarded in a better world, Heaven has sent you to me!'). The serenity of the music is to be short-lived, for Pizarro is about to appear to kill his prisoner, until once again Leonora intervenes, holding him at bay at first with her body and then with a pistol, until a trumpet sounds announcing that the Minister has arrived to find out who is being held in Pizarro's prison. A brief verbal exchange takes place between Florestan and Leonora:

FLORESTAN: O meine Leonora, was hast du für mich getan?
LEONORA: Nichts, nichts, mein Florestan!
FLORESTAN: My Leonora, what have you done for me?
LEONORA: Nothing, nothing, my Florestan!

And then at once like the sun bursting out in this dark place, they sing together: 'O namenlose Freude! . . . Nach unnennbaren Leiden so übergrosse Lust!' ('O nameless joy . . . after such unspeakable suffering, such surpassing Joy!') Here, Beethoven's music expresses a joy which is 'nameless', beyond language in its harmony and confidence, because light has triumphed over darkness, justice over tyranny, love over cruelty, bearing witness to Leonora's assertion (also spoken) before she challenges Pizarro, that a Providence governs all things ('Ja, ja, es gibt eine Forsehung').

The magnitude of the effect comes from its following upon the unsung 'melodrama', as though music breaks the bondage of words at the moment when Leonora also secures Florestan's release from the bondage of his chains. Both here, and in the equally jubilant duet and chorus in the final act, the power of music confirms a faith in a world where all is possible when loyalty, courage and hope remain unshaken. The concentration of the music charges the whole scene with an electric tension which returns to the audience magnified and life-affirming, made more plausible than in the Ninth Symphony because of the rescue which we have seen achieved with desperation and daring. The words locate in the particular what the music transforms into an expression of human hope at the instability of evil, when confronted with courage. The music alone (for the characters as such lack any great weight or subtlety) makes it impossible to leave the theatre without that feeling of having been renewed.

In Wagner's *Tristan und Isolde* (1865) the relation between words and music becomes even more extreme. In Act II, language is strained to the point at which it disappears into non-meaning. Night and death are invoked by the two lovers who see daylight as hostile and deceitful. Night, it is claimed, can set them free from the world, which is delusion, and liberate them into ecstasy.

> TRISTAN and ISOLDE (*together*):
> O sink hernieder, Nacht der Liebe.
> Gib Vergessen, dass ich lebe;
> Nimm mich auf in deinem Schoss
> Löse von der Welt mich los!
>
> O sink down upon us, Night of Love
> Make me forget that I live
> Take me into your keeping
> Free me from the world.

The world as 'maya' or 'illusion' has become entangled with a mystical rapture in which the lovers, as in John Donne's poem 'The Ecstasy' are temporarily removed from their bodies. Death is invoked as loving, because in death Tristan will become Isolde and Isolde Tristan. Sexual ecstasy is interwoven with desire for release from a world in which daylight perception deludes, and where night-time expression remains ineffable. In John Donne's poem, 'The Ecstasy', the lovers know they must return to their bodies (souls and bodies are intertwined); in *Tristan und Isolde* all such realism is extinguished. When, in Act III, Isolde reaches Careol where Tristan is dying, he rises from his bed, causing the wound she has come to heal to burst open, and greets her in death with the blood flowing from him. Isolde in her *liebestod* ('love-death') which ends the opera expresses this ecstasy as a union in death beyond the limits of the world:

> Mild und leise wie er lächelt
> wie das Auge hold er öffnet,
> Seht ihr's, Freunde? Seht ihr's nicht?
> Immer lichter, wie er leuchtet,
> stern-umstrahlet hoch she hebt?

In dem wogendem Schwall, in dem tonenden Schall,
in des Welt-Atems wehendem All,
ertrinken, versinken
unbewuss, höchste Lust!

How gently and quietly he smiles
How fondly he opens his eyes!
Do you see, friends? Don't you see?
How he shines, always more brightly
Rises ever higher, surrounded by stars . . .

. . . In the surging swell, in the ringing sound
In the vast wave of the world's breath
To drown, to sink
Unconscious, highest bliss!

As in much of Act II, the exorbitance of expression, drawn
from a mish-mash of Oriental philosophy and Christian mys-
ticism, might lead to the conclusion that Wagner wrote less
meaningful lyrics than Cole Porter. (One of Strindberg's cra-
zier projects in his Intimate Theatre was to perform *Tristan
und Isolde* without the music.) The melody, and harmonies of
the *liebestod* can be heard in the head; but no one in their right
mind would go down the street singing the words. The words
cannot say what the music is about; and in their attempts, as
T.S. Eliot put it in *Four Quartets*, they 'slip, slide, crack, perish'.
In their perishing they give birth to music which has no
verbal equivalent. The music expresses what words cannot say.
At the close of *Tristan*, it hovers at that point where sound
itself becomes transcendence, the physical disappears into
what can no longer be heard, and the silence which follows
the final note is the silence of something reluctantly relin-
quished, as the physics of music becomes the metaphysics of
silence.

If the music is felt here as a liberating counter-balance to
the destructive effect of human actions, there are some operas
where the music works in the opposite direction to confirm
and generalize a world from which human beings can find no

release or freedom, where their actions confirm their imprisonment within a set of conditions, social, economic, sexual and genetic which cannot be changed. The orchestra as actor assumes a much darker role: the inner drive of the music expresses what is irresistible and inevitable, a fatality that cannot be denied. In different ways this is true of Debussy's *Pelléas et Mélisande* (1892); and Alban Berg's *Wozzeck* (1925). Both operas have had memorable productions which by creating a visual poetry on an uncluttered stage where every object 'tells', succeeded in relating the complexity of what the music was expressing to a stage action which was simple and unobtrusive. *Wozzeck* (1952) at the Royal Opera House was designed by Caspar Neher, who worked with Bertolt Brecht at the Berliner Ensemble, and found a visual language which brought out individual chacterization, and the symbolic significance of the plot in images of striking beauty. Peter Stein produced *Pelléas et Mélisande* (1992), with sets by Karl-Ernest Hermann and costumes by Moidele Bickel, for the Welsh National Opera, using various areas of the stage vertically and horizontally, to create a stage action reflecting a plot where the characters go down into the dark in caves and cellars, but also climb in search of light to terraces and towers. The performances were conducted by Pierre Boulez.

The opera is about the jealousy of Golaud, when he discovers the love between his wife Mélisande and his half-brother, Pelléas. Golaud has found the mysterious Mélisande beside a spring in a forest, into which she has dropped her crown. Mélisande refuses to tell Golaud why she is there, or where she has come from. Golaud takes her away, marries her, and returns with her to the court of his grandfather, Arkel. There, Pelléas falls in love with her, arousing Golaud's jealous rage. Golaud kills Pelléas, and fatally wounds Mélisande before turning his sword on himself. As Arkel says at one moment in despair at what is unfolding before him, 'Si j'étais Dieu, J'aurais pitié sur les coeurs des hommes'('If I was God, I would have pity on the hearts of men'). In the music, as in the words at this moment, there exists an 'infinite sadness'.

The depth of the opera comes from questions which cannot be answered. The mystery and mysteriousness in Maeterlinck's original play which Debussy follows closely has been transformed into a work about the fatality of human lives. These characters lack a sure sense of their own identity, are lost in forests by day and surrounded by darkness at night. They cannot answer the questions which others ask of them, or of life. The truth about ourselves and others is unknowable. In the world of matter there is no light. The demand to know, like the belief that through action events can be controlled, adds to the sum of human unhappiness. When Golaud demands to know if Mélisande's love for Pelléas has been guilty, she cannot tell him. As Golaud has proved, the more you act, the greater the harm you do. At best, as the ageing Arkel reflects, one can acquire a sort of faith in the fidelity of events.

The action of the whole work is expressed in music which remains enigmatic and unconcluded, drawn on by its own constantly shifting moods and colours, suggestive of all that human beings cannot control, and expressive of the fatality within which they live. The child (whose child?) which Mélisande has given birth to on her death-bed 'must live now. It's her turn': her turn to try to find answers to the questions (whatever they are) in a world which does not provide answers. The marriage between the music and the words in this great work comes from the inscrutability of music itself. Even when we attach words to it, music remains unreadable. It has no programme, and speaks only of itself, as life does too, unless we impose a programme upon it.

Berg's *Wozzeck* like Debussy's *Pelléas* is closely based on an existing play. In this case, written by Georg Büchner in 1836. Like *Pelléas* too, it is written in a series of short scenes, whose connection expresses a view of how things are. Büchner writes about the life of poor people, of the impossibility of virtue without money, and of the terror of trying to work for thirty years, with only the prospect of poverty, abuse and violence. From the start, Wozzeck is haunted by fantasies, hallucinations, voices and premonitions of disaster. The music is an expression of this inner score; but it also enlarges upon the individual fate of Wozzeck who is driven to murder when his woman, by whom he has a child, is seduced by the Drum-Major. To Wozzeck, 'man is an abyss'. 'One grows dizzy looking into his depths.' As others notice, he tears through the world like an open razor. But it is Marie who suggests to him how he must solve his problems. 'Rather a knife in me than a hand on me.' It is with a knife that Wozzeck will stab Marie to death, and drown himself in the pool where he has thrown the knife.

The music of the score frequently sounds 'askew', using rhythms and dances from more traditional forms of opera and folk-dance, but twisting them to reflect the way in which the increasingly tormented and psychotic Wozzeck hears them. The world outside torments him – the Doctor uses him as a guinea-pig, persuading him he must live entirely on beans – making his inner world increasingly impossible to live, or endure. The music expresses all this but also the tenderness of which Wozzeck and Marie are capable. At the start of Act III, Marie reads from the Bible to her child, telling him the story of Mary Magdalene. Only Dostoevsky equalls Berg in his awareness of the need for pity in a world where so much savagery and cruelty exists. At the opera's end he expresses the cruelty and the tenderness in the figure of the abandoned child, whose parents are dead, left alone on the stage to sing the fragment of a song: 'Hop, Hop! Hop, Hop!' Like all great moments of theatre, it only expresses its vision glancingly. Its effectiveness depends as always on colour and lighting which create a focus of intensity for the boy, and his words.

As in all drama, performance counts for everything in that only when the audience is present can that unitive action between performer and listener occur. The diversity of that experience, in revivals and new works, in theatres, halls, streets, pubs, open spaces, in reviews, plays, musicals, operas is constantly creating moments of shared experience and intuited community. The theatre is not a pulpit, and it makes no claims for what happens after the lights go out. Its ghosts remain palpable presences, of living people in actual relationships; it always exemplifies through the concrete. Conflict is of its essence, making us more aware of that 'dark mass of factors whose general drift we perceive but whose precise interrelations we cannot formulate.'

Actors, directors, designers of costume and lighting and music are engaged in a shared act of illustrating the shadows, of drawing into the area of light, which is the stage, what was less clearly seen before. Their talents in the last fifty years have been prodigious. But in theatre, there always exists an element of luck, of right timing, of conjuring out of what exists off-stage from that whole entangled mass of different perspectives, of conflicting wills, and roles, an image which clarifies: an action abstracted from experience.

Hans Sachs in his Monologue in *Die Meistersinger* (1868) reflects on the madness which underlies so much human activity, on the way in which people torment each other in useless foolish anger. No one has a reward or thanks for it, or knows quite how it started, or what brings it to rest. But nothing ever happens without such madness. As in life, so on the stage: a kind of wrestling occurs, to bring roles out of words, people out of what exists on paper: rooms, streets, landscapes out of descriptions, gestures out of silence, movements out of stillness, till a pattern is formed. No one knows at a rehearsal by what alchemy something organic will be created from diverse talents; whether the performance will fall on deaf ears or, as with Chekhov's *The Seagull*, when it was performed by the Moscow Art Theatre, be greeted first with silence, and then with a roar of applause as spontaneous as it was unexpected. The theatre in making us applaud like this involves a mutual act of recognition; and in this spontaneous, intuitive act learn not only to love the theatre and its players but also, perhaps, a little more the shadow-play in which we are involved for the two or three hours traffic of our stage.

Index

Achurch, Janet, 29, 30
Admiral's Men, 5
Aeschylus, *Agamemnon*, 3;
  Oresteia, 59
Almeida Theatre, 137
Andrews, Harry, 141
Annals, Michael, 147
Anouilh, Jean, *Antigone*, 14;
  L'Invitation au Château,
  139
Appia, Adolph, 158, 159, 162
Aristotle, 11
Arnold, Janet, 105
Ashcroft, Peggy, 16–17, 32, 34,
  37–8, 69, 76, 90, 110, 145,
  171, 172, 183, 195
Auden, W. H., 168; and
  Christopher Isherwood, *The
  Ascent of F.6*, 175
Ayckbourn, Alan, 81, 86–8;
  Absurd Person Singular, 88;
  Man of the Moment, 86–8; *A
  Small Family Business*, 88,
  156

Badel, Alan, 75, 189
Barrault, Jean-Louis, 101
Barrie, J. M., *Peter Pan*, 149
Barton, Lucy, 105
Beaumarchais, Pierre Augustin
  Caron de, 216
Beckett, Samuel, 11, 103, 143,
  146, 156, 172; *Act without
  Words II*, 19, 152; *Happy
  Days*, 35, 172; *Not I*, 103;

Play, 9–10, 157; *Waiting for
  Godot*, 24, 53, 83–4, 104,
  111–13
Beethoven, Ludwig van, *Fidelio*,
  220–1; Fifth Symphony, 22,
  197, 198; Ninth Symphony,
  221; Opus, 111, 220
Bennett, Alan, 148
Benson, Frank, 66
Berg, Alban, *Wozzeck*, 224,
  225–6
Berger, John, *Pig Earth*, 130
Berkoff, Steven, 25, 33
Berlin, Irving, *Annie Get Your
  Gun*, 203
Berlin, Isaiah, 215–16
Berliner Ensemble, 21, 224
Bernstein, Leonard, *West Side
  Story*, 165, 206
Bickel, Moidele, 224
Billington, Michael, 124
Binoche, Juliette, 39
Birtwistle, Harrison, 149, 198
Bizet, Georges, 219
Blackford, Richard, *Gawain and
  the Green Knight*, 149
Blake, William, 108
Bloom, Claire, 29
Böhm, Karl, 210
Boublil, Alain, and Claude-
  Michel Schonberg, *Les
  Misérables*, 5, 209
Boulez, Pierre, 224
Brecht, Bertolt, 15, 21, 47, 50,
  92–5, 131, 135, 224; *The*

Caucasian Chalk Circle, 94, 99, 131; *The Good Woman of Setzuan*, 145; *The Life of Galileo*, 146–7; *Mother Courage*, 21, 104; and Kurt Weill, *Die Dreigroschenoper*, 93, 205–6
Brendel, Alfred, 27
Briers, Richard, 132
Brook, Peter, 23–4, 25, 34, 36, 100, 101, 102–3, 115, 132, 139, 144, 169, 172, 180
Browning, Robert, 71
Büchner, Georg, 225
Burton, Richard, 141, 180
Bury, John, 183
Byron, Lord, 71, 203

Cadell, Simon, 28
Calder-Marshall, Anna, 125, 195
Callas, Maria, 210, 219
Callow, Simon, 28, 34, 39, 147, 169
Campbell, Mrs Patrick, 75
Carrière, Jean-Claude, 132
Charon, Jacques, 126, 127
Cheek by Jowl, 25, 129
Chekhov, Anton, 54–7, 66, 71, 143, 194, 195; *The Bear*, 194; *The Cherry Orchard*, 12, 28, 56–7, 107, 108, 192–3, 195; *Ivanov*, 55; *Platonov*, 55, 143; *The Proposal*, 194; *The Seagull*, 32, 54–6, 144, 227; *Three Sisters*, 56, 190–2; *Uncle Vanya*, 26, 100, 124–5, 193–4
Chichester Festival Theatre, 181
Christoff, Boris, 210
Cilento, Diane, 39
'Cirque du Soleil', 152

Claudel, Paul, *Partage de Midi*, 101
Comédie Française, 127
Congreve, William, *Love for Love*, 26; *The Way of the World*, 40–1
Courtenay, Tom, 195
Coward, Noel, 31, 89, 134, 209; *Hay Fever*, 78–80, 128
Cox, Murray, 121
Craig, Edward Gordon, 158, 162
Criterion Theatre, 112

Da Ponte, Lorenzo, 216
Daldry, Stephen, 128–9
de Filippo, Eduardo, *La Grande Magia*, 40
de la Tour, Frances, 164
Debussy, Claude, *Pelléas et Mélisande*, 224–5
Dench, Judi, 35, 75, 106, 164, 195
Dewhurst, Keith, 48
Dexter, John, 140, 145, 146, 147, 180
Diary of Anne Frank, The, 57
Dickens, Charles, *David Copperfield*, 14
Domingo, Placido, 210
Donington, Robert, 159–60
Donizetti, Gaetano, 219
Donmar Warehouse, 137
Donne, John, 184; 'The Ecstasy', 222
Dostoevsky, Fyodor, 226
D'Oyly Carte Opera Company, 202
Drury Lane Theatre, 34
Dudley, William, 112
Dürrenmatt, Friedrich, *The Visit*, 33, 130
Duse, Eleonara, 29

Eddison, Robert, 185
Elgar, Edward, 198
Eliot, George, *The Mill on the Floss*, 33
Eliot, T. S., 67, 166; *The Cocktail Party*, 176, 178–80; *The Family Reunion*, 176, 177–8; *Four Quartets*, 223; *Murder in the Cathedral*, 176–7; 'The Music of Poetry', 180; 'The Naming of Cats', 209; *Sweeney Agonistes*, 175; 'The Use of Poetry', 175
Elliott, Michael, 177
English Shakespeare Company, 72
Epidauros, 4, 59, 151
Espert, Nuria, 150
Esslin, Martin, 50
Evans, Edith, 32, 37, 41, 75, 164, 180
Evans, Geraint, 210
Eyre, Richard, 45, 96, 166, 170, 206, 208

Farquhar, George, *The Recruiting Officer*, 22, 197
Feuillière, Edwige, 101
Feydeau, Georges, 126; *Un Fil à la Patte*, 127; *A Flea in Her Ear*, 126, 127; *Hotel Paradiso*, 127; *A Little Hotel of the Side*, 126
Fiennes, Ralph, 195
Finney, Albert, 164, 195
Fonda, Jane, 29
Fontanne, Lynn, 33
Ford, John, *'Tis Pity She's a Whore*, 154
Fox, Edward, 178
Frank, Anne, 58
Frayn, Michael, 46; *Wild Honey*, 143

Freud, Sigmund, 69
Friedrich, Götz, 160, 162
Friel, Brian, *Dancing at Lughnasa*, 181, 182–3; *Translations*, 98–100
Frigerio, Ernesto, 150
Fry, Christopher, 71, 180–1; *The Dark is Light Enough*, 180; *The Lady's Not for Burning*, 139, 180, 181; *Ring Round the Moon*, 139; *Tiger at the Gates*, 77; *Venus Observed*, 181

Gambon, Michael, 39, 86, 87, 97, 164, 195
Garnier, Charles, 3
Gershwin, Ira, 200; George and Ira, *Porgy and Bess*, 206
Gheorghiu, Angela, 210
Gielgud, John, 25, 31, 34, 48, 156, 180, 195
Gilbert, W. S., and Sir Arthur Sullivan, 202; *The Mikado*, 202; *The Yeomen of the Guard*, 202
Giraudoux, Jean, *The Trojan War will not Take Place*, 77
Giulini, Carlo Maria, 210
Globe Theatre, 4, 6
Glyndebourne, 150, 218
Gobbi, Tito, 210, 219
Grahame, Kenneth, 148
Granville Barker, Harley, 75, 143
Green, Martyn, 202
Greene, Graham, *The Complaisant Lover*, 169
Greenwood, Joan, 29
Grieg, Edvard, 166
Griffiths, Trevor, *Comedians*, 95
Guinness, Alec, 32–3, 127, 164, 179, 185
Gunter, John, 135, 143, 208

Guthrie, Tyrone, 7, 26, 36, 66, 138

Haitink, Bernard, 210
Hall, Peter, 8, 24, 25, 31, 34, 53, 59, 75, 111, 113, 140, 171, 185, 198, 199; Company, 143
Hampton, Christopher, *Tales from Hollywood*, 142
Handel, George Friedrich, *Samson*, 138
Hare, David, 101, 164; *The Absence of War*, 72, 96; *Amy's View*, 35, 45, 52; *Murmuring Judges*, 72, 96; *Racing Demon*, 72, 96; *Skylight*, 96–8
Harris, Richard, 64, 65
Harrison, Rex, 64, 65, 145–6, 175
Heiress, The, 168
Herbert, Jocelyn, 136, 144–7
Hermann, Karl-Ernst, 224
Hersey, David, 137
Hill, Geoffrey, 67
Hirsch, Robert, 127
Hobson, Harold, 168
Hochhuth, Rolf, *The Representative*, 104
Hoheisel, Tobias, 150
Holm, Ian, 122
Hopkins, Anthony, 164, 190
Hotter, Hans, 210
Howard, Alan, 75, 164
Hudson, Richard, 108
Hunter, Kathryn, 33
Hunter, N. C., 134; *A Day by the Sea*, 89; *Waters of the Moon*, 89
Hutchinson, Jeremy, 17
Hytner, Nicholas, 148

Ibsen, Henrik, 30, 39, 66, 68–9, 71, 78; *A Doll's House*, 29–31, 190; *An Enemy of the People*, 137; *Ghosts*, 68, 155; *Hedda Gabler*, 109–10; *John Gabriel Borkman*, 69, 155; *The Lady from the Sea*, 69; *Little Eyolf*, 69; *The Master Builder*, 26; *Peer Gynt*, 13–14, 138; *Rosmersholm*, 155
Ionesco, Eugène, 81, 82, 100, 132; *The Bald Prima Donna*, 80; *The Chairs*, 131–2
Irons, Jeremy, 63
Irving, Sir Henry, 3

Jacob, Sally, 115
James, Henry, *Washington Square*, 168
Janáček, Leoš, 219; *Jenufa*, 150
Johnson, Samuel, 122
Jones, Richard, 127, 162
Jones, Robert Edward, 152–3

Kafka, Franz, *Metamorphosis*, 33
Kaufman, George, 207
Keats, John, 71
Kedrova, Lil, 195
Kerr, Walter, 43
Kipling, Rudyard, 29; *Barrack-Room Ballads*, 93, 205
Klemperer, Otto, 210
Koltai, Ralph, 104, 154
Komisarjevsky, Theodore, 32
Kustow, Michael, 108

Lehnhoff, Nicholas, 150
Leigh, Vivien, 75, 90
Lepage, Robert, 33
Lerner, Alan Jay, and Frederick Loewe, *My Fair Lady*, 75, 204–5, 206
Lewis, Cecil Day, 35
Liszt, Franz, 198
Livesey, Roger, 75, 175
Lloyd Webber, Andrew, 208–9;

Cats, 5, 209; *The Phantom of the Opera*, 5
Loesser, Frank, *Guys and Dolls*, 203, 206–8
Lorca, Federico García, *The House of Bernarda Alba*, 150
Lord Chamberlain's Men, 5
Lowery, Nigel, 162
Lunt, Alfred, 33

McBurney, Simon, 131
McCowan, Alec, 164, 180, 195
McEwan, Geraldine, 132
McKellen, Ian, 36, 38, 137, 143, 164, 195
McTeer, Janet, 29–31
Maeterlinck, Maurice, 225
Mahabharata, The, 24, 132–4
Mahler, Gustav, 198
Mamet, David, 53
Man Who, The, 24
Marber, Patrick, *Closer*, 49, 53
Mason, Brewster, 75
Massey, Anna, 29
Massey, Daniel, 164
Messel, Oliver, 139–40, 180
Mifune, Toshiro, 38
Miller, Arthur, 11, 42; *Death of a Salesman*, 9, 11, 13, 196–7, 207; *A View from the Bridge*, 39
Miller, Jonathan, 124
Milton, John, *Comus*, 72
Moiseiwitsch, Tanya, 141
Morahan, Christopher, 143
Mortimer, John, 127
Moscow Art Theatre, 2, 135, 171, 195, 227
Mozart, Wolfgang Amadeus, 198–200; *Don Giovanni*, 173, 218; *The Marriage of Figaro*, 154, 216–17; *Die Zauberflöte*, 214–15

Napier, John, 137, 209
National Theatre, 40, 59, 111, 124, 127, 143, 149, 192, 206; Cottesloe Theatre, 8, 69, 137; Lyttelton Theatre, 8; Olivier Theatre, 8, 17, 131, 135, 137, 146, 148
Neher, Caspar, 224
Neville, John, 187
New London Theatre, 209
Nighy, Bill, 52
Nilsson, Birgit, 210
Noble, Adrian, 108
Nunn, Trevor, 137

Obolensky, Chloe, 133
Old Vic, 72, 127, 143, 155
Olivier, Laurence, 16, 25, 27, 34, 38, 75, 91, 120, 137, 164, 180, 190, 192, 195
O'Neill, Eugene, 14; *Long Day's Journey into Night*, 26
Opéra, 3
Orton, Joe, 81–2; *Loot*, 81; *What the Butler Saw*, 82
Osborne, John, 95; *The Entertainer*, 91–2, 137; *Look Back in Anger*, 89, 91; *Luther*, 92
Other Place, The, 137, 142
O'Toole, Peter, 93

Page, Anthony, 30, 125
Parry, Natasha, 172
Pascal, Blaise, 100
Pasco, Richard, 17, 164
Pater, Walter, 219
Pemberton, Reece, 138
Pilbrow, Richard, 150, 152
Pinnock, Winsom, *Leave Taking*, 48
Pinter, Harold, 46, 49, 50, 57–8, 96; *The Birthday Party*, 48–50;

The Caretaker, 53; *The Dumb Waiter*, 19; *Landscape*, 181, 183–4; *No Man's Land*, 156

Pirandello, Luigi, 66, 163; *Henry IV*, 64–5; *It is so, if you think so!*, 63 *Naked*, 39; *The Rules of the Game*, 17; *Six Characters in Search of an Author*, 17–18

Playhouse Theatre, 185

Plowright, Joan, 150, 192

Pope, Alexander, *The Dunciad*, 77

Porter, Cole, 223; *Kiss me Kate*, 203–4

Pozzi, Elizabetta, 125

Priestley, J. B., *An Inspector Calls*, 128–9

Proust, Marcel, 163

Prowse, Philip, 140

Pryce, Jonathan, 55, 95, 195

Puccini, Giacomo, 219; *La Bohème*, 202, 218–19; *Tosca*, 219

Purcell, Henry, *Dido and Aeneas*, 211–12; *King Arthur*, 212–13

Pyant, Paul, 149

Quay Brothers, 127, 131

Rattigan, Terence, 89–91, 134; *The Deep Blue Sea*, 16, 90–1

Ravenhill, Mark, *Shopping and Fxxxxxg*, 53

Redgrave, Lynne, 15

Redgrave, Michael, 63, 111, 141, 195

Redgrave, Vanessa, 55, 68, 69, 195

Richardson, Ralph, 16, 28–9, 31, 32, 48, 69–70, 75, 82, 138, 156, 164, 168, 169, 173

Ricks, Christopher, 67

Rodgers, Richard, and Oscar Hammerstein, *Carousel*, 200–1, 206; *The King and I*, 206; *Oklahoma*, 202, 206; *South Pacific*, 206

Rogers, Paul, 155

Ross, David, 40

Rossini, Gioacchino Antonio, *The Italian Girl in Algiers*, 213

Round House, 177

Routledge, Patricia, 164

Royal Court Theatre, 75, 89, 137, 144, 146

Royal National Theatre, *see* National Theatre

Royal Opera House, 149, 224

Royal Shakespeare Company, 25, 108, 121, 136, 154, 171

Rudman, Michael, 112

Runyon, Damon, 207, 208

Rutherford, Margaret, 40–1

Sachs, Hans, *Die Meistersinger*, 227

Sacks, Oliver, 24

Schoenberg, Arnold, *Moses and Aaron*, 100

Schumann, Robert, 211, 218

Scofield, Paul, 69–70, 75, 125, 139, 164, 169, 175, 178, 199

Seven Streams of the River Ota, 33

Shaffer, Peter, *Amadeus*, 198–200; *The Royal Hunt of the Sun*, 147–8

Shakespeare Memorial Theatre, 7

Shakespeare William, 13, 21, 23, 70, 101, 136, 143, 195, 214; music, 166, 184–9; objects, 114–23; theatre, 5, 9, 164; words, 34, 35, 36, 50, 52, 53, 66, 72; *Antony and Cleopatra*, 11, 67; *As You Like It*, 17, 37, 60; *Coriolanus*, 17; *Hamlet*, 12,

33, 51, 119, 155; *Julius Caesar*, 118–19; *King Henry IV, Part One*, 60–1, 141; *King Henry IV, Part Two*, 61, 141; *King Henry V*, 6, 9, 71, 141; *King John*, 142; *King Lear*, 13, 24, 112–13, 117, 122–3, 136, 144, 155, 165–6; *Love's Labour's Lost*, 51, 59, 102–3, 154, 186; *Measure for Measure*, 60, 186–7; *The Merchant of Venice*, 116–18, 119, 189; *A Midsummer Night's Dream*, 35–6, 114–16, 185–6, 189, 205; *Much Ado about Nothing*, 35, 59, 60; *Othello*, 12, 27, 62, 104, 106, 154; *Richard II*, 62–3, 71, 141; *Romeo and Juliet*, 33, 36, 59; *The Taming of the Shrew*, 203; *The Tempest*, 34, 67–8, 116, 188–9, 215; *Twelfth Night*, 60, 119–20, 184–5, 188; *The Winter's Tale*, 166

Shared Experience, 33, 129

Shaw, Fiona, 164

Shaw, George Bernard, 29, 75–8, 164, 172; *Arms and the Man*, 173; *Back to Methuselah*, 76; *Caesar and Cleopatra*, 76; *Heartbreak House*, 76, 145, 173–5; *Major Barbara*, 76, 77–8; *Man and Superman*, 75, 76, 173; *Pygmalion*, 75, 205; *Saint Joan*, 78, 176

Shelley, Percy Bysshe, 71

Sheridan, Richard Brinsley, 78, 164; *The Critic*, 40, 49; *The Rivals*, 32, 135; *The School for Scandal*, 73–4, 123–4

Silja, Anya, 210

Sinden, Donald, 37, 164, 181

Smith, Maggie, 41, 75, 80, 164

Sondheim, Stephen, 205, 208; *Company*, 208; *A Little Night Music*, 208

Sophocles, 13; *Ajax*, 13; *Antigone*, 144; *Philoctetes*, 11

Stanislavsky, Konstantin, 15, 27, 146, 171

Stein, Peter, 125, 224

Stephens, Robert, 164, 192, 195

Stevenson, Juliet, 29

Stoppard, Tom, 35, 81, 86; *Arcadia*, 52, 84; *The Real Inspector Hound*, 40; *Rosencrantz and Guildenstern Are Dead*, 82–4

Storey, David, *Home*, 48

Strauss, Richard, *Capriccio*, 213–14, 215

Strehler, Giorgio, 108

Strindberg, August, 66, 70, 97, 136; *The Dance of Death*, 16, 26, 190; *The Father*, 70–1; Intimate Theatre, 223

Suchet, David, 199

Sutcliffe, Tom, 162

Svoboda, Josef, 160–2, 192

Swan Theatre, 8, 69, 108

Tate, Nahum, 211

Taylor, Laurette, 41–3

Teatro di Roma, 125

Teatro Stabile di Parma, 125

Tennyson, Alfred Lord, 71

Terfel, Bryn, 210

Theater Guild, 206

Théâtre de Complicité, 25, 33, 129–31

Théâtre le Ranelagh, 33

Theatre of the Absurd, 24

Theatre Projects, 150

Thomson, Mark, 148

Thorndike, Sybil, 75, 164

Three Lives of Lucie Cabrol, The,
  130–1
Tiepolo, Giambattista, 151
Tolstoy, Leo, *War and Peace,* 33
Tomlinson, John, 210
Turgenev, Ivan, *A Month in the
  Country,* 55
Tutin, Dorothy, 164, 195
Tynan, Kenneth, 38, 40–1, 89,
  91, 207

Vahey, Brian, 180
Vanbrugh, Sir John, *The
  Provok'd Wife,* 143
Verdi, Giuseppe, 219; *Falstaff,*
  219; *Otello,* 202, 219; *La
  Traviata,* 202
Visconti, Luchino, 154
Vitruvius, 4

Wagner, Cosima, 158
Wagner, Richard, 7, 104, 167,
  198; *Götterdämmerung,* 160;
  Das Rheingold, 159, 161; *The
  Ring,* 157, 159–62; *Tristan und
  Isolde,* 221–3
Wagner, Wieland, 158–9, 162
Waller, David, 183
Wanamaker, Zoe, 43
Warner, Deborah, 136, 142,
  218
Wars of the Roses, The, 37
Watteau, Antoine, 103
Waugh, Evelyn, *Vile Bodies,* 45

Welsh National Opera, 224
Wertenbaker, Timberlake, *Our
  Country's Good,* 21–2, 99, 197
Wesker, Arnold, *Roots,* 95
Westminster Theatre, 128
Whitelaw, Billie, 103
Wilde, Oscar, 35, 48, 49, 66, 77,
  78, 81; *An Ideal Husband,* 114
  *The Importance of Being
  Earnest,* 41, 74–5, 82, 113–14,
  168; *Lady Windermere's Fan,*
  114; *Salome,* 33; *A Woman of
  No Importance,* 140
Wilder, Thornton, 2; *Our Town,*
  181
Wilkinson, Tom, 68
Williams, Lia, 97
Williams, Tennessee, 42–3, 48;
  The Glass Menagerie, 13, 41–3,
  181–2; *A Streetcar Named
  Desire,* 9
Wilton, Penelope, 90, 164
Withers, Googie, 90
Wittgenstein, Ludwig, 17, 100
Wodehouse, P. G., 207
Wolfit, Donald, 164
Wood, John, 164
Wordsworth, William, 8, 153
Worth, Katharine, 178

Yeats, W. B., 136
Young Vic, 68

Zeffirelli, Franco, 18